I0151946

Blow the Cap off your Capability

Be Unstoppable

Yomi Akinpelu

PNEUMA SPRINGS PUBLISHING UK

First Published in 2020 by:
Pneuma Springs Publishing

British Library Cataloguing in Publication Data. A catalogue record for this book is available from the British Library.

Pneuma Springs Publishing
A Subsidiary of Pneuma Springs Ltd.
7 Groveherst Road, Dartford Kent, DA1 5JD.
E: admin@pneumasprings.co.uk
W: www.pneumasprings.co.uk

Sol de Gloria - For His glory alone

Contents

A fine collection of contemporary and ancient wisdom designed to provoke thought and induce action.

Expel the status quo
Embrace the stellar quotes

Foreword

Everything begins with an idea. Quotes are idea capsules. Sayings that distil very complex human conditions into a few simple words have the ability to inspire and energise. Quotes can generate new ideas, perspectives and ways of thinking in your mind. When you read famous quotes from notable people such as Mark Twain, Mother Teresa or Winston Churchill, you cannot help being stirred up. In just a few condensed words, quotes can encapsulate a philosophy, strategy or approach to life. Pithy quotes are small capsules of wisdom easy to swallow and digest; they stick to your mind and if they don't stick to your mind you can stick them on to the place you visit often; that will be the refrigerator for some, the toilet door for others, and the mirror for the vain ones.

I've always felt I must write a book off the back of some powerful quotes that have motivated me to higher heights; so here it is: A book guaranteed to inspire you to action; enable you to succeed personally and professionally and at the same time stimulate your grey matter and reading palette. This book contains many stories; real life and imagined. Why so many stories? Because long after the lessons are forgotten, the stories will remain.

You don't put your valuables within easy reach of children. Similarly life puts valuable things on higher levels, so you can reach them by the books you stand upon. Success is not what you achieve, it's what you attract by the person you have become; the person you become through reading, learning, self-development and personal growth.

As you read, make notes about the actions you will take and underline and highlight everything that resonates with you. Then review those notes and underlined sections again and again. Repetition is the key to real learning. As you reread these portions, you'll be reminding yourself of what you need to do to get from where you are to where you desire to be. It takes repetitive contact with a new idea before it becomes a part of your thinking and way of life. Authentic learning actually occurs only when you assimilate and apply the new information, i.e. when there is a change in your behaviour.

This book is based on the wisdom, teachings and quotes of men and women like Jim Rohn, John Maxwell, Terry Savelle Foy, Keith Moore, Myles Monroe, David Oyedepo, Sam Adeyemi, Joyce Myer, Gloria Copeland, Nicky Gumbel, Steve Harvey, John Mason, Paul Enenche, Brian Tracy, Rick Warren, Oprah Winfrey, David Oyedepo Jnr., Les Brown and a bevy of sages and leaders through the ages. These wise men and women have been my mentors from far and near.

This book takes a stellar quote, expounds it, breaks it down to simple thoughts so you can use it to challenge the status quo and blow the cap off your cap-ability!

Don't let the status quo put a limit on your ability: No more limits, blow the cap off! Be unstoppable!

1. Action! Action!

The secret of getting started is breaking your complex everyday tasks into small manageable tasks and then starting with the first one. (Mark Twain)

On a cold December evening, after a tiring day working as a department store seamstress, a young lady stepped on to the Cleveland Avenue bus for the ride home. She found a seat on the fifth row and rested her weary legs. This should be a relaxing journey home. It turned out not to be. As the bus filled up, Montgomery bus driver James Blake ordered the lady and three others on the fifth row to relinquish their seats and move to the back of the bus. This was 1955, Montgomery, Alabama USA. In Montgomery, Alabama, segregation was rife, the whites sat on the front rows of the bus and the coloured sat from the fifth row onwards. When a bus became full, coloured passengers were asked to give-up their seats to white passengers. At the demand of the driver, three riders complied. The lady Rosa Parks did not. The following is an excerpt of what happened:

'Are you going to stand up?' the driver demanded. Rosa Parks looked straight at him and said:

'No.' Flustered, and not quite sure what to do, Blake retorted,

'Well, I'm going to have you arrested.' And Parks, still sitting next to the window, replied softly,

'You may do that.'

She was arrested and jailed and fined $10.

Civil rights activists organized a one-day bus boycott on the day of her trial. With its success, they founded the Montgomery Improvement Association (MIA), and began a citywide bus boycott, led by a new local minister, Dr Martin Luther King, Jr. The boycott lasted 381 days. Many African-American citizens made sacrifices of time and energy to walk to work and other destinations. As they comprised the majority of bus passengers, the boycott greatly reduced the profits the bus company earned. Eventually on November 23, 1956, the United States Supreme Court ruled in favour of the MIA. Bus segregation was declared unconstitutional. The boycott was important for mobilising people in the civil rights movement both in the Deep South and on a nationwide basis across the United States. What seemed like a small act by a quiet, unassuming woman who just wanted to sit down and relax after a long day of work triggered and inspired a year-long boycott action of Montgomery's bus system by many others. The boycott led to the rise of the civil rights movement and this chain of events changed the United States. On a cold winter day, somewhere in the universe, a gear in the machinery shifted; action, decisive action, saved the day[1].

The test of a person lies in action. Knowledge does not lead to success, application of knowledge (i.e. action) does! Action is the real measure of intelligence. The litmus test for wisdom is action. Action is the proper fruit of knowledge. One right action is more valuable than a thousand good intentions. Faith without corresponding works is like gold within the earth - it is of very little value until it's mined. It is not enough to know that you know. It's more important to *show* that you know.

The key required to achieve your goal in life is: action, action, action, yes massive action! Success comes as a result of an accumulation of actions performed by you every single day that will put you one step closer to achieving your overall goal.

Have you heard the popular riddle about five friendly frogs sitting on a log? Four of the five decided to jump off into the pond below. How many are left? Still five. The moral: there's a lot of difference between deciding and actually doing. Good intentions are not enough, so strike a course and begin — and begin again, if necessary. Your true convictions are seen not in the words you speak, but in the actions you take. Actions are always the true measure of your beliefs.

What great accomplishments we'd have in the world if everybody had done what they intended to do! (Frank Clark - American politician)

The secret of getting ahead is getting started. Prolonged idleness paralyses initiative; to the hesitant mind everything is impossible because it seems so. What you can do now is the only influence you have over your future. Everything great begins with something insignificant. Don't be afraid to take small steps. Many times; the impossible is simply the untried. Take the steps that get you beyond the starting point. Soon you'll get to a point of no return. Don't let what you can't do stop you from what you can do. So don't just sit there, get moving, put legs to those dreams.

Even if you're on the right track, you will get run over if you just sit there. (Will Roger)

A good battle plan that you act on today can be better than a perfect one tomorrow. (General George S. Patton)

The courage to begin is the same courage it takes to succeed. Winning starts with beginning. The beginning is a crucial part of any endeavour, without beginning there can be no end-result. Worse than a quitter is anyone who is afraid to begin! In my opinion, 80% of success is showing up and starting. You will be disappointed if you fail, but you are doomed if you don't try. To win - you must begin! Dare to begin. No endeavour is worse than that which is not attempted.

Life is 10% of what happens to you, and it's 90% what you do about it. (Steve Harvey)

Do every day all that can be done that day. You cannot foresee the result of even the most trivial act; you do not know the workings of all the forces that have been set moving in your behalf. Much may be depending on your doing some simple act; it may be the very thing which is to open the door of opportunity to very great possibilities. You can never know all the combinations which supreme intelligence is making for you in the realm of the unseen or natural. Your neglect or failure to do some small thing may cause a long delay in getting what you want.

A week of neglect could cost you a year of regret. (Jim Rohn)

You actually feel a sense of relief when you do what you should do, instead of carrying around the stress of what you ought to do but have not done! Not doing what you ought to do in a timely manner is like a sword of Damocles hanging over your head, and this is what causes stress.

If you persist you will win - you may never know what results will come from your action, but if you do nothing there will be no results. No one ever stumbles on to something big while sitting down. Sitting still and wishing makes no person great. You don't have to be great to start, but you have to start to be great. You earn respect only by action; inaction earns disrespect. You will be exactly the same today as in five years' time except for three things: the company you keep or associate with, the books you read and the actions you take.

The most difficult thing is to act, the rest is merely tenacity. (Amelia Earhart)

According to Jesus it is more blessed to be a doer of the word of God than being a relative (mother, sister or brother) of Jesus. It is by action that we build a solid foundation for success. The fact is that if you don't act, you don't really believe it. The longer we take to act on a good or divine direction, the more unclear it becomes. 'Well done' is a better commendation than 'well said'. So take action now!

Timely action, immediate action - action is king! Don't fail to act. Think, plan, reflect, don't be impulsive, but then jump! Act immediately. Never waste time planning, analysing and over thinking on small straightforward ideas. It's smarter to spend more time on decisions and ideas that are irreversible and less time on those that reversible. Avoid the paralysis of analysis.

The best helping hand you will ever find is at the end of your own arm. (Swedish proverb)

Don't wait for your ship to come in: swim to meet it! (Gary Wood)

Action not only helps us achieve our objectives speedily, but it also helps us learn faster by reinforcing the knowledge we've acquired. It is said that we usually remember only 20% of what we read, 30% of what we hear, 40% of what we see, 50% of what we say but 60 %

of what we do. This shows the most effective way to learn or imbibe new information or material is to take relevant action on it. In my postgraduate and undergraduate studies, some twenty-five to thirty years ago, I can still remember quite clearly experiments carried out in the science laboratory, though I have long forgotten the lectures that preceded them. Action reinforces learning. And when we combine hearing, seeing, saying and doing we remember a whopping 90%! The best way to learn is through ACTION! We learn by doing because learning is an active process. Only knowledge that is used or acted upon sticks to your mind.

When you start taking action steps, your dreams become more visible. Things start happening, momentum builds, opportunities reveal themselves and relationships are formed to help bring about your dreams. As you initiate action, new ideas will come to life. It's like a baby beginning to walk. She's shaky at first, but eventually those baby-steps become a steady stride and soon enough the baby begins to run. As this happens a whole new vista opens up, and she sees the world from a totally different vantage point.

No one goes forward sitting down. (Dr David Oyedepo)

It is said if you don't act within twenty-four hours of the inspiration to do something chances are that you never will. You have to act on whatever is stirring in you today. Your entire destiny can change today because you acted on an idea. According to John Maxwell, most people are subject to 'the law of diminishing intent' which states: the longer you wait to do something you should do now, the greater odds that you will never actually do it. The law of diminishing intent sets in if you don't act straight away. When the emotion is hot and the idea and passion are fresh capture the moment by making yourself do it pronto!

Life can be compared with a do-it-yourself project. You get your life package flat-packed, but you have to open the box, get the parts out and assemble the parts by faith, action and imagination. Action reveals faith, faith without corresponding action is useless.

In Hebrew the word for faith is emunah, which is less about knowing and more about doing. Emunah literally means to take firm action. The Hebrew word for artisan is 'uman' — because artisans have practised their craft repeatedly until it becomes natural. So to have faith is to act. It's kind of like a staircase: you may intellectually know the stairs go up to the next level, but until you climb the stairs you won't experience the next level. What you do is more important than what you know.

All you can do is all you can do, and all you can do is enough, just make sure you do *all* you can do. Take action now before you feel like it. Do you want to jump, or do you want life to push you? I say jump and jump now!

Jump, then grow wings on the way down. (Jack Canfield)

2. Attitude

Some people freeze in the winter; others ski! (Unknown)

Nick is a remarkable man. Those who have met him are always inspired and challenged by his life. Nick was born without arms or legs, yet he writes, 'I am truly blessed. I am ridiculously happy.' Many times as a child he prayed for arms and legs. He did not get arms and legs, yet he writes, 'God used me to reach people in countless schools, churches, prisons, orphanages, hospitals, stadiums and meeting halls. Even better, I've hugged thousands of people in face-to-face encounters that allow me to tell them how very precious they are ... God took my unusual body and invested me with the ability to uplift hearts and encourage spirits.'[2]

What a great outlook! It's not the cards you've been dealt in life that determine the outcome of your life, it's your attitude to it.

Jim Rohn tells the story of two salesmen: they look out of the window and it's pouring. One says, 'With weather like this they can't expect you to go out and make sales calls.' The other says, 'With weather like this I must go out and make sales calls because everyone will be at home, especially the salesmen.'

Psychologists tell us that it is the way we choose to interpret what happens in our lives, more than the actual circumstances and experiences, that determines our destiny. Bitter or better — we get to decide! Our attitude is the determinant of our outcome. It is not our position but our disposition that makes us happy! Our attitude determines our altitude. When we have the right attitude every experience - positive and negative becomes an opportunity for progress. When facing a huge, Goliath-sized challenge in life there are two possible attitudes you can adopt: one is to say, 'It's so big, there's nothing I can do.' The other is to say, 'It's so big, I can't miss!'

Whether you are a success or a failure in life has little to do with your circumstances; it has much more to do with your attitude. When you change your attitude regarding a problem, you open up many opportunities for growth and solutions to the problem.

Whether you think you can. Or think you can't. You are right. (Henry Ford)

Between you and anything great will be giants. You cannot bring about change without confrontation. If you like things easy you will have difficulties. If you are not intimidated by problems you will succeed. Circumstances are the rulers of the weak; but they are the instruments of the wise. Therefore it's not what happens to you in life that determines the outcome or quality of your life, it's what you do about it.

What you do in trouble can make you bitter or better. It all depends on your attitude. Why don't you decide to turn your trouble into a classroom and learn some valuable lessons? Someone once said, a bad attitude is like a flat tyre: if you don't change it, you're not going anywhere.

Any fact facing us is not as important as our attitude towards it, for that (our attitude) is what determines our success or failure. (Norman V. Peale)

And we have complete control over our own attitude. We are the ones who decide how we feel, how we look at things, how we react. (Catherine Pulsifer)

3. Belief (self-belief)

Believe you can and you're halfway there. (Theodore Roosevelt)

'The Eagle has landed,' said Neil Armstrong. President Nixon, watching the events on television, described it as 'one of the greatest moments of our time'. The Pope greeted the news by exclaiming, 'Glory to God in the highest and peace on earth to men of good will!' At 3:56 am on 20 July 1969, Neil Armstrong stepped off the ladder from the Eagle and on to the moon's surface. 'That's one small step for a man, one giant leap for mankind,' he said, as he became the first man to walk on the moon. Due to the recent invention of television, this remarkable event was the first of such historic significance to be seen so widely and known so immediately. The whole world watched with awe and amazement. They believed they could put a man on the moon and they did.

Until Roger Bannister came on the scene in 1954, some experts said it was physically impossible to break the four-minute mile. The thinking was, if it hasn't been done before, it's because it can't be done. But Bannister not only did it, he started a new trend. History continues to prove that records are made to be broken.

One of the main weaknesses of humankind is the average person's familiarity with the word 'impossible'. We know all the rules which will not work. We know all the things which cannot be done. Success comes to those who become success-conscious. Failure comes to those who indifferently allow themselves to become failure-conscious.[3] You become what you believe. Whatever you attach consistently to the words ' I am,' you'll become. Believe and act as if it were impossible to fail.

Have you ever seen trained fleas in a jar? You don't need a lid to keep them in. That's because when the trainer first places them in the jar, he puts the lid on it, and the fleas jump up and down frantically hitting their heads against it. Finally, after a lot of headaches, they stop jumping and settle in to enjoy their newfound comfort. Now when the lid is removed the fleas are held captive by a mindset that says, ' So high and no higher.' What a picture!

Self-Belief

No successful person ever became wealthy without the firm conviction that he or she would succeed one day. Some people of incredible talent have fallen by the wayside, while others with less talent, but with a firm belief in their own abilities, succeed beyond their wildest dreams. The key is knowing how to get the most out of what we have been given at birth. Why is it that many first-class people fail in life? They do extremely well in school, get a degree or two, then fall into some crack and disappear - you hear nothing more about them. Others muddle through school with average or less than average grades but end up building spectacular careers and making a fortune.

Often being handed a pile of money, being born with a silver spoon in your mouth as they say, kills all the qualities you need to succeed in the real world. Many successful people had to struggle and overcome terrific obstacles, but it was precisely because they had to struggle so hard that they were able to mould their talent, their financial astuteness, into a razor sharp instrument that has served them more than someone who simply inherited a million bucks at birth. If someone gave you a million pounds would that make you a success? Would you be able to develop that capital into something of your own, make it grow? Or would you just sit on it, watch it lose value through inflation, live off the interest you could get from someone else, someone who would really be doing something with it? Your talent is like a million dollars. It just fell into your lap. Now you have to manage it, make it grow and prosper.

Belief is the thermostat that regulates what we accomplish in life. A person is a product of his own thought. Believe Big. Adjust your thermostat forward. Launch your success offensive with honest sincere belief that you can succeed. Believe big and grow big.

Success is determined not so much by the size of one's brain as it is by the size of one's thinking. Poor thinking habits keeps more people poor than poor working habits. [4]

Many things appear hard until they have been achieved. Many things are scary until they are understood. (Ola-Vincent Odulele)

Many times the impossible is often the un-dared small opportunity. Every great idea is impossible from where you are starting today - but small baby-steps add up rapidly - so take that step today! Nothing is impossible. Everything you need to flourish is in you already. Trust the talents and gifts you've been blessed with and use them to propel you forward.

Do what you can, with what you have, where you are. (Theodore Roosevelt)

Develop your gifts as you go along, grow as an individual and take hold of every opportunity to use your gift/talent, do it scared if you have to, but just do it! You don't have to be the smartest to succeed. You just have to be focused, determined, motivated, persistent and have tons of self-belief.

Self-esteem is the single most significant key to a person's behaviour. No factor is more important in people's psychological development and motivation than the value judgements they make about themselves. Every aspect of my life is impacted by the way I see myself. A person who believes they are worthless won't add value to themselves. You cannot outperform your self-image. People are never able to outperform their self-image. The value we place on ourselves is usually the value others place on us. If you place a small value on yourself, don't expect someone else to put a higher value on you; rest assured nobody will raise the price. If you want to become the person you have the potential to be, you must believe you can! It is hard to feel bad about yourself when you're adding value to others. We tend to get in life what we are willing to tolerate, if we allow others to disrespect us, we get disrespected; if we tolerate abuse we get abused.

The easiest thing to be is you! The most difficult thing to be is what someone else wants you to be. Be the best of yourself!

Self-worth and net worth are not the same! Your value in life is not determined by your valuables. The most valuable things in life are not things!

4. Books / reading

You are the same today as you'll be in five years except for two things: the books you read and the people you meet. (Charlie 'Tremendous' Jones)

Jack Canfield, the author of *Chicken Soup for the Soul*, said he had read over 3000 books by reading a small daily 'dose' every day. He is in the Guinness Book of World Records for the most number-one books on the Best Seller's List at the same time. The daily habit of reading transformed the life of Terri Savelle from having no goals, no vision, no money. Less than ten years later, she is an author of many books, international speaking engagements, a YouTube channel with millions of viewers, money in the bank, lovely home and much more. She is not alone; many thousands have had their lives transformed by the simple habit of reading great books.

The book you don't read won't help. (Jim Rohn)

Brian Tracy once said, if you read 30-60 minutes a day, five days a week, you will read on average a book in a week. That will translate to about thirty to fifty books a year. If you read about fifty books a year on a subject, you will get the equivalent of a PhD in that field in about a year. You can get the equivalent of a million pound idea just from a book but you never know which book will give you the insight unless you read widely. All you have to do is keep reading lots of material and ever so often, one observation will jump off the page and your whole life will change. One idea from a book combined with a thought in your mind plus the right opportunity can totally transform your life.

Over a decade ago, while holidaying abroad, I woke up one morning with this thought ringing in my head: 'books are ladders ... books are ladders'. As I pondered on this phrase I realised the acuity of these words. Books provide us with the insight and inspiration we need to climb swiftly in order to reach our goals in life. A good book will draw out from within you courage and perception that you never knew you possessed. Books are ladders for advancement to greatness.

If we say we want to be great leaders, according to Jim Rohn, the first thing we must do is to check our library. Why? Because what we read pours massive ingredients into our mental factory and the fabric of our life is built on those ingredients.

It doesn't matter how huge a door is: if you have the right key, the door will open. The habit of reading is the key that will open many doors. Books are idea containers, books are liberators. Countries ruled by oppressors try to prevent people from reading or monitor what people can read. You maintain oppression by maintaining ignorance. Knowledge is light. Therefore if you want to keep people in darkness, keep knowledge away from them; keep books away from them; in other words keep them ignorant. The saying: if you want to keep something away from a fool, hide it in a book, comes to mind.

Research shows that mental activity boosts resistance to dementia. Study after study has found that older people who were mentally engaged doing things like reading and writing, or taking part in hobbies or games, stayed mentally sharper and were less at risk of Alzheimer's than those who were not. While keeping your mind active generally seemed to go together with greater mental sharpness, this does not apply to watching television. Watching television over long periods tends to sap mental energies. Studies show that watching television reduces arousal while reading boosts arousal and this arousal of the brain protects it. Other brain-arousing and -protecting activities include mentally demanding jobs (not excessively stressful), education and maintaining a social network. Many hundreds of studies have shown that mice and rats which are kept in cages with a variety of objects to explore show much better memory and cognitive abilities than those kept in standard, relatively austere environment. What's more, they also grow extra brain cells! When we face challenges, including mental challenges, our brains release a chemical called noradrenaline to help sharpen our perception and decision-making process.

Noradrenaline is a brain-enhancing disease-combating chemical that is released in tiny doses hundreds of millions of times over a lifetime. This 'wonder drug' is produced naturally in our brains as a result of environmental factors like mental stimulation or challenge, a novel situation, social interactions and memories retrieved (e.g. through studying for exams).   Brain connections are strengthened and brain networks grow as a result of the beneficial effects of millions of mini-infusions of noradrenaline triggered by mental stimulation or challenge. If mental challenge builds brains through noradrenaline release, then anything that diminishes that challenge (e.g. television) could do the opposite.[5]

Reading is life-transforming and can help us achieve our full potential and lead a richer life. Reading can transform your life because the more you read, the more you know. The more you read, the more you can imagine. The more you read, the better you understand other people and this can help enhance your relationships and consequently improve your life.

When the message of a book is rightly phrased, it could pass your defences, enter your heart and explode silently and effectively within your mind and change you from inside out. The Bible is generally accepted by Christians as God's word to humankind. That being the case, one could say God chose to communicate his thoughts to humanity through a book. Millions are known to have been greatly inspired and transformed by it.

There are a few simple habits you can cultivate in life that really have a potential to change your life; reading good books is one of such habits. Reading has such a capacity to transform a life; it has the ability to unlock a wealth of treasure and greatness from within an individual. Through reading you can rub minds with the greatest thinkers of all time. You can share in the wisdom of the greatest minds that ever walked the surface of the earth simply by reading their books. Through reading you access the knowledge and wealth of wisdom of the author's mind. You also become a partaker of the rapturous moments of inspiration enjoyed by the writer. You can even experience and enjoy 'divine' moments of insight akin to a spiritual experience, simply by reading a book.

David Oyedepo Jnr. once commented that the value of books is that you benefit from the experiences of others and gain access to their insight without having to go through the process they passed through. Others have made the discoveries and you can benefit from it just by reading their books. What has taken others years to discover can become yours in a few hours of reading. These individuals could be your contemporaries or those who have gone before you including individuals from previous generations.

Books are magical, people can find a new world through the power of the written word. Books have a certain kind of enchantment about them; they are able to catapult you to a different world in the twinkling of an eye. Between the covers of a book exists a sort of paradise. All you have to do is add a little ingredient called imagination and you can feel the magic everywhere. You don't have to be a child to enjoy the thrill of reading; you need only the imagination and enthusiasm of youth and you're halfway there.

The ability to read is an awesome gift, enabling you not just to perform tasks like reading the instructions for the use of new electrical equipment, or reading the signs to where you're going or reading the label on a can of food in the supermarket, but so you can enjoy life through reading jokes, letters, prose, poetry etc.

I love reading, and paradise for me is settling down in front of the fireplace on a cold winter evening (with a sweet snack and a hot cup of decaffeinated green tea) to read a good book. I love to suck out the life and marrow from a good book like a dog with a juicy bone. There is nothing that I enjoy more than gleaning wisdom from writings of wise men and women. For me this is like a conference of great minds being ignited and exploding in revelation. Or it could just be getting captivated in a fascinating story; riding the waves, feeling the breeze, and enjoying the thrill of a good adventure novel.

Reading is one of the most enjoyable activities in life, but in case you have not discovered the joys of reading, this chapter shares some benefits of reading. Reading novels, short stories, poems, and plays provide good quality lasting entertainment. As you read through the pages you may well find that a kind of peaceful paradise exists between the covers of books.

Some people never pick up a book to read after their formal education; what a waste! I heard that if you put your arm in a sling for six months without using it; it will atrophy. What do you think will happen to your brain if you don't read challenging, thought-provoking or stimulating books in a year?

You cannot think more deeply than your vocabulary will allow you to. (Robert Niederholer)

Reading can make you a more interesting individual. Those who are well-read are likely to be quite knowledgeable and interesting. The book-knowledge just seeps from them. Even if they don't always know all the details, they can often converse on some of the most interesting literary topics! It's true! If you've read a great deal, you'll have a conversation piece on many topics wherever you find yourself. Another benefit of reading which is probably quite obvious is that you become a better scholar or writer when you read. It is a fact that reading more will improve your writing skills and develop your knowledge. In addition, reading excellent books improves your vocabulary by adding to the 'word-bank' in your brain and deepens your thinking.

A word is a condensed thought, therefore the more words you know the better you can think because you have more tools to think with. With more words you can think with greater subtlety. You can analyse better and make better decisions. According to Brian Tracy, the more words you know, the smarter you become. This is because every brain cell is connected with 22,000 other brain cells. So as you learn more words you connect those with other words which enable you to see things, sense things, develop your intuition to a higher level and this makes you more successful. When you read you also learn new concepts and ideas that you might not have previously known before.

Reading is one of the soundest investments you can make in yourself. Soak-up-facts method of education is not what we are talking about. Real education is that which develops and cultivates the mind. Anything which improves thinking ability is good education. The word educate is said to be derived from the Latin word 'educo' meaning to educe, to draw out, to develop from within. An educated man is therefore not one who has an abundance of knowledge, but one who has developed the faculties of his mind that he may acquire anything he wants, without violating the rights of others. An educated man is one who knows what information he needs, where to get that knowledge when he needs it, and how to organise and utilise this knowledge to accomplish his objectives.[6]

If you want to travel but can't afford the ticket, through reading you can imagine walking along a sandy and sunny seashore, skiing down snowy mountain slopes, sleeping in a field of flowers, adventuring in an African Safari. Your holiday destinations are quite frankly practically limitless.

Buy truth – don't sell it for love or money; buy wisdom, buy education, buy insight. (Pr 23:23 MSG).

There is no mountain anywhere, every man's ignorance is his mountain. (Dr David Oyedepo)

We like to spend money on comfort or entertainment, but it is wiser to invest in our personal growth and character. God wants us to take some of our money and invest it in ourselves – in personal and spiritual improvement. He wants you to develop skills and educate yourself so that you can become the kind of person he has designed you to be. Every time you buy a book or a CD that helps you grow, you've invested in yourself. Investment in your personal growth is using your money the right way and it's an investment that yields a bountiful return. There are many skills you can acquire through reading. For example, if you want to be an articulate person or a speaker, develop the habit of reading daily for about thirty minutes and writing for at least twenty minutes.

The difference between your life today and your life in the next few years will depend upon the decisions you make, the actions you take and the people you associate with personally or through reading their books or listening to their audio messages. I've been privileged to rub minds with the greatest thinkers and wealthiest people in the world - not personally, but by reading their books.

If you are not committed to mental work, you will do menial work - you choose!

Fantastic book quotes

Books are the perfect entertainment: no commercials, no batteries, hours of enjoyment for each dollar spent. What I wonder is why everybody doesn't carry a book around for those inevitable dead spots in life. (Stephen King)

When I read great literature, great drama, speeches, or sermons, I feel that the human mind has not achieved anything greater than the ability to share feelings and thoughts through language. (James Earl Jones)

No entertainment is so cheap as reading, nor any pleasure so lasting. (Mary Wortley Montagu)

At the end of the day a man's most valuable possessions are his books and journals which contain not just chronicles of the days lived but his greatest insights and deepest thoughts plus his reflections upon the collected books and upon his life. (Andrew Eyeoyibo)

A book is a mirror: if an ass peers into it, you can't expect an apostle to look out. (G. C. Lichtenberg)

The man who does not read good books has no advantage over the man who can't read them. (Mark Twain)

A real book is not one that we read, but one that reads us. (W. H. Auden)

Reading is a basic tool in the living of a good life. (Mortimer Adler)

When I am dead, I hope it may be said: 'His sins were scarlet, but his books were read.' (Hilaire Belloc)

I suggest that the only books that influence us are those for which we are ready and which have gone a little further down our particular path than we have gone ourselves. (E. M. Forster)

A reader today; a leader tomorrow. (W. Fusselman)

5. Boundaries

A life without boundaries is like a house without walls - nobody feels safe.
(Unknown)

I recently read a story of a football (soccer) match that was arranged for twenty-two young boys. After waiting for what seemed like ages, the referee still did not show up. The boys could wait no longer, so one of the parents was asked to act as referee in order to avoid the huge emotional meltdown that would result from disappointing twenty-two energetic youngsters. The substitute referee was more or less press-ganged into the role. He had no whistle, nor did he make any boundary markings for the limits of the pitch and according to him, he did not even know the rules of the game nearly as well as some of the boys. The game soon descended into complete chaos. Some shouted that the ball was in. Others said that it was out. The pseudo-referee wasn't at all sure what was in or out, so he let things run. Then the fouls started. Some cried, 'Foul.' Others said, 'No foul.' The referee didn't know who was right. So he let them play on. Then the kids began to get hurt. By the time the real referee arrived, there were three boys lying injured on the ground and all the rest were shouting at the substitute referee! However, the moment the referee arrived, he blew his whistle, arranged the teams, told them where the boundaries were and had them under complete control. The boys then enjoyed a great game of football.

Were the boys freer without the rules, or were they in fact less free? Without any effective authority, chaos was the result. Although they could do exactly what they wanted, the game ended in mayhem and consequently the result was confusion and the kids got hurt. The boys undoubtedly preferred that the game was played according to the rules. The boundary lines allowed the boys the freedom to enjoy the game. The rules of football did not diminish the pleasure of the game but rather enhanced it and at the same time kept the children safe.[7]

Boundaries are not designed to take away the fun in life, but they are designed to enable the 'game' of life to be enjoyed to the full without hurting or trampling on the rights of others.

God's rules are his boundaries for life, given out of his love for us. His boundaries are not designed to restrict our freedom but rather to give us freedom. Like the rules of football, they do not stop the enjoyment of the game. Rather, they enable the game of life to be enjoyed to the full and to minimise the chaos and mayhem that comes with a life without boundaries.

The ten commandments were given not to restrict our freedom but rather to safeguard it.

God loves you. He does not want you to get hurt and mess up your life and the lives of other people. That is why he gives you his instruction manual (the Bible) and warns of the dangers of living outside of his loving boundaries. God's boundaries are intended to bring blessing.

A boundary is a line which marks the limits of an area. Boundaries can also be guidelines, rules or limits that a person creates to identify for themselves what are reasonable, safe and permissible ways for other people to behave around them. Boundaries must be set in relationships and indeed in every area of our lives. Don't ask the question: 'How close can I get to the fire without burning?' Instead, we should be asking, 'How do I stay as far away from the fire as I can?'

Children especially need boundaries to flourish in life. Without boundaries and discipline, children are subjected to a life of heartache: the support structure required for them to thrive is missing. If you don't set boundaries for your children because you're afraid they won't like you for enforcing discipline or you're afraid of confrontation, then you're setting them up for a life of pain and regret. The stress of enduring a tantrum now and enforcing boundaries is nothing compared to the shame and pain of regret they (and you) will have to face when they become adults and they're stopped by the police for not keeping to the safe boundaries of speed limits, evicted by a landlord because they're in arrears or contacted by the bank for defaulting on a loan due to not keeping to their spending limits. Throwing a tantrum at that point in their lives won't get them off the hook! Enforce the boundaries and discipline now, please think of their future and maybe yours too!

6. Challenges / adversity

When suffering knocks at your door and you say there is no seat for him, he tells you not to worry because he has brought his own stool. (Chinue Achebe)

Circumstance does not make the man; it reveals him to himself. (James Allen)

Dr G. Campbell Morgan tells of a man whose shop burned to the ground in the Great Chicago Fire of 1871. Next morning he arrived at work carrying a table which he set up amid the charred ruins. On it he placed a sign that read, 'Everything lost except wife, children, and hope. Business as usual tomorrow morning.'

A seedling tree has to fight its way up through rocks to get to sunlight and air, then wrestle with storms and frost to survive. You can be sure of one thing: its root system will be strong and its timber resilient. Nature itself teaches us that it's impossible to succeed without going through adversity.

In a sense, this life is a series of problem-solving exercises. We will never be without problems in this life. If you cannot learn to thrive in the midst of all the challenges in which you find yourself, you will never find contentment.

Nearly all men can stand adversity, but if you want to test a man's character, give him power. (Abraham Lincoln)

You can do well only under either of two conditions: desperation or inspiration. Your setback is a setup. Eagles use storms to reach a higher altitude. You will never be the person you can be if pressure, tension and discipline are taken out of your life. Show me someone who has done something worthwhile and I'll show you someone who has overcome adversity. Difficulties always present opportunities to learn and grow. Always treat and see difficulties as a growth opportunity. Facing adversity or difficulties is inevitable, learning from it is optional. Consistent victories over your problems are important steps on your stairway to success. Difficulties give birth to opportunity and every opportunity, every difficulty, has an opportunity.

Your mind is the sharpest when faced with hard times. Threat of death, failure, defeat makes strong people a lot more aware of their lives and brings out deep wisdom, direction or innovation. On the other hand such threats make weak people cave in and go under.

Goliath was the means to announce David - therefore every adversity can be a means to reveal you to your world. Your adversity, if handled well can really be a great opportunity to announce your greatness. A faith that cannot be shaken comes only from a faith that has been so severely shaken that it is now sure, certain and steadfast. Only melted gold can be used for minting. Only crushed roses can bring out fragrance.

The story is told of some bumble-bees taken to space: they were allowed to fly for several days in space without the resistance of gravity, they did this for several days but on the fourth day they all dropped down dead. What happened? Bees are not designed to fly without resistance! We grow when there is resistance and even in adversity if we have the right attitude.

The ultimate measure of a person is not where they stand in moments of convenience, but where they stand in moments of challenge, moments of great crisis and controversy. (Martin Luther King)

When we are hit by adversity, we may feel as if we belong to the brotherhood (or sisterhood) of the bedraggled, beat-up and burnt-out. You may feel like a charred log in a fireplace, totally drained of energy, and unable to light a fire in yourself. Your personal inner resources appear to be exhausted. Sometimes when you're in a dark place you think you've been buried, but actually you've been planted. And if you've been planted, then the next stage in life will be a period of personal growth for you. That's because God uses the tough times of life to stretch us, and to draw new life out of us … so we can reach our full potential.

We must understand that life-challenges don't make us who we are: they reveal who we are. We can take what is revealed through our troubles or challenges and use that as an opportunity to point us in a new direction to bring about necessary change in our lives. And if we trust in God, the challenge will strengthen our faith.

Your problem is your promotion. The way you look at any obstacle in your life makes all the difference. No obstacle will ever leave you the way it found you. You will be better, or you will be worse (or bitter). Every obstacle has a limited life-span. Obstacles subdue mediocre people, but help great leaders emerge.

Sweet are the uses of adversity. (William Shakespeare)

If there is a silver lining to bad times, it is this: when facing severe challenges your mind is normally at its sharpest. (John Osborn)

Mountaintops inspire us, but valleys mature us. (Nicky Gumbel)

Humans seldom have created anything of lasting value unless they were tried or hurting (John Osborn)

It is the tests that create credibility. (Myles Munroe)

Humorist Erma Bombeck once said, 'If life is a bowl of cherries then what am I doing in the pits.' Life is not always a bowl of cherries, sometimes it's the pits. You're going to encounter a few pit-stops on the journey to your dream, and what you do when you are in the pit can determine whether it is just a pit-stop or a pit-stay.

In 1978 a young man ran into trouble. He was working at a local hardware store and he got fired from his job. Getting fired is the pits, but instead of staying in that pit, he decided that he would use the situation as an opportunity to start his own business. He found a business partner and together they dreamed of opening a hardware store. They opened their first store in 1979, and today they have over 2000 stores worldwide. The name of that young man was Bernard Marcus and the name of the store that opened was the Home Depot.[8]

In one 'Peanuts' comic, Linus says, 'You know Charlie Brown, they say we learn more from losing than from winning.' Charlie Brown responds, 'Then that must make me the smartest person in the world.'

Adversity can be downright discouraging and yet some of the most important lessons that we need to learn in life can only be learned from adversity. The Bible says in Hebrews 5:8 that Jesus himself 'learned obedience through the things that He suffered.' This amazing verse tells us that some things can be learned only through suffering. It's not that you want to suffer, or seek to suffer, but there are some things that you can learn only through adversity.

We often stare at our giant-sized problems instead of at our God. Our adversity can turn out to be our advantage. Problems and trials don't automatically produce what God intends - some people become bitter, rather than better and never grow up. When facing trials or trouble, don't give up, grow up!

Kintsugi is a Japanese art-form in which broken ceramics are carefully mended by artisans with a lacquer resin mixed with powdered gold, silver or platinum. The repairs are visible — yet somehow beautiful. Kintsugi means 'golden joinery' in Japanese. They repair to such a point that its brokenness becomes part of the beautiful history. The brokenness is not disguised but enhanced, so that the past has more beauty than it did before. In the same way, God takes our brokenness, and preciously repairs it with strength and beauty. We are Kintsugi – a golden repair.

Ernest Hemingway said, 'The world breaks everyone and afterward many are strong at the broken places.' All of us can identify with that statement. The truth is that life throws a lot of curves at us that can break us. But, like broken bones that heal stronger than before and scar tissue that is stronger than skin, God can bring strength out of brokenness.

I read a fictional story about two friends who were baseball fanatics. They loved the game. One day they were talking about heaven and they wondered if there would be baseball in heaven. So they hatched a plan. Whoever died first would come back to earth and tell the other if there was baseball in heaven. One day, one of the men died, and true to his word he returned in the middle of the night and woke up his friend and said, 'I've got some good news and I've got some bad news. The good news is, there is baseball in heaven. The bad news is, you're pitching tomorrow.'

The journey to your dream will be like a breakthrough (good news) and challenge (bad news): a rollercoaster. There will be ebbs and flows, ups and downs, prosperous seasons and lean seasons.

On the journey to your dream you are going to run into problems; it's inevitable. People who achieve their dreams are people who see more than just the problem, they see solutions to the problem and they think of creative ways to solve problems. In fact, many of the great inventions of the world came as a solution to a problem.

One day, a salesman was closing a deal. He handed his pen to the customer to sign on the dotted line. When the pen didn't work, he was so frustrated that he decided to invent a pen that would write every time he needed it. Thus, the Waterman pen, one of the finest pens, was conceived.

Every problem is really an opportunity to come up with a solution. Problems are inevitable on the journey to your dream. Expect them.

What is your first port of call when conflict comes in your life? If you make prayer your default mode, adversity and attacks can actually draw you closer to God. Joyce Meyer wrote 'When trouble comes do you run to the phone or rather 'run to the throne'? [9]

Al Davis, who owned the Oakland Raiders American football team, said: 'A great leader doesn't treat problems as special. He treats them as normal. If you're working, expect problems. If you're dealing with family, expect problems. If you're just minding your own business and trying to relax, expect problems. If everything goes according to plan, then be pleasantly surprised. If it doesn't, and you've planned accordingly, you won't get frustrated. A problem not anticipated is a problem. A problem anticipated is an opportunity.' This doesn't mean you should hope for problems it simply means you should be ready for them and always have contingency plans in place.

Challenges are what make life interesting and overcoming them is what makes life meaningful. (Joshua J Marine)

7. Change

If you keep on doing what you've always done, you will keep getting what you've always got. (Tony Robbins)

In the year 2000 a man wheedled his way into a meeting with John Antioco, the CEO of Blockbuster, and proposed a partnership to manage Blockbuster's fledgling online business. The CEO declined an offer to purchase the newer company for 50 million dollars. John laughed him out of the room, saying that he had millions of existing customers and thousands of successful retail stores. The other man was Reed Hastings, the CEO of Netflix. In 2018 Netflix turned out a profit of 15.8 Billion Dollars while Blockbuster filed for bankruptcy in 2010 exactly ten years after that meeting. The CEO of Blockbuster was so focussed on exploiting his current success, he could not see around the next corner. In that way his previous success became the enemy of his future success and ability to change and adapt to new trends and technology.

A similar scenario played out with the Blackberry and iphone. BlackBerry's global market share was around 50% in 2009 but collapsed to less than 3% by 2013. At its peak in 2008, the company that invented the smartphone had a stockmarket value of $55bn. By 2013 it was worth just $6bn. BlackBerry executives continued to believe the consumer research that nobody wanted Apple's iPhone with its 'many shortcomings'. They made no effort to improve their technology; failed to change and ended up going out of business.

Your life doesn't get better by chance, it gets better by change. (Jim Rohn)

At 211°F water is hot. At 212°F it boils. Boiling water produces steam, and steam can actually power a locomotive. Raising the temperature of water by merely one degree means the difference between something being extremely hot and something generating enough force to power a massive machine. One small change in your life could produce tremendous results.

According to Jim Rohn, nothing will change, unless you change. For things to change, you've got to change. To change my life, I need to change. You can have more than you have because you can become more than you are. Unless you change how you are, you'll always have what you've got.

When we are no longer able to change a situation, we are challenged to change ourselves. (Victor Frankl)

Change doesn't come easily, but unless you make a start it won't come at all. Minuscule changes in input can make macroscopic differences in output. Many people fail in life because they are unwilling to change. Correction and change always result in fruit. Anything worth having is worth working for. Change is worth the effort. When you begin to change, you'll discover a world of opportunity you never dreamed possible. If you resist change, you'll find yourself living far below your potential. Refusing to change has dire consequences. Here is the hard fact of life: if you keep doing what you've always done, your future will always look like your past.

Until your misery factor (disgust with your present location or condition) exceeds your fear (fear of change) you won't change.

You cannot change your destination overnight but you can change your direction. (Jim Rohn)

The difference between where we are and where we want to be is created by the changes we are willing to make in our lives. To change my life, I need to change. Change is profitable - I will be rewarded when I change. You cannot go back and make a brand new start, but you can start now and make a brand new ending. When you're at the bottom you change because of desperation; as you rise in the ranks, you change because of inspiration.

Human beings can alter the course of their lives by making the choice to change. Only human beings can do this. Geese can't do it, trees can't do it; only human beings can do it. Five years from now you will arrive, the question is where. Will you arrive at a well-designed, desirable destination or an undesirable destination? We go in the direction we face, we face the direction we design. Destination is determined by direction. A small change in direction daily can lead you to a great destination in five years' time. Little disciplines help you change destination. Little decisions made daily can really make a huge difference in destination. It's only a small change daily that leads to a new destination. It's a small journey to a new direction, e.g. an apple a day instead of a chocolate bar. You don't need a big revolution or a huge change: start with an apple a day. Just munch on that first apple and you start a new direction to a healthier you. Start going to bed a little earlier, start reading a chapter a day, start walking for thirty minutes a day. You cannot make an omelette without breaking eggs. Accomplishment automatically results in change. One change makes way for the next just start … Everyone can change.

The Grace to Change

John Newton (1725–1801) was a militant atheist, bully and blasphemer. He was a wild and angry young man. He was press-ganged into the navy at the age of eighteen where he broke the rules so recklessly that he was publicly flogged for desertion. He was hated and feared by his crewmates and himself became a slave-trader. When he was twenty-three, Newton's ship encountered a severe storm off the coast of Donegal and almost sank. As a result of this adversity, he called out to God in prayer as the ship filled with water and on that day, 10 March 1748, God rescued him. He began a new life. He started to pray and read the Bible. Eventually he became an abolitionist and joined William Wilberforce in the campaign to abolish the slave trade and became a leading light in that campaign. What a dramatic change! Everyone can change, there is no one beyond change; even a radical life change, if they decide to do so and are willing to pay the price.[7]

Newton is best known as the author of the hymn 'Amazing Grace' (and also 'Glorious Things of Thee Are Spoken'):

Amazing grace! How sweet the sound
That saved a wretch like me!
I once was lost but now I'm found,
Was blind, but now I see.

*If you want to see changes in your life, change something you do daily.
(John Maxwell)*

8. Character

Many a man's reputation would not know his character if they met on the street. (Elbert Hubbard)

I heard the story of a rock-band called Van Halen. It is said that they would make outrageous demands when they were touring. One of their demands was quite strange. They requested there be a bowl filled with M&M's candy-coated chocolate in their dressing room, but all the brown M&Ms had to be removed. Weird request! Lead singer David Lee Roth explained that this was not because the band wanted to make capricious demands, but rather a test of whether or not the contract had actually been thoroughly read and honoured, as it contained other requirements involving legitimate safety concerns. If the bowl was present, then the band members could safely assume the other, legitimate items in the technical rider were being fulfilled to their satisfaction. The band felt that if the fickle M&M request was not met correctly then they would have to line-check the entire production and it was a guarantee that they would run into trouble. But if that little thing was taken care of, then the bigger things would be taken care of as well.[7]

Jesus said in Luke 16:10, 'If you are faithful in little things, you will be faithful in large ones.' Putting it another way, if you're trustworthy in the little things, you're likely to be in the great things. Bloom wherever you are currently planted. On the way to your God-sized dream, do your best at whatever your work is today, because being faithful and fruitful today opens the door for your dreams tomorrow. On the way to your God-sized dream, be faithful and fruitful with the little you have today and it will open the door to your tomorrow.

What little thing do you need to improve on in order for God to open the door to bigger things?

Would your reputation recognise your character if they met in the dark? (Nwabueze Pleroma Temple)

Personality, charisma, talent and can open doors, but character will keep the door open because character delivers; people of character do what they say they will do, they show up. Character is what you are in the dark.

Excellence in character is shown by doing unobserved what we would be doing with the whole world watching. More harm has been done by weak people than by wicked people. The right train of thought will bring you to the best station in life. Nothing costs more than doing the wrong thing. The best way to escape evil is to pursue good.

A little sin is like being a little pregnant, it will eventually show. (Unknown)

Character building is a slow process. Whenever we try to avoid or escape the difficulties of life, we short-circuit the process, delay our growth and actually end up with the worse kind of pain - the worthless type that accompanies denial, avoidance or regret. When we grasp the eternal consequence of character development, we'll pray fewer 'comfort-me-Lord' prayers and more 'conform-me-Lord' prayers.

On the path to maturity, even temptation becomes a stepping-stone rather than a stumbling-block when we realise that in the temptation is a chance to do the right thing as much as it is to do wrong. Character development always involves a choice, and temptation provides that wonderful opportunity to choose right and grow in maturity.

Life is a test; a trust and temporary assignment. Therefore nothing is insignificant in your life. Even the smallest incident has significance for your character development. The more God gives you the more responsible he expects you to be. If you treat everything as a trust, God promises you His affirmation, promotion and celebration in the world to come: well done, good and faithful servant! You have been faithful over little, I will put you in charge over many things. Enter into the joy…

A silversmith was asked - 'How do you know when the silver is pure?'

'When I see my reflection in it,' was the reply. When we've been refined by trials people can see God's reflection in us.

Opportunity may knock once, but temptation leans on the door bell.

Temptation means to temper, i.e. to test for, weakness. The only way to test character is by temptation. Your character is as strong as the temptation you fell for. You are as safe as your character. Don't fight a tempting thought, just refocus your attention on something else. Change the channel of your mind and get interested in another idea. Temptation begins by capturing your attention; what gets your attention arouses your emotions and your emotions activate your behaviour. Ignoring temptation is far effective than fighting it. Once your mind is on something else the temptation loses its power. When temptation calls you on the phone, don't argue with it just hang up! You defeat bad thoughts by thinking of something better.

According to John Maxwell, character growth determines the height of your personal growth. And without personal growth, you can never reach your full potential. Good character, with honesty and integrity at its core, is essential to success in any area of life. Without it, a person is building on shifting sand. Character growth determines the height of your personal growth. Character is the strength and material of the ladder of success, if the material is brittle, the higher you go the bigger the crash, because the material cannot sustain the height. Character is what we really are or who we are on the inside. If you focus on being better on the inside than on the outside, over time you will also become better on the outside.

Character cannot be summoned at the moment of crisis if it has been squandered by years of compromise and rationalization. The only testing ground for the heroic is the mundane. The only preparation for that one profound decision which can change a life, or even a nation, is those hundreds of half-conscious, self-defining, seemingly insignificant decisions made in private. Habit is the daily battleground of character. (Dan Coats)

43

9. Choices

We all make choices but in the end our choices make us.

There are three things that make or break us: habits, choices and routines. Many of us don't even realise the importance of the choices we make or that we are in control of our choices. We need to understand that each and every day, we make numerous choices and that these choices are actually responsible for the outcome or state of all areas of our lives. We should learn from our blunders or wrong choices and we can build on our strengths.

Choice, not chance determines destiny. Your life is a sum total of the choices, decisions and actions you've taken up to date. Your choice of a spouse will seriously impact the outcome of your life, your choice of lifestyle, e.g. a healthy lifestyle, will greatly affect your longevity, energy levels and accomplishments. The choice of habits, e.g. to read or not to read, to watch television for hours on end, smoke or drink, all have positive and negative consequences. Your choice of friends also will significantly influence the outcome of your life. Your choice to save, invest or accumulate debt will massively impinge on not only your bank balance but your future wealth. You have a choice as to the street where you live. You choose not only your home but those who will live next door. It is not our abilities that show what we truly are. It is our choices. The light I have is as a result of my choices.

It is our choices...that show what we truly are, far more than our abilities. (J.K. Rowling)

Every decision, no matter how small, alters the trajectory of your life. Everything in your life exists because you first made a choice. Each choice starts a behaviour that over time becomes a habit. Your choices can move you swiftly to your goal or hurl you far away to a distant galaxy. If you make poor choices then you have to live with the dire consequences as well as go back to the drawing board to make a more difficult choice. And if you fail to make a choice at all, then you have chosen to be a passive receiver of the consequence of not making a good choice. What is more insidious, though, is the frequent series of small seemingly harmless decisions which you make unconsciously every day that sabotage your success because of the compound effect of this daily habit. You've been sleep-walking into these choices. It's insidious because it's unconscious, so not easy to tackle head-on and change.[10]

To remind you of the import of your choices in determining the outcome of your life, here are some inspirational and thought-provoking quotes:

Choose your life's mate carefully. From this one decision will come 90 percent of all your happiness or misery. (H. Jackson Brown Jr.)

You always do what you want to do. This is true with every act. You may say that you had to do something, or that you were forced to, but actually, whatever you do, you do by choice. Only you have the power to choose for yourself. (W. Clement Stone)

You are free to make whatever choice you want, but you are not free from the consequences of the choice. (Unknown)

Decisions are the hardest things to make, especially when it is a choice between where you should be and where you want to be. (Unknown)

May your choices reflect your hopes, not your fears. (Nelson Mandela)

Life is all about making choices. Always do your best to make the right ones, and always do your best to learn from the wrong ones. (Unknown)

Life is a matter of choices, and every choice you make makes you. (John C. Maxwell)

In every single thing you do, you are choosing a direction. Your life is a product of choices. (Dr Kathleen Hall)

Life is full of choices. What you choose to live for is the most important choice of all. Once you have made this choice, it will help you to make every other choice in life. Your choices affect your relationship with your creator, the outcome of everything you do and indeed your eternal destination.

What new choices can you make that will have a positive impact on your future?

If our lives are defined by our choices, the all-important question becomes: How do we make good ones? A key way to make right choices is to ensure you make choices that are consistent with your core beliefs and values. Also learn from others in similar situations. Learn from experience: yours and others' i.e. successes and failures. Seek input and advice if you are not knowledgeable in the situation. Try to view the issue from various perspective before you choose and don't be hasty: if you don't have to make the choice now, then give it time.

Making the right choices every day is the key to having the life we envision. Whatever your goals may be, it is the small choices and corresponding actions repeated daily that will make or break you. When you make good choices today you won't have regrets tomorrow. If you develop your abilities, grow in your awareness and make the right choices, you can reach your capacity. Right choices made daily will compound and eventually lead to success. According to Darren Hardy, the editor of *Success Magazine* and the book *The Compound Effect,* the principle is one of reaping huge rewards from a series of small smart choices.[10]

10. Comfort-zones

The place between your comfort zone and your dream is where life takes place. (Nick Vujicic)

Bill was on a roll. He had a great and secure job; annual bonuses, stock options, fringe benefits, comfortable lifestyle - the works; everything was on track. On Monday January 7th 2008 at 3pm the president of his company called him into his office for a meeting and fired him. Bill said his words sucked the breath out of him. He obviously had not seen this coming. He left the meeting in a dazed state and went home and curled up in bed in the foetal position for three hours. That event created the greatest amount of discomfort he had ever felt: the departure from his ordered life; but it forever changed his life for the better. Getting fired is never a good thing but it can bring about a radical change which can bring the greatest amount of growth. In his TedX Talk, 'Why comfort will ruin your life', Bill Eckstrom explains that what makes you uncomfortable is the only way to grow. Only by discomfort do you continually grow. What dictates the size of a goldfish is its environment. When a goldfish lives in a fish-bowl it is in a safe comfortable environment; it is also a very limiting environment in a lot of ways and doesn't grow beyond a certain size for several reasons. However, when it is placed in a more robust environment like a pond, it can really grow to its full potential. Living in the big pond also means that it can be eaten, but this complex state of discomfort is how growth occurs. You are the goldfish: the environment in which you work, live and play are the proverbial fish-bowl that dictates your growth.[11]

Life begins at the end of your comfort-zone. (Neale Donald Walsch)

Comfort-zones are predictable. Science shows that any time you continually do something or think of something in the same way you'll eventually stop growing, and this applies to every living thing. Substantial growth occurs only in a state of discomfort. Unpredictability makes us uncomfortable but this is the only place sustained and exponential growth occurs.

You'll never fly if you're too comfortable. You will never change that which you are willing to tolerate. But life has a way of making us move out. It's called discomfort. Continually focus on making the next stretch. Leave your comfort zone and stretch toward your true potential. To live a meaningful life we must push outside your comfort zone. Designing a life that includes meaningful work, financial security, and a healthy family-life takes work and a willingness to be flexible and creative — pushing outside our comfortable boundaries into uncertainty. Limiting ourselves to only what feels comfortable is self-sabotage. Pushing past our doubts is a spiritual battle. When we begin to envision our possibilities, fear is inevitable, but it is not a stop-sign. A meaningful life means saying 'no' even when it is hard and saying 'yes' to what is purposeful, even when it is frightening.

Comfort and convenience run the lives of unsuccessful people. (Unknown)

To be successful we must step outside our comfort zone and learn to manage pressures, stress and challenges well, otherwise we will be limited. Pressures and stress are all parts of life. There is no such thing as a stress-free life. You cannot get rid of stress, you can only become better at handling it. When you approach stress in the right way, it can motivate you towards your dreams and goals. You will see that you don't really have a stress problem, you have a capacity issue. If you run from pressure you will step away from the path of purpose and live an unfulfilled or dissatisfied life. The key to increasing your capacity is to decide you will allow God to work in your life to stretch you beyond your comfort zone and enlarge your capacity to overcome challenges.

A possibility is a hint from God. One must follow it. That possible path is God giving us an opportunity to make a difference. As we follow it, we stop asking ourselves what we are and start asking ourselves what we can become. What we did yesterday might be great, even awesome, but we don't put it on a pedestal. It is small in comparison with the possibilities in the future. Looking forward to greater accomplishment fills us with energy. Significance is birthed within each of us, if we are willing to stretch. The change and growth within us challenge us to make changes around us. And that's how we begin to change our world!

Growth stops when you lose the tension between where you are and where you could be. Having less tension makes people less productive. You have to give up to grow up, according to John Maxwell. Be motivated by the possibility of success more than by the fear of failure. Trade-offs are opportunities for growth. While we don't always get what we want, we get what we choose. When you face the opportunity for a trade-off ask these questions: What are the advantages and disadvantages of this opportunity; will I go through this change or grow through this change?

There is no comfort in the growth-zone and no growth in the comfort-zone. (Unknown)

We must be aware of the gap that stands between us and our potential and let the tension of that gap motivate us to keep striving to become better. Don't choose comfort over fulfilling your full potential. If you plan on being anything less than you are capable of being, you will probably be unhappy all the days of your life. You must realise that you will only reach your potential if you're willing to push yourself outside your comfort zone and break the mind-set of mediocrity. Face the tension that comes from stretching towards your potential.

There are two types of people in our world when it comes to a comfort-zone. There are those who live in the comfort-zone where they feel safe. There are also those who reach outside their comfort-zone and grow and achieve more. In your comfort-zone, life is monotonous. Everything is predictable. There is no potential to learn and grow. However, the moment you step out of your comfort-zone you are exposed to a whole new set of emotions – emotions you never previously experienced; some amazing, some downright hair-raising but thrilling nonetheless. Outside your comfort-zone you are able to learn and develop. You understand your true self better, you become more self-aware. You discover things about yourself you never knew; strengths and virtues you never knew existed within you.

Move out of your comfort-zone. You can grow if you are willing to feel awkward and uncomfortable when you try something new. (Brian Tracy)

The paradox of the comfort zone is that people are uncomfortable in their comfort-zones. They are bored, anxious, depressed or insecure. There is no excitement in a comfort-zone. On the other hand we don't want to live on the edge or in a risky uncomfortable zone which creates constant anxiety and self-doubt. If we're too comfortable, we're not productive. And if we're too uncomfortable, we're fearful and doubtful and not productive. Therefore we need to look for a productive discomfort, where we are constantly challenged to stretch, grow, develop or learn new skills. This requires stepping out, trying new things, consistently achieving small goals and pressing on towards bigger dreams.

Where do you need to push outside your comfort-zone to pursue what is meaningful and timeless?

You are only confined by the walls you build around yourself. (Unknown)

11. Communication

The single biggest problem in communication is the illusion that it has taken place. (George Bernard Shaw)

In October 1962, there was a standoff between President Kennedy of the United States and Premier Khrushchev of the Soviet Union over planting missiles in Cuba. The Cuban Missile Crisis was probably the closest we have ever been to World War III, but it was averted because communication was established.

In the days before mobile phones and modern ways of instant messaging, it was decided to put one red telephone on the desk of the President of the United States, and another on the desk of the Premier of Soviet Russia. The communication link was called the 'hotline'. If at any time there was a danger of misunderstanding they could simply lift up the phone and communicate. [7, 12]

Communication is vital to all relationships; between nations, organisations and individuals. Communication breakdown leads to the breakdown of relationships. Therefore setting aside time to build and nurture communication is essential to the well-being of all relationships. Effective communication involves asking the right (intelligent) questions, using the right tone of voice, active listening, and, before responding, mirroring back what you think they said. Emotional intelligence i.e. understanding your own feelings and at the same time being sensitive to those of the other party greatly improves communication. Communication and emotional intelligence are inextricably linked.

Communication can be verbal or non-verbal communication. For example, looking people in the eyes, arm movement, posture, smiling, the tilt of the head etc. are all non-verbal means of communication. Parents have been known to communicate non-verbally with the eyes with their children when they are in public

51

places. It is said that your eyes show the strength of your soul, so be bold enough to look people in the eyes.

Listening and writing are also essential communication skills. In business, it is generally accepted that there are seven main components of effective communication, that is, when you're clear, concise, concrete, correct, considerate, complete and courteous with your message. This is also applicable in all other relationships.

Communication is not just about speaking words, it is about listening and taking responsibility for ensuring that what we have in mind - the content and intent - has been understood by the other party. Relationships thrive where communication is kind, considerate and courteous. Two people can convey a message to you; one person's message is received with grace and the other person's message infuriates you. In essence they have both spoken words but the difference is that one has communicated and the other has simply uttered words. When we speak with consideration and respect our words are more easily received. It is a reflection of wisdom to be able to correct someone and leave them smiling on the inside and appreciative of your instruction. Effective communication diffuses feuds and is like water that quenches wildfires.

A soft answer turns away wrath, but harsh words stir up anger. Gentle words can break a bone, but offensive words are like the gates of a city. Harsh words are like the piercing of the sword, but calm words sooth the soul. (Jewish proverb)

Example of how to communicate: Don't say: 'You have disappointed me', instead say: 'I am disappointed by what has happened.'

The ability to communicate effectively is an indispensable skill for success and life. Effective communication occurs when the receiver comprehends the information or idea that the sender intends to convey. Any fool can make utterances; but only the wise communicate.

12. Confidence

Self-confidence is the best outfit, own it, wear it well and rock it.

I heard a humorous story of a mayor of a town in the US. The mayor and his wife were going on a parade of the town in a carriage. As they passed the local gas-station he saw a man who had been the former boyfriend of his wife. He said to his wife smugly, 'Aren't you glad you didn't marry him? You would have been working in a gas-station.' The wife smiled and said, 'If I had married him, he'd be the mayor.'

Optimism is the faith that leads to achievement. Nothing can be done without hope and confidence. (Helen Keller)

Self-confidence is the belief that you can accomplish any task no matter the odds or difficulty. It is a skill because it can be developed. Self-confidence can be developed by repetition, repetition, repetition. When you have done it over and over and practised and practised you have confidence. Persistence gives you confidence. Positive self -talk also builds your confidence: speak well about yourself to yourself, ponder on all the things you have achieved and done well, relish them, magnify them in your mind and congratulate yourself continually for them. Avoid negative and critical people who put you down.

Be yourself; everyone else is already taken! (Oscar Wilde)

People with self-esteem are comfortable in their own skin, they don't have a need to impress others or try to be what they are not. There is great power in authenticity. You are at your most effective when you are being yourself.

Be who God meant you to be and you will set the world on fire. (St Catherine of Siena)

Self-confidence comes from not neglecting to do the small daily disciplines. Confidence does not come from a pill, from a seminar, it comes as a result of doing certain activities over and over again. When you do these daily, you feel happy with yourself and this builds your confidence. If you are a business person or professional, to have confidence in yourself and win and hold the confidence of others, an essential rule is to know your business and keep on knowing your business.

Successful people are not necessarily more intelligent than others who are less successful: it is their confidence and determination that make them stand out. Confidence is an essential quality for every leader. Great leaders are confident in themselves, their vision and their people. Great leaders help their people feel confident. Confidence is the core of charisma. According to John Maxwell, 'Nothing sells like confidence.'

Confidence is a requirement in order to be an effective communicator or speaker. The main keys to effective public speaking are to know your subject and believe in your message. When you are preparing for a talk, don't ask yourself: will they believe? The key issue is: do you believe what you are saying? Believe it - really believe it – and that conviction will show through.

Despite what society and social media tell you, your worth is not determined by how many twitter followers you have, or Facebook friends you have, or how many pounds you weigh, or what sports team you play for. If we find our worth and identity in temporary things, then our satisfaction and joy will also be temporary.

No one can make you feel inferior without your permission. (Eleanor Roosevelt)

As previously mentioned, self-esteem is the single most significant key to a person's behaviour. No factor is more important in people's psychological development and motivation than the value judgements they make about themselves. Every aspect of my life is impacted by the way I see myself. Self-esteem is at the root of self confidence. Self-esteem is the ability to say no to the good so you can say yes to the great. It is the ability to say no without feeling guilty. There is power in the word no. No is an 'anointed' word. No can break the yoke of over-commitment and weakness. No can be used to turn a situation from bad to good, from wrong to right. Don't let your mouth overload your back, feel free to say no. Yes and no are the two most important words that you will ever say. These two words can determine your destiny in life. Who you marry, what job you accept, what position you accept, what opportunities you embrace, what challenges you accept etc.

Someone humorously said confidence is the uplifting feeling you have before you truly understand the situation.

We must not measure our meaning and value by the yardstick of others. Being confident in who you are (inside and out) starts with your recognizing your worth. When we recognize that the source of our worth is infinite, our satisfaction and joy will be infinite too.

You no longer need to find worth in dating, appearance, popularity, or personality because you already have worth in an infinite God who created you uniquely like Himself. If you are struggling with insecurities, or are constantly striving to be more, weigh less, and do better so that you feel better about yourself, then you might not have recognised your true worth as a unique human being – or you may just need a reminder!

What others think is not my problem unless I make it so.

To think confidently, act confidently and speak confidently. Motions are the precursors of emotions. You can't control the emotions directly, but through your choice of motions, words or actions you can change our attitudes.

Class is just confidence dressed in humility. (Ann Landers)

13. Consistency

In consistency lies the power. (Gloria Copeland)

Jim Ryun was track- and field-runner who, after becoming the first high-school runner to break the four-minute mile in 1964, emerged as the greatest middle-distance runner in the history of the sport during a decade notable for producing great running stars. Jim did not lose hope after being dropped from the basketball and baseball team but went on to make his life in athletics. He was three times Olympian former world record-holder in the mile, 1500 metres and half-mile. He knew the power of consistency and he reaped the benefits of multitudes of hours invested over a long period of time. He knew he could not become a world-class runner without a lot of practice and self-discipline. Rarely does anything of great worth come easily, even to the very gifted.

His story showed that his personal life paralleled his running career. While running he was consistently building his life in other areas. The day came when Jim's record was finally broken by an eighteen-year-old from Virginia. If all Jim Ryun had to be proud of was a thirty-six-year-old running record that now had been broken by a high-school senior he would have been shattered. His running career would be over as well as his feeling of accomplishment. But Jim Ryun had something more—consistent service to God and his community that has spanned a lifetime. He also ran for public office and was a five-term US congressman. Yes, his fame gave him a platform, but it could have been a very shaky place to stand if it was all he had ever accomplished. By hard work and consistency he was on much firmer and safer ground surrounded by a lifetime of achievement.

In real life, strategy is actually very straightforward. You pick a general direction and implement like hell. (Jack Welch)

The doubling penny

Darren Hardy, in his book *The compound effect*, illustrates the compounding effect of consistency with the penny principle. Here is my version of the principle: If you were offered £3m and your friend is given a penny which doubles daily over thirty-one days, who will have more money at the end of thirty-one days? On day two, the penny will be worth 2p and 4p on day three. On day ten, the penny is £5, on day twenty you have £5000. The doubling penny will be worth 2.9m by day twenty-nine, £5.3m on day thirty, and by day thirty-one, the very last day; your friend blows you out of the water with over a whopping £10.7m! That is the magic of consistency in any area of life as it compounds over time.[10]

The power of consistency is further illustrated by what some call the 'Angle Principle'. It is the principle that if you only get half a degree away from the centre, ten years down the line, you will be way off course and never even know it. This is applicable in the positive as well as the negative. Little disciplines practised consistently every day will take you places you never dreamed of. Success does not happen overnight. It is the result of faithfulness in little things over a lifetime. The small unnoticed things can add up to great achievement and a crescendo of success—if you are consistent. You can build your life on a consistent body of small achievements, not just a single giant success.

Little by little, a little leads to a lot! People are rewarded in public for what they practise in private. Success is a result of small habits repeated day in, day out. (Terry Savelle Foy)

Your future is dependent upon your personal growth. Improving yourself consistently; little by little every day guarantees you a future filled with possibilities. When you expand yourself by your daily growth habit, you expand your horizons, your options, your opportunities and potential. Consistency is more important than perfection.

If you want to gain momentum and improve your motivation, begin by setting goals that are worthwhile but highly achievable. Master the basics, then practise them every day without fail. Small disciplines repeated with consistency every day lead to great achievement gained slowly over time. Success in most things comes not from some gigantic stroke of fate but from simple, incremental progress. Everything worthwhile in life takes dedication and time.

Small steps are powerful and life-changing. Don't feel you have to undergo an instant extreme makeover to get where you need to be. Just focus on minor improvement every day, every week and every month. Over time, you will be amazed at the cumulative effect of your small efforts. Repetition is the mother of skill. The way to extraordinary results is knowing what matters to you and taking daily doses of actions in alignment with it.

Judge each day not by the harvest you reap but by the seeds you sow. (Robert Stevenson)

Success according to Darren Hardy is not doing five thousand things really well. Success is doing half-a-dozen things really well five thousand times. That is the power of consistency.

The hallmark of excellence, the test of greatness, is consistency. (Unknown)

14. Courage / Boldness

I learned that courage was not the absence of fear but the triumph over it.
The brave man is not he who does not feel afraid but he who conquers that
fear. (Nelson Mandela [13])

'The emperor's new clothes' is a short tale written by Danish author
Hans Christian Andersen, about two weavers who promise an
emperor a new suit of clothes that they say is invisible to those who
are unwise or unfit for their positions. In reality they are conmen
but because the King is too proud to admit he can't see the said
clothes, he pretends he can rather than be thought unfit or unwise.
The thieves take advantage of the king's weakness. The wise men in
the king's court also cannot bring themselves to admit they can't see
these clothes. Not until the king goes on a parade through the town
in his 'invisible' garb does a child cry out from the crowd that the
king is naked.

Cowards die many times before their deaths, The valiant never taste of
death but once. (Julius Caesar, Shakespeare)

We all want to be loved, to fit in, to be accepted and this is good.
But a time will come in your life when you have to stand alone,
speak out and be different. Will you be that courageous person who
shuns the status quo and says the king is not wearing any clothes?
Be sure you will be thought stupid or strange or slightly insane by
those who are too fearful to admit their failings. So be it. Only dead
fish go with the flow of the river.

It is better to be a lion for a day, than a sheep all your life. (Elizabeth
Kenny)

An 1828 copy of Webster's dictionary defines courage as 'that
quality which enables us to face difficulty and danger ... without
fear or depression'. An ancient proverb says: success favours the

bold and daring. Courage is stepping out of your comfort-zone and letting go of the familiar. Boldness is choosing to act despite the fear you feel, despite the butterflies in the pit of your stomach. It is following your heart and persevering in the face of hardship. Courage is standing up for what you know is right. Living your conviction in the face of fear. People follow courage. Life expands or shrinks for you depending on your courage. Your past will be your future until you have the courage to create a new one.

What you can do or think you can do, begin it. For boldness has magic, power and genius in it. (Johann Wolfgang von Goethe)

You get in life what you have the courage to ask for. (Oprah Winfrey)

If you avoid conflict to keep the peace, you start a war inside yourself. So be bold and courageous. Confront your fears and you just never know what amazing things might be on the other side waiting for you.

The only thing necessary for the triumph of evil is for good men to do nothing. (Edmund Burke)

Success is not final, failure is not fatal: it is the courage to continue that counts. (Winston Churchill)

It's not the size of the dog in the fight, it's the size of the fight in the dog. (Mark Twain)

There is no living thing that is not afraid when it faces danger. The true courage is in facing danger when you are afraid. (L.Frank Baum, The Wonderful Wizard of Oz)

Encouragement

The root word for encouragement is courage. We all need encouragers, those who build our courage and inspire us to be more and do more. Encouragement is not flattery or empty praise; it is like verbal sunshine. It costs nothing and warms other people's hearts and inspires them with hope and confidence.

Whatever tries to steal or take away your courage is discouragement. Never allow discouragement: it is harmful, it makes you sit down, pity yourself and do nothing. According to

Keith Moore, never, never, never allow self-pity in your life. The answer to discouragement is intelligent action. Failure is only delay not defeat - it is a temporary detour, not a dead end. Setback and failure mean little: it is what we make of them.

Being terrified but going ahead and doing what must be done – that's courage. The one who feels no fear is a fool, and the one who lets fear rule him is a coward. (Piers Anthony)

Courage doesn't always roar. Sometimes courage is the little voice at the end of the day that says I'll try again tomorrow. (Mary Anne Radmacher)

15. Creativity

Creativity is intelligence having fun. (Albert Einstein)

Murray Spangller was a janitor at a department store in Canton, Ohio. He decided that the only way to overcome the boredom of his job, which consisted of sweeping floors, was to find a more innovative way to do it. In addition to the boredom, he had the added incentive of being allergic to the dust he was sweeping every day. Then the thought came to him: 'Instead of sweeping up the dust, maybe there is a way to suck it up.' Spangller's question led him to invent a crude but workable portable electrical vacuum cleaner. He found an old friend who was married to his cousin to finance the manufacturing of his invention. The friend's name was H. W. Hoover. Hoovering became a name synonymous with sweeping floors.

Built into every obstacle is an opportunity; into every question, an answer; into every problem, a solution. So ask questions. Question methods, systems, equipment and ask, 'Is there a better way? The world has been enriched by people who asked that question. YOU can be one of them.

Creativity is a wild mind and a disciplined eye. (Dorothy Parker)

The first step towards success is becoming good at what you know how to do. The more you do what you know how to do, the more you discover additional worthy things you could do, when this occurs do the new things. Doing new things leads to innovations and new discoveries and among the new discoveries is the realisation of things you should do on a constant basis. If you do these it will lead to growth and expansion of your potential. If you don't - you will plateau.

I am always doing that which I cannot do, in order to learn how to do it. (Pablo Picasso)

A former president of Yale pointed out that Hamlet could never have been written by a committee, or the Mona Lisa painted by a club, or the New Testament composed by a conference. Creative ideas usually come from individuals.

Creativity is seeing what everyone else has seen, and thinking what no one else has thought. (Albert Einstein)

There are no such things as creative people and non-creative people. There are only people who use their creativity and people who don't. Unused creativity doesn't just disappear. It lives within us until it's expressed, neglected to death or suffocated by resentment and fear.

Creativity is just connecting things and presenting them in a unique or different way. Asking questions about what you see or read spurs creativity and leads you to make discoveries. Consider this silly poem. The writer is unknown, but it displays creativity. It's a silly version of the nursery rhyme 'Three blind mice,' but I think it is wonderfully creative:

Three myopic rodents, three myopic rodents.

Observe how they perambulate, observe how they perambulate.

They all circumnavigated the gardener's spouse.

She excised their extremities with a sharp utensil.

Did you ever regard such an occurrence in your existence

As three myopic rodents?

What a silly poem, but oh, so creative!

Creativity is knowing how to hide your sources (Albert Einstein)

16. Criticism

Criticism is something we can avoid easily by saying nothing, doing nothing, and being nothing. (Aristotle)

As Rick Warren pointed out, 'Criticism is the cost of influence. As long as you don't influence anybody, nobody is going to say a peep about you. But the greater your influence ... the more critics you are going to have.' Don't lose sleep over it and don't be surprised if you're on the receiving end of criticism. Remember: no one ever built a monument to a critic.

He who throws dirt always loses ground. (Unknown)

While criticism can be useful for growth and improvement, we should be very careful of what we say about other people. Don't criticise, condemn or complain. Instead instruct, advise, counsel and encourage. Reward for good behaviour helps learning more than punishment for bad behaviour. By criticising we do not make lasting changes and often incur resentment. Sharp criticism and rebukes almost invariably end in futility. Do you know someone you would like to change, regulate and improve? Good - why not begin on yourself?!

Any fool can criticise, condemn and complain - and most fools do! (Benjamin Franklin)

Don't be distracted by criticism. Remember, the only taste of success some people have is when they take a bite out of you. (Zig Ziglar)

If you need to respond to criticism or offer your criticism, do it with sensitivity and remember a soft answer is always better than a sarcastic one. If you say it offensively, it will be received defensively. The more pleasant your words the more persuasive you are. You are never persuasive when you are abrasive. It is usually best to be generous with praise, but cautious with criticism.

He has a right to criticise who has a heart to help. (Abraham Lincoln)

The trouble with most of us is that we'd rather be ruined by praise than saved by criticism. (Norman Vincent Peale)

Being criticised is not something that anyone enjoys and looks for; it hurts and stings. However, if you look at people who are successful versus people who are average, a key difference is often their willingness to listen to criticism and learn from it. While not all criticism is valid, some surely is. If the hat fits, wear it; learn from it and let the rest go. Self-analysis, self-education, reviewing and appraisal are important for success. It takes character, maturity and self-control to be understanding and forgiving when we feel we have been harshly or wrongly criticised.

Criticism may not be agreeable, but it is necessary. It fulfils the same function as pain in the human body. It calls attention to an unhealthy state of things. (Winston Churchill)

We need very strong ears to hear ourselves judged frankly, and because there are few who can endure frank criticism without being stung by it, those who venture to criticise us perform a remarkable act of friendship, for to undertake to wound or offend a man for his own good is to have a healthy love for him. (Michel de Montaigne)

The final proof of greatness lies in being able to endure criticism without resentment. (Elbert Hubbard)

17. Debt

Debt kills options - period! (Yomi Akinpelu)

A couple of decades ago, a friend of mine had a small credit-card balance of a few hundred pounds and was paying just about the minimum payment monthly. He also had a payment-protection insurance which he paid monthly. The trouble was, despite paying the minimum monthly payment and the payment-protection insurance, the balance was not reducing at all. My friend was flummoxed. He did not realise that paying the minimum monthly payment barely covered the extortionate interest rate, and, if not for timely intervention, it would take decades to pay off just a few hundred pounds. When he told me about it, I volunteered to pay off the debt if he would cut up the credit card and become financially literate. He agreed. The first thing I did was cancel the useless payment-protection insurance and then paid off the balance in about three instalments. Since then, my friend has become quite financially astute. He has one or two credit cards now but pays the full balance monthly.

A lot of people struggle with debt. Generally speaking, spending more than you earn automatically creates debt no matter how much you earn. Debt destroys your options. Nevertheless, no matter how bad it is, you can get rid of debt. It might take time but it can be dealt with. To get rid of debt you must first stop adding new debt to your debt, decide to live **well** below your means, develop a spending plan or budget which includes payment of debt. You must not pay the minimum payment because it will take you almost forever to pay it off. Pay off your debts first before you start saving. Try and find ways to increase your income. When you have cleared your debts then divert all the money budgeted for debt repayment into your savings account.

Broke is too much month at the end of the money.

So let's get a handle on your financial situation and start the process of eliminating debt in five steps. Remember: for this to work, you must not create any new debts! Trying to keep up with the Joneses will keep you perpetually in debt. Stop spending money you don't have, to buy stuff you don't need, to impress people you don't like!

List All Debt - The first step to reeling in your debt is to list everything you owe.

Set Goals - Write and communicate the short and long-term goals.

Work Hard - Work diligently and find creative ways to increase your income. This is a necessary component of prosperity.

Live Well Below Your Means - Reduce expenses wherever possible and renegotiate any remaining debt.

Become financially literate - Learn everything you can about finances.

Consumer debt has grown (in trillions) owing to lack of financial literacy. Instead of passing on a good inheritance to the next generation, we are passing on debt and bad fiscal habits. To combat such, we first must clarify the difference between assets and liabilities. For example, many understand that liabilities are anything that takes money out of their pockets, while assets put money in. However, some of the very things people consider assets are actually liabilities. For instance, our houses can be a liability (unless they are generating income), but a necessary liability because, if you are renting you still have to pay rent. However, if you have bought more house than you can afford, you might be better off down-sizing or letting out a room in your home or taking in a lodger. Not at all convenient; but it may well be a temporary solution if you are deeply in debt. We should be leveraging our gifts and talents to multiply our resources so that we can expand our ability to reach the world and be a blessing.

Proverbs 13:22 reads, 'A good man leaves an inheritance to his children's children, but the wealth of the sinner is stored up for the righteous.' The proverb suggests that, if there is no responsibility in the management of resources, then your wealth will be shifted to those who are responsible.

You may have really messed up financially in the past. But it doesn't matter where you've been. What matters is the direction your feet are going right now.

The borrower is servant to the lender. (Jewish proverb)

18. Decisions

Your life changes the moment you make a new, congruent and committed decision. (Anthony Robbins)

An ancient story is told about a great warrior who, facing a grave situation, had to make a decision which would ensure his success on the battlefield. He was about to send his soldiers against a powerful foe whose numbers and military might exceeded his own. He loaded his soldiers into boats, sailed to the enemy's country, unloaded the soldiers and equipment, then ordered his soldiers to burn the ships that had carried them to the shore. Addressing his men before the first battle, he said, 'You see the boats going up in smoke. That means there is no possible chance of retreat: we cannot leave these shores alive unless we win. We now have no choice; we win or we perish.' They won.

Every person who intends to succeed in any undertaking must be willing to make a decision to burn his bridges and ships and cut off all strings to retreat. The decisions we make determine our success or failure.

I'm not a product of circumstances. I'm a product of my decisions. (Stephen Convey)

Decision-making is ineluctable: it can't be avoided, you can't escape from it. We cannot avoid responsibility by indecision. Indecision is itself a decision not to act. It is a decision to maintain the status quo. It is an action with consequences. *You* are the boss of you, so you must make decisions about your life, you can't pass the buck, the buck stops with you. Indecision robs you of the future and can deprive you of opportunities. Don't be dithering and indecisive. Don't use delay as a device to avoid making a decision. Avoiding a decision is a decision in itself.

To decide means to cut off alternative options. Being decisive is essential for a successful life because every accomplishment, great or small starts with a decision. Decide to do something now today to make your life better. The moment you definitely commit yourself, God moves as well. All sorts of things happen to help you that would otherwise have not if you hadn't made the decision. One decision, one change, one risk, one idea - that's all it takes.

One way to make decisions is to very carefully consider the consequence of that decision if we acted upon it and then seriously consider the consequence if we did not make that decision or take the step based on the decision. If the risks outweigh the potential benefits and have far-reaching consequences, then you should not take that risk. However, if the risks are moderate and manageable without far-reaching consequences if things don't work out, but with a potentially substantial beneficial outcome if it all works out, then we should take the step.

A good decision is one that is made deliberately and thoughtfully, considers and includes all relevant factors, is consistent with the individual's values and generally moves you closer to the achievement of your goal.

When it comes to life-altering decisions proceed with caution. Haste can be dangerous. 'When in doubt do nothing.' It takes more time to repair the damage caused by a bad decision than to make the right choice. A couple of minutes more never killed anyone. Do you have a tendency to leap into situations without weighing them carefully? That can be a good thing if a person is lying on the side of the road, bleeding to death, and in need of immediate assistance. However, being impulsive can be fatal if in your haste you are run over by oncoming traffic. Control your impulses and respond prudently. Remember the instruction to stop, look, listen before you take action.

Nothing is so exhausting as indecision, and nothing is so futile. (Bertrand Russell)

The writer of *Proverbs* warns against being imprudent. A careful person will not be right in every decision he or she makes but will not enter into any decision too lightly either. The prudent person understands that not everything turns out the way it seems it will at first glance. So think your decisions through, especially the ones with wider implications.

It is wise to exercise prudence and be cautious, as the *Book of Proverbs* advises. Weigh your decisions carefully. You can smear a lifetime of accomplishment with doubt in a moment of haste.

Today's decisions are tomorrow's sadness or celebration. The decision of choosing a spouse is especially imperative. Right now your decisions are determining who your spouse wakes up to down the road. A decision to live a pure life now determines the kind of person your spouse has to live with. Fight for them even if you have no idea who they are. Yesterday you said tomorrow. Today is the day to put God first. Be who he made you to be. You will attract the right one by protecting the right things. Life attracts life. If you are filling your life with tinder while you're single, it will lead to a forest fire down the road.

Managed motions can change emotions. Action cures fear. Hesitation only enlarges and magnifies the fear, therefore take prompt action, be decisive.

We are the creative force of our life, and, through our own decisions rather than our conditions, if we carefully learn to do certain things, we can accomplish those goals. (Stephen Covey)

19. Delayed Gratification

The ability to discipline yourself to delay gratification in the short term in order to enjoy greater rewards in the long term is the indispensable prerequisite for success. (Brian Tracy)

In the late 1960s and early 1970s psychologist Walter Mischel, then a professor in Stanford University carried out a study which involved 500 children - it was called the 'Marshmallow Test'. Kids were offered one Marshmallow (or some other desirable treat) and they were told that the researcher would step away for 15 minutes, if the child could wait until the researcher returned, he'd be awarded a second treat. In other words one treat now or two treats later. Left alone with a marshmallow they couldn't eat, kids engaged all kinds of delay strategies, from closing their eyes, pulling their hair, and turning away to hovering over, smelling and even caressing their treats. On average kids held out less than three minutes. Only three out of ten managed to delay their gratification until the researcher returned. It was quite clear most kids struggled with delayed gratification. It was discovered later that children who had successfully waited for the second treat seemed to be doing a lot better than those who had not. Starting from 1981 Mischel began systematically tracking down the original subjects of the study. He measured academic and social progress. His hunch was correct: ability to delay gratification was a huge indicator of future success. Success in the experiment predicted higher general academic achievement and better stress management. On the other hand the ones who could not delay gratification were more likely to be overweight and later suffered higher rates of drug-addiction. The adage, 'Good things come to those who wait', has an element of truth. Nevertheless more recent research has shown that delaying gratification is not a unique lever to pull to positively influence other aspects of a person's life. One has to consider the bigger picture, harder-to-change components of a person, like their intelligence and environment they live in. Still, it makes for interesting reading.[14]

A wealthy and influential patriarch had twin boys, and one of the boys is to receive a great inheritance. The inheritance is this: out of his family will come great nations, great kings. Based on ancient tradition, the bequest would go to the firstborn: Esau. However, one night in a fit of hunger, Esau trades his decisive birthright with Jacob, his twin brother, for a measly bowl of stew. The story of Esau and Jacob illustrates the tragedy of instant gratification. Afterwards Esau wept bitterly trying to undo what had been done, but it was too late, his fate had been sealed.

Delaying gratification is a process of scheduling the pain and pleasure of life in such a way as to enhance the pleasure by meeting and experiencing the pain first and getting it over with. It is the only decent way to live. (M. Scott Peck)

Terry Savelle Foy tells the story about a lady known for making delicious homemade biscuits. People would drive great distances just to get a taste. You could smell them in the driveway. Your mouth would water as she pulled these warm softball-sized biscuits out of the oven. One day she said, 'Just consider what goes into making these biscuits. The flour itself doesn't taste good, neither does the baking powder. Can you imagine drinking the shortening or having a tablespoon of salt or two tablespoons of butter straight off the spoon? 'But,' she said, 'when you mix them all together and put them in the oven, it all comes out just right.'

Why have I recounted this story? The story reminded me of delayed gratification. You see, if you were really very hungry and decided to eat the biscuit ingredients because you couldn't wait for the process of mixing and baking, the ingredients would taste absolutely disgusting and almost impossible to swallow. They are the correct ingredients needed for making the biscuits all right, but they would not be enjoyable or satisfying until they have been mixed together and baked in the oven. Eating the individual ingredients before they have been properly prepared will give you a tummy-ache. On the other hand, if you waited just a little while, the same ingredients mixed and then baked are completely transformed to a delicious treat.

When you choose a half-baked reward because you can't wait, you deny yourself the wonderful benefits of delayed gratification. Once you've consumed the cake ingredients, you have deprived yourself of the delicious baked product because you can't have your cake and eat it.

Delayed gratification describes the process where a person chooses to defer pleasure or reward to the future or a later more appropriate period when the reward will be of more value. Delayed gratification means you refuse the temptation to take an immediate smaller reward in preference for a later better reward. Generally, delayed gratification is associated with saying no to a lesser but immediate reward in order to receive a more enduring reward later. Delayed gratification is relevant in a wide range of life situations and is a quality associated with a host of other positive outcomes, which include financial success and physical health.

Don't give up what you want most for what you want now. (Richard G. Scott)

Red pill, blue pill. Swipe left, swipe right. Click on the link or shut down the browser. Say no, say yes. Two options were on the table: would you like to have it right now, or would you like to see great things through your life down the road? Don't give up your inheritance for something that will make you feel good for a night. Don't sell your virtue for momentary pleasure.

Delayed gratification will enable you say no to the chocolate cream cake and go for the carrot sticks instead, the benefits of healthy eating far outweigh the fleeting pleasure of that scrumptious dessert. The ability to delay gratification will enable you to say no to that shopping spree and yes to the investment opportunity. When the investment begins to yield you can shop till you drop on the profits and not your capital. Delayed gratification will help you burn the midnight oil while your friends are relaxing and chilling; your diligence in studying and personal development helps you become more valuable in the market-place.

A person's ability to delay gratification relates to other similar skills such as endurance, patience and self-control, all of which are involved in self-discipline. Self-discipline basically enables you to make yourself do what needs to be done when it needs to be done, irrespective of your feelings. It is a person's capacity to adapt themselves as and when necessary to effectively meet the demands of life.

This quality of self-denial in pursuit of a longer-term goal and, indeed, the willpower to maintain the denial, is excellent training for the boardroom. (John Viney)

If you do what you have to as quickly as you can, you can do what you want to as long as you want. Instant gratification and personal growth are incompatible. Immediate gratification is almost always the enemy of growth. If you delay gratification, you grow! Here's the truth, getting what you want immediately may not be best for you. Sometimes waiting is the best thing because it helps develop character and resilience.

Levi Lusko says, 'Don't you dare trade your calling for something that's one-and-done. Don't you believe the lie that sleeping with someone before marriage will make you feel loved. You are already loved by an almighty God. Don't believe the lie that you have to compromise your values to be successful. Don't you believe the lie that you are missing out on fun by not doing what your friends are doing. You will be missing out for sure by delaying gratification, but what will you miss out on? You will be missing out on heartache, regret, guilt, shame and a truck load of misery.'[15]

Don't succumb to what the devil's got in his crock-pot. Instead, decide that when he tempts you, you're going to throw that bowl of stew off the table.

Now yells louder, but later lasts longer. (Levi Lusko)

75

20. Diligence

The heights by great men reached and kept
were not attained in sudden flight.
But they, while their companions slept,
were toiling upwards in the night. (Longfellow)

He started out working hard as a labourer for a railway company. When he was given the opportunity to work in the shipping office for a few days, he jumped at it. During that time his supervisor asked him for some vital facts and figures. He was given three days to come up with the information. The young man had no clue about book-keeping but he worked three days and nights without sleep and, at the end of three days, he had the facts and figures ready. This won the respect and admiration of his supervisor, and, as soon as a permanent position opened up, he recommended the young man for the job. Over time the young man was promoted several times and applauded for his thoroughness and trustworthiness. Eventually he ended up as a vice president of one of the world's largest manufacturers of pet food.

A man was building a primitive car (quadracycle) in a shed. When he finished building the car, he realised that it would not fit the entrance and so he could not bring it out of the shed. What did he do? He knocked down some of the shed wall to bring it out. Nothing was going to deter him. That man was Henry Ford.

Napoleon was born in poverty. His classmates made fun of him in school. But he devoted himself to his books, excelled in his studies and became the brightest student in class. Before his life was over, he conquered much of the world!

Diligence is the mother of good luck. (Benjamin Franklin)

Good things don't come to those who wait, it goes to those who hustle. All good things come to those who persistently go after them.

A genius is someone who shoots at a target no one else sees and hits it. (Unknown)

The more you sweat in training, the less you bleed in combat. (Richard Marcinko)

If we judge ourselves only by our aspirations and everyone else only by their conduct, we shall soon reach a very false conclusion. (Calvin Coolidge)

The dream is free, but the hustle is sold separately. (Steve Harvey)

Genius is 1% inspiration and 99% perspiration. (Thomas Edison)

Only a mediocre person is always at his best. (W. Somerset Maugham)

Average is the opposite of diligence. Being average is the lazy person's cop-out, it's lacking the guts to take a stand in life, it's to live by default! Being average is to take up space for no purpose; to take the trip through life but never pay the fare; to return no interest for God's investment in you. Being average is to kill time, rather than to work it to death. To be average is to commit the greatest crime against oneself, humanity and God - no contribution to life!

If you won't be better tomorrow than you were today, then what do you need tomorrow for? (Rabbi Nachman of Bratslav)

You cannot grow within and be stagnant without. Our station in life is mainly due to the choices we make and the actions we take or fail to take. The way to get ahead is to over-deliver. To get ahead in business you have to fully meet the client's needs and questions and then provide answers to a slew of questions the client has not asked or thought of, in other words, exceed your client's expectations because of your energy, passion, creativity, insight and optimism! Successful people set themselves apart because they initiate the improvement others need. When we stop stretching, we stop growing.

Nature has everywhere written her protest against idleness; everything which ceases to struggle, which remains inactive,

77

rapidly deteriorates. It is the struggle towards an ideal, the constant effort to get higher and further, which develops character. God's gift to us is our potential, our gift to God is to develop it.

Someone said, 'Too many people are dead but haven't made it official yet.' Don't be one of them! I don't know how true this is, but someone said no one has ever made a significant impact after they won the Nobel Prize!

The greatest enemy of tomorrow is today's success. (Peter Drucker)

Rubber bands are useful only when they are stretched. (John Maxwell)

According to Jim Rohn, if you do something long enough, a ratio will appear. You learn more by losing than winning. You can make up in numbers what you lack in skill. Be diligent: always do more than is required of you. Laziness is waiting for what you want, without doing what you can do. It is a well-known fact that the man who consistently does more than he is paid for will soon be paid for more than he does. There are no traffic jams along the extra mile.

If you want to get something done, give it to a busy person. Why is that? People who can get a lot done seem to be able to take on even more and remain productive.

21. Excellence

Mastery lives quietly atop a mountain of mistakes or failures.

When you become so skilled, so flat-out fantastic, your talent cannot be ignored. When you are excellent at what you do, you become unforgettable. In the words of Oprah Winfrey, let excellence be your brand! When excellence is your habit, you become unforgettable.

Excellence is doing ordinary things extraordinarily well. (John W. Gardner)

One writer put it this way: 'There is a remarkable difference between 99% and 100% commitment. At 100% you see your problems all the way through to their solution. At 99% you can still find a way to take the path of least resistance.' [16, 17]

People will gauge your character by the height of your ideals, the breadth of your compassion, the depth of your convictions, and the length of your persistence. Leaders know excellence when they see it. What is the value of excellence? Excellence inspires trust, loyalty, and respect and establishes a reputation that will follow you wherever you go and as long as you live.

Aim for perfection but settle for excellence.

Don't make excellence an idol, do what you can now! 'Whatever is worth doing is worth doing well' is not a passage of Scripture! Jesus didn't say: 'If it can't be done with excellence, don't do it.' Just do it and you will become better at it. You get better by doing. Doing mundane menial tasks is part of your character-development curriculum. Don't worry about hitting the target or perfection, focus on the trajectory: is this moving me towards my goals? Are you doing your very best, in everything, in every way? Stop doing important things occasionally and start doing important things daily. The slightest lack of doing your best always affects your psyche, philosophy and conscience.

The excellent fail more than the mediocre because they start more, try more and do more.

Your capacity is not set once you become aware of the possibilities that can make you better. Developing self-awareness will enable you to see yourself clearly. It informs your decisions and helps you weigh opportunities. It allows you to test your limits, maximise your strength and minimise your weaknesses. When you discover things about yourself you must decide which areas to focus your attention on and develop your strengths in. Excellence comes from focusing on your strengths. When you become excellent at what do, a sea of opportunities opens up to you. When you are excellent at what you do, you come to the attention of more people.

It's not the hours you put in but what you put in the hours. (Jim Rohn)

22. Excuses

An excuse is a way of promising ourselves that we will have the same issue again. (Henry Cloud)

Abraham Lincoln was faced with many opportunities to give up on his dream of being president of the United States. Between the ages of twenty-two and twenty-four, he failed in two business ventures. During that time, he ran for state legislature and lost. Two years later, the woman he loved died, and then he had a nervous breakdown. Over the next twenty years, Lincoln lost seven more political races. Finally, at fifty-one years old, Abraham Lincoln was elected president of the United States. He had more than enough excuses to give up on his dream but he didn't take any of the excuses. Instead he pursued his dreams relentlessly.

Roosevelt could have hidden behind his paralysed legs. Truman could have used the no-college-education' excuse. Kennedy could have said, 'I'm too young to be president.' Johnson and Eisenhower could have ducked behind heart attacks. Don't make excuses: make progress.

You can have results or excuses, not both. (Anonymous)

The person who really wants to do something finds a way: the others find an excuse. When you make a mistake and then make an excuse for it, you have made two mistakes. Most failures come from people who have the habit of making excuses. Excuses are a crutch for lack of commitment and a smoke-screen for self-justification. You cannot help someone until they are willing to take responsibility for their life and apply the given solutions.

There are a thousand excuses for failure but never good reason. (Mark Twain)

You choose. Excuses change nothing but make everyone feel better. The origin of every excuse is the failure to do something. Excuses are nothing more than a reason to fail. The lazy man finds an excuse, the diligent man finds a way. Find a way, don't find an excuse.

When you're good at making excuses, it's hard to excel at anything else. (John L. Mason)

Each time you make an excuse, the excuse becomes embedded more deeply into your subconscious mind. Thoughts, positive or negative, grow stronger when fertilized with constant repetition. After a while you actually believe the excuse to be the truth. When you habitually make excuses you never learn anything because you're justifying the unjustifiable. The excuses cloud your mind and you don't see the truth of your situation; it's a vicious circle.

To be completely honest, there really isn't much more to write about excuses, except that they stink, make you sink and keep you stuck in self-pity and mediocrity. So snap out of it and soar into success!

Do you find yourself making excuses when you do not perform? Shed the excuses and face reality. Excuses are the loser's way out. They will mar your credibility and stunt your personal growth. (Alexander Pope)

We've all heard excuses from kids who said the dog ate their homework or the employee who got to work late and his excuse was that an iguana ate his car key. Oh, please! Someone sent me a really funny poem titled *All My Great Excuses* by Kenn Nesbitt. It's about a child who, instead of doing his homework, decides to make lame and ridiculous excuses about how his pen ran out of ink, the hamster ate his homework, he accidentally dropped the homework in the soup, how it dropped in the toilet and how an aeroplane crashed into his house and the homework caught fire, how aliens and an evil clown abducted him and so on. I love the response of the teacher to the excuses. She said, 'I think you'll find it's easier to do the work instead.'

Don't make excuses. Make things happen. Make changes. Then make history. (Doug Hall)

23. Failure

I have not failed. I've just found 10,000 ways that won't work.
(Thomas Edison)

Warren Buffet is known to have said that he would not invest in any business where the owner hasn't failed at least twice. Why? Because you're much stronger and more prepared for the trials and challenges that come with greater success!

Terry Savelle Foy said that the accidents, the mistakes, the painful experiences she'd been through have turned into nine books, online courses, speaking engagements to thousands all over the world, TV shows, and a weekly podcast.

Failure, according to Napoleon Hill, is a trickster with a keen sense of irony and cunning. It takes great delight in tripping one when success is almost within reach. Many successful people have stated that their greatest success came just one step beyond the point at which defeat had overtaken them.

The person who never made a mistake never tried anything. (Albert Einstein)

Failure is a part of life. In life, sometimes we win and sometimes we learn. Every mistake or failure is a chance to grow and learn, and, if you understand that, then you'll never lose: you either win or you learn. Both of these outcomes are worthwhile; both of them are valuable. I know it's more easily said than done, but if you adopt this mind-set it can save you from a lot of heartache, because you won't view failure as a negative outcome, but rather an opportunity to learn, grow and become better. There is really no failure: there is only learning what works and what doesn't. Failure is there to point you in the right direction. Failure is life saying, 'Excuse me, you're going in the wrong direction.' Failure is inevitable, but learning is optional. Failure is not your enemy unless you fail to learn from it. It is impossible not to fail at something if you're continually trying new things and growing. So make failure your friend by learning fast and getting to try again fast. That leads to growth and future success faster. No idea is perfect. No matter how good, it can be improved. Most revolutionary ideas were disruptive violations of existing rules. Failure should be another name for success if we learn from it. You cannot travel the road to success without a puncture or two, said a wise man.

Every master was once a disaster. (T. Harv Eker)

A bend in the road is not the end of the road, unless you fail to make the turn. (Helen Keller)

It has been said that, 'The greatest mistake you could make in life is to be continually fearing you will make one.' A man is not a failure when he is defeated, he is a failure when he quits. No one is ever truly defeated until he has accepted defeat as a reality. When you experience failure, don't wallow in regret: learn from it and get going again. Regret is an appalling waste of energy: you can't build on it!

Have you been embarrassed or ashamed only to discover later that your experience was supremely valuable? Maybe your failure turned your life in an important way that nothing else could have accomplished. We don't seem to learn very much when everything is going great. It is usually in failures that we pay more attention and learn.

Anyone can handle success. How you handle failure is a sign of greatness. Most leaders will suffer setbacks and discouragement; it goes with the territory if you are trying to accomplish something great. The one who is always playing it safe will never find out what kind of stuff they are made of.

Our failures and disappointments are not always what they appear to be, either. Maybe they are really just momentary set-backs. Failure does not mean that nothing has been accomplished. Successful people have more failure in their lives than average people do. Great people throughout history have all failed at some point. Those who do not expect anything are never disappointed, those who never try never fail. It is better to fail at doing something than excel at doing nothing. People who have no failures also have few victories. All people get knocked down. It is how fast they get up that counts. There is a positive correlation between spiritual maturity and how quickly a person responds to failure and setbacks. Failure is a situation, never a person.

Mistakes are often the best teachers. You can profit from your errors if you are reflective. Failure is not falling down but staying down and not learning from the fall. If you can learn from them, mistakes are invaluable. We fail only when we do not learn from an experience. Learn the lessons and forget the details. Don't listen to the negative voices when you make a mistake. They remind you only of the gory details, not the lessons learnt that can make you better.

There are many kinds of fears that can hold you back. One of them is self-doubt. You've failed in the past, so you're never going to try again. But just because you fail doesn't mean you give up. Everybody fails. It's the only way you learn what works!

There were two disciples who denied Jesus at the cross — Judas and Peter. They committed the same sin, but the difference was the way they reacted to their failure. Judas had a pity party, got depressed and took his life. Peter, however, realized what he did was wrong, so he prayed and repented and asked God for forgiveness. Then, Jesus chose Peter to preach on Pentecost, and 3,000 people were saved the first day. Jesus chose the biggest failure in the bunch to lead the church. What a God! God never sees us as failure: he sees us as learners. He didn't choose the superstar. He chose the guy who had blown it the most. God uses ordinary people who just keep on going instead of giving up.

Failure is a natural part of life. Show me someone who has not failed at least once and I'll show you someone who has not dared to succeed. All great personalities have failed, some many times, but every time they fall, they get up and try again, driven by their inner faith. Problem is, we hear about them only after they attain success.

A few failures, a few obstacles, a few setbacks should not throw you off the path of success. Simply consider them as minor nuisances, little tests of character. Have complete confidence that you will eventually succeed and attain your goals. And do you know what? Life has strange ways. When it realises that we are not going to quit or submit, no matter what obstacles it places in our path, when it sees that nothing can drain our determination and enthusiasm, then, like a maiden giving in to a persistent suitor, it gives us everything we ask for.

As you drive towards your destiny, you're sure to hit potholes along the way, or take some wrong turns, or forget to check your fuel-gauge and run out of fuel. The truth is, the only way to avoid failure is not to leave your driveway! The real issue in life isn't whether or not you're going to fail, but whether you're going to learn from your experience and turn it into the wisdom needed to succeed. In a survey of successful people, not one of them viewed their mistakes as failures. They considered them 'learning experiences', or tuition paid, or 'opportunities for growth'. That's the winning attitude!

It's defeat that turns bone to flint, gristle into muscle, and makes men invincible. Do not then be afraid of defeat. You are never so near victory as when you're defeated in a good course. (Henry Ward Beecher)

So the next time you fail at something, stop and ask yourself, What have I learned? am I grateful for this experience? how can I turn it into success? where do I go from here? and so on. If you do, you'll grow stronger and wiser because of what you've been through.

Failure means nothing at all if success comes eventually. The issue is not whether you have failed but whether you are content with failure. The secret of life is to fall seven times and get up eight times. Failure is simply what points you in the track of a better direction. Failure is not falling and getting up. Failure is falling and not trying and trying to get up again and again. It is only when you stop trying that you fail.

Failure (Folding Arms In Laziness Uttering Ridiculous Excuses)

How to Handle Failure

I read an interesting article doing the rounds on social media recently I don't know whether it was true or made-up, but it illustrates my point perfectly. Here it is:

"There was a very brilliant boy. He always scored 100% in science. Got selected for IIT Madras and scored excellently in IIT. He went to the University of California for MBA. Got a high paying job in America and settled there. Married a beautiful Tamil girl. Bought a big house and luxury cars. He had everything that made him successful; but a few years ago he committed suicide after shooting his wife and children. So, what went wrong? California Institute of Clinical Psychology Studied his case and found what went wrong. The researcher met the boy's friends and family and found that he lost his job due to America's economic crisis and he had to sit without a job for a long time. After reducing his previous salary, he didn't get any job. Then his house instalment broke and he and his family lost the home. They survived a few months with little money and then he and his wife together decided to commit suicide. He first shot his wife and children and then shot himself. The case concluded that the man was programmed for successes but not trained for handling failures.

Now let us come to the question: What are the habits of highly successful people? First of all, there are many people who will talk to you about the habits that lead to success, but today I am saying to you: even when you have achieved everything, there is a chance to lose everything; nobody knows when the next economic crisis will hit the world. The best success-habit according to me is getting trained for handling failures. I also request every parent not to program their child to be successful but to teach them also how to handle failures and the proper lessons about life. Learning high-level science and maths will help them to clear competitive exams, but a knowledge about life will help them to face every problem. Teach them about how money works, I say, instead of teaching them how to work for money. Help them find their passion, because these degrees might not help them in the next economic crisis."

Take action even if you fail, you are learning more ways not to do it and there is a greater chance of doing it right. Doing it wrong or badly is useful.

What would you do if you believed you could not fail? Now go do it!

24. Fear

Everything you want is on the other side of fear. (Jack Canfield)

The story is told about a man who approached a farm-house, and every few yards he noticed signs that read, 'Beware of Dog'. When he finally reached the farm-house he discovered the dog was a tiny Chihuahua. 'You mean to tell me that little dog keeps people away?' he asked. The farmer smiled and said, 'No, but the signs do!' Fear roars like a lion, but much of the time when we confront it, it's just a Chihuahua!

If you're going to be successful in life, you must move against your fears. You have to do the very thing that you fear the most! To fear the future is to waste the present, so don't fear the future - God is already there! Fear God and nothing else. The truth is, you can face anything when you know God has promised: 'I, the Lord thy God, will hold thy right hand, saying unto thee, Fear not; I will help thee' (Isaiah 41: 13 KJV). So instead of fearing the worst, start believing God for the best. And you do that by personalising His promises.

Fear knocked at my door. Faith answered ... and there was no one there! (Billy Sunday)

Bullies are scared people living inside scary people. (Michelle Obama)

Don't let fear in

What we give attention to, we also give authority to. Even if fear is present in your heart, you don't need to allow it to be president of our mind. You don't have to allow it to fill your windscreen. Don't get on the train of thought that focuses on the situation and doubt, fear or negativity: this will lead to failure and defeat. Shift your focus on the promises of God, on the faithfulness and goodness of

God - that is the train of faith and hope, and the destination is victory and success. The greatest enemies of the peace within are worry and fear. We have no control over the reality that in this world we will have trouble, but we have control over whether we decide to allow our hearts to be troubled. While worry will rob our joy, fear will steal our freedom, for what we fear establishes the boundaries of our freedom. What we fear has mastery over our souls. When we are fearful, we lose our strength; when we are anxious, we lose our courage. When we have found peace, we have both the strength and courage to live life to the full.

Peace does not come because we have everything under control. On the contrary, peace comes when we understand that we don't need to be in control to enjoy a full life. You cannot control your circumstances, but you can control your character. You cannot control the actions of others, but you can control the choices you make. You cannot control the outcome, but you can control the process. When you refuse to allow yourself to be paralysed by the uncertainty of tomorrow and choose to live with courage and faith, you begin to live an abundant life.

Fear will make you surrender to a condition where we simply just exist, paralysed by apathy or despair or discouragement. Worry consumes your energy without productivity. Fear consumes our energy, while faith restores it. Don't let fear have mastery over your soul; don't allow fear to create boundaries to your freedom. Refuse to be subjected to the tyranny of fear. Live fearlessly.

We gain strength and courage and confidence by each experience in which we really stop to look fear in the face ... we must do that which we think we cannot. (Eleanor Roosevelt)

Stand up to the bullies, but never stoop down to their level. (Michelle Obama)[18]

25. Feelings and emotions

A man in a passion rides a mad horse. (Benjamin Franklin)

On 16 August 2018, severe floods affected the south Indian state of Kerala, owing to unusually high rainfall during the monsoon season. Kerala received heavy monsoon rainfall, which was about 116% more than the usual rainfall, resulting in dams filling to their maximum capacities. It was the worst flood in Kerala in nearly a century. According to reports, over 480 people died, and about 140 are missing. Floods are among the most terrifying forces on Earth. They have led to countless disasters throughout history. Interestingly, the same heavy rain that causes floods can be harnessed in dams for the benefit of humanity. Dams are used not only to suppress and control floods but can also generate hydroelectricity and provide water for activities such as irrigation, human consumption and industrial use. Emotions are a bit like floods: well harnessed they will do much good; left untamed they will wreak untold havoc. Anger is like a river. Controlled, it can generate enough electricity to power an entire city. Uncontrolled, it can overflow its banks and become a raging flood that destroys everything in its path.

Anger, love, lust, envy, fear, happiness and sorrow are strong emotions that can propel us to the uttermost of virtues or make us plunge into the guttermost of vices. Emotions can vacillate between two extremes in such a short space of time that you will be a basket-case if you relied solely on them. Our feelings can infuse us with incredible ability to perform the noblest endeavours or the most despicable acts. Our feelings can elevate us to the celestial or dump us in the cesspit of life. Feelings are fickle, fleeting and floundering. Emotions are ephemeral, erratic and misleading; following them can lead to error. Our emotions have the capacity to make us or break us. Allowing them to take the lead can lead to disaster.

Anger and madness are brothers. (African proverb)

A popular cliché says: 'Just follow your heart.' Blindly following your heart is not a good idea. Our greatest achievements and our worst mistakes all come from the same place: the human heart. Just as a pilot needs instruments he can trust, you need objective filters for your soul. Your feelings aren't irrelevant; they just can't be the lord, master and director of your life. Scrutinize them, study them, monitor them, but don't trust them. Rather, sift them through an objective sieve, so that even when you feel like doing wrong, you can spot the danger and choose to avoid it.

Control your anger, because it's only one letter away from danger.

Strong emotions definitely have a great capacity for good. When people's feelings are strong about a worthy cause, they are stirred up and inspired to do a lot of good to help the poor and ensure that they get justice; to campaign for worthy causes, become activists to change the plight of the down-trodden. It was Wilberforce's passionate hatred of slavery that eventually led to the abolition of the slave-trade. So strong emotions can be directed to do a lot of good. When you feel passionate about a cause, take advantage of that powerful emotion and ride the waves of your emotion by being a voice for the voiceless, oppressed and needy in our society. An emotion like anger gives you a stronger hand in the game of life; it increases your chances of getting your way. For anger to have a resilience-building purpose it most have a purpose: to fight injustice, poverty etc.

Never make an important decision when you are angry or tired.

One of the best ways to control our feelings so we don't wreck our reputation or relationships is to react slowly or delay our response just a bit - if at all possible till the next day. In the heat of the moment, if you don't have to make the decision, don't. If you don't have to reply now, then don't.

The best cure for anger is delay.

I don't want to be at the mercy of my emotions.

Reading the bible can keep you from being fooled by the haze of our emotions, and it prevents us from being ruled by every thought and desire. God's rules are there for a reason—not to kill your joy but to enhance it. He has so much more in store for you than you could ever know. But to get there, you must relinquish your desire to navigate on your own, lest you lose your way. When you put your trust in the instruments God has given you, you set yourself up to soar. Don't simply follow your feelings and emotions, put them through an objective filter.

We are shaped and fashioned by what we love. (Johann Wolfgang von Goethe)

Anger rests in the bosom of fools. (Ecclesiastes 7:9)

Don't allow others' actions to affect your spirit. Impulsive actions can get you into trouble.

A man who has no rule or control over his emotions is like a city that broken down and without walls. (Pr 25:28)

Anybody can become angry - that is easy, but to be angry with the right person and to the right degree and at the right time and for the right purpose, and in the right way - that is not within everybody's power and is not easy. (Aristotle)

Anger is an acid that can do more harm to the vessel in which it is stored than to anything on which it is poured. (Mark Twain)

Anger is not like a dam behind which pressure inexorably rises as it fills up leading to catastrophe unless it is released. Emotion arises, partly out of how we think about a situation we are responding to. If we are able to reinterpret or re-engineer the situation, i.e. change our thinking about it, then the anger or emotion can be abated. Our thinking or mental state determines what we feel and to quite a remarkable extent. By a simple mental flip or reappraisal of a situation, anxiety can be transformed to excitement. Anger for instance can be transformed into an energy-giving invigoration. You will be made stronger emotionally to the extent you re-interpret and reappraise rather than suppress your emotion. For instance, you are in a queue at the train station and all of a sudden you feel a sharp elbow and push in your back which sends you careering into the people in front of you. What rudeness! You turn round in rage, nostrils flaring, ready to rebuke your assailant, only to discover it's a blind person who has lost her bearing in the crowd. Your anger abates faster than a balloon losing air. Your anger is assuaged by the act of reinterpreting or appraising the situation.[5]

I think this is a skill that can be practised or simulated in a variety of other scenarios. I know it's more easily said than done, but if we decide to practise reinterpreting potentially volatile situations perhaps we can get a better handle on our negative emotions and improve our relationships with our loved ones who often bear the brunt of our anger. I believe we can actually control our reaction because the reaction we exhibit towards a subordinate or a weaker person is usually different from the reaction we would display towards a stronger more threatening person, even if the offence from both parties is exactly the same. Miraculously, owing to the self-preservation instinct, we are more controlled in reacting to the stronger opponent.

Wisdom says "wait," emotions say, "Hurry!" (Joyce Meyer)

When your temper gets the best of you, it brings out the worst in you.

26. Focus

If you have more than three priorities, you don't have any. (Jim Collins)

Several years ago an airline crashed into the Florida Everglades. On its approach to Miami airport, the light indicator for proper deployment of the landing gear failed. While the crew checked the light assembly, none of them noticed that the aircraft was losing altitude. As a result the plane flew right into the swamp, killing 101 people on board. All was lost because the crew were distracted by a cheap light bulb and took their eyes off what mattered most. In life you'll be tempted to choose what seemed urgent over what seems important. [19]

Chase two rabbits and you will catch neither. (Confucius)

Blessed are the single-hearted, for they shall enjoy much peace. (Amy Carmichael)

One thought driven home is better than three left on base. (James Liter)

One clear example of someone who has harnessed the power of focus to build an extraordinary life is Bill Gates. Bill's one passion in high school was computers. He developed one skill: computer programming. While in high school he met Paul Allen, who gave him his first job and became his partner in forming Microsoft. Extraordinary results are directly determined by how narrow you can make your focus. Success comes when we do a few things very well. You need to be doing fewer things for more effect instead of doing more things with side effects.[20]

Focus gives you peace and tranquillity. Without focus, there is no peace. What are you aiming for? Delegate, simplify or eliminate low priorities as soon as possible. Do more by doing less. What you set your heart on will determine how you will spend your life. People who want to be everywhere get nowhere. The saying: Jack of all trades master of none, is true. To get what you want in life. Keep it in view and go for it, never let your eyes wander to the right or the left or up or down and never look back.

Put your eggs in one basket - and watch that basket! (Andrew Carnegie)

It is claimed that Andrew Carnegie in a speech made the following statement:

> 'Don't put all your eggs in one basket' is all wrong. I tell you, 'Put all your eggs in one basket, and then watch that basket.' Look round you and take notice; men who do that do not often fail. It is easy to watch and carry the one basket. It is trying to carry too many baskets that breaks most eggs in this country. He who carries three baskets must put one on his head, which is apt to tumble and trip him up. One fault of the American businessman is lack of concentration.'

*Follow One Course Until Successful- **FOCUS***

When you have a dozen different things to do, pick the most important one and stick with it until it's complete. Then pick the second most important and do the same thing, until you're done. The quickest way to do many things is to do only one thing at a time. You become effective by being selective. The power of focusing can be seen in a characteristic of light. Diffused light has little power or impact, but you can concentrate its energy by focusing it. With a magnifying glass, the rays of the sun can be focused to set paper on fire. When light is focused even more as a laser beam, it can cut through steel. There is nothing quite as potent as a focused life lived on purpose. If you want your life to have impact - focus it! Prune away even good activities and do only that which matters most. Never confuse activity with productivity.

Preoccupation with a good thing is no substitute for the right thing. Wherever focus goes, energy goes. Be ruthless with distractions. Constantly changing gear from one focus to the next without time to pause makes us unproductive, fatigued, and blurs our purpose and vision for timeless living.

Learning how to rein in your thoughts and focus is going to help you to achieve your goals in life. Without focus, you can never achieve anything. (Eric Phillips)

A 100-year-old millionaire, asked for his advice on how to succeed, wrote: 'Do fewer things more often and get better at them.' It is said that millionaires have three things in common: 1) a passion to succeed 2) an obsessive attention to detail: focus, alertness of mind; 3) eagerness to learn, to improve, to discover success secrets, principles.

The only reason men fail is because of broken focus. (Mike Murdock)

Our focus is our future, and what we focus on will multiply in our life. (David DeNotaris)

27. Forgiveness

Resentment is like drinking poison and waiting for your enemy to die.
(Nelson Mandela)

On Wednesday, 13 May 1981, in St. Peter's Square in Vatican City, four bullets hit Pope John Paul II – two of them lodging in his lower intestine, the others hitting his left hand and right arm. This assassination attempt on the pope left him severely wounded and with considerable blood loss. In July 1981, the perpetrator, Ali Ağca, was sentenced to life imprisonment. Pope John Paul II asked people to pray 'for my brother Ağca, whom I have sincerely forgiven'. Two years later, he was to take the hand of Ali Ağca, then in prison, and quietly tell him that he had forgiven him for what he had done (even though his would-be killer had not asked for forgiveness). He developed a friendship over the years, meeting Ağca's mother in 1987 and his brother a decade later. In June 2000 Ağca was pardoned by the Italian President at the pope's request. In February 2005 Ağca sent a letter to the pope wishing him well. When the pope died on 2 April 2005, Ağca's brother, Adrian, gave an interview saying that Ağca and his entire family were grieving and that the pope had been a great friend to them. [7]

Forgiveness is not an occasional act; it is a permanent attitude. (Martin Luther King)

In 1956 Martin Luther King Jr. was speaking at a rally when around 9pm a boy interrupted him and shouted that King's house had been firebombed by the Klu Klux Klan. King ran out of the rally and found his house still on fire! The police and fire department were there, along with a large angry mob of citizens from Montgomery, Alabama, there to support King. They surrounded the house with rifles, baseball bats, and other weapons ready to retaliate. The people were looking to get an eye for an eye! King stepped on to the porch of his home and said these words, 'I want you to love your enemies. Be good to them, love them, and let them know that you love them. We must meet hate with love. What we are doing is right, what we are doing is just, and God is with us. Go home with love in our hearts, with faith, and, with God in front, we cannot lose.' As he spoke these words the angry mob put down their guns and baseball bats and spontaneously broke into singing Amazing Grace. They sang, they cried, and they peacefully went back to their homes.

When we return hate with hate it never ends well, but when we turn the other cheek - even to our enemies - that's when change is on the way! MLK brought change to the world by seeing things as Jesus saw them.

It is said that holding a grudge is like letting someone live rent free in your head. If someone has offended you, don't return the offence: instead return hatred with love. Speak well of the other person even behind their back and you may find that your love puts an end to the bickering and heals the relationship. Guard your friendships. When there is a fallout, always seek reconciliation.

Author Max Lucado says: 'Revenge builds a lonely, narrow house. Space enough for one person. The lives of its tenants are reduced to one goal: Make someone miserable. They do - themselves.

Jesus said, 'Forgive, and you will be forgiven.' Forgive people even if they are not sorry. Forgiveness saves the expense of anger, the cost of hatred and the waste of energy. The forgiveness that God gives you should be a virtuous circle that overflows into your relationships with others. Lack of forgiveness is a barrier to prayer and to your relationship with God. He says, 'And when you stand praying, if you hold anything against anyone, forgive them, so that your Father in heaven may forgive you your sins.' Jesus says we are not to hold 'anything against anyone'. There are no limits to forgiveness. Lack of forgiveness destroys relationships. Jesus also said in Matthew 5:44, 'Do good to them that hate you.' In other words, learn to travel light, without the heavy baggage of resentment and bitterness.

Forgiveness sometimes takes great courage but it restores relationships and brings great joy. Forgiveness doesn't diminish justice; it entrusts it to God. He guarantees the right amount of retribution. We give too much or too little, but He has the precise prescription. Also long after we have moved on, God is still there probing the conscience, stirring conviction, orchestrating redemption.

A man was having his portrait painted by a successful artist. When the portrait was finished it was unveiled. The man was most unhappy with the result. When asked whether he liked it, he replied, 'I don't think it does me justice.' To which the artist replied, 'Sir, it is not justice you need, but mercy!' We all need mercy, so let's be sure we are quick to dispense it.

Do you ever find it difficult to forgive other people or even to forgive yourself for something you have done? The key to forgiving others and yourself is knowing how much God has forgiven you. Forgiven people forgive. As C.S. Lewis pointed out, 'To be a Christian means to forgive the inexcusable because God has forgiven the inexcusable in you.' As far as forgiving yourself is concerned, he wrote, 'If God forgives us we must forgive ourselves. Otherwise, it is almost like setting up ourselves as a higher tribunal than him.' Unforgiveness is extra unnecessary baggage. Things like resentment and bitterness will weigh us down and can sabotage our dream. When it comes to the past, it may not be possible to forget it, but it is possible not to dwell on it.

The memory may be there, but the sting is gone. (Archibald Hart)

When we feel we have been cheated by life, we make a choice to allow ourselves to become bitter and withdrawn or we can decide to learn from the experience and become better. When your world appears to come apart at the seams due to circumstances that are not your doing, it makes you angry to think that you have been cheated out of your right to be happy. But this should not be the end of your life. Let it be merely a temporary detour that will eventually help you move in a more positive direction. The truth is that it is the one who has been wronged who has all the power, not the one who does the wrong. And our power comes in the form of forgiveness. When we forgive, we liberate ourselves to live the life God has given us. Forgiveness is a powerful force in the hands of those who have been wronged. Forgiveness does not take away the consequences of our actions, though.

It is not what others do or even our own mistakes that hurt us the most: it is our response to those things. Chasing after the poisonous snake that bites you will only drive the poison through your system more quickly. It is far better to take immediate measures to take the poison out. We are free to choose our response in any situation, but in doing so, we choose the attendant consequences. When you pick up one end of the stick, you pick up the other. When you make a mistake, admit it, correct it, learn from it and turn a failure into success. It is inspiring to realise that in choosing our response to circumstances, we powerfully affect our circumstances. When we change one part of chemical formulae, we change the nature of the results. The most effective and positive way I can influence any situation in my life is to work on me.

When you're insulted, you can retaliate with a stinging comeback or see it as a growth opportunity. One could say the person who insults us is a teacher that has come to help us reduce our ego, develop patience and compassion, practise unconditional forgiveness, and teach us about life and relationships. They are friends in disguise. If you don't perceive an insult as such, but as a teaching or a gift, it loses its power to hurt you. On a practical level, if you're insulted, say nothing. Give yourself time. Much harm is created by lashing back escalating the situation and saying things you will regret later. Recognise this: it's your ego - that false sense of pride acting up. You don't have to go along with it! Take pleasure in insults (it's not easy), let it build character and push you to be better and to do better but never become bitter.

Being able to apologise without it being demanded is a sign of maturity and growth. The ability to apologise quickly when you've done wrong is a sign of a bigger person. Those who cannot apologise when they are wrong and know it are small people. So don't be a small person, be a big person. Don't mess with small people - they will bring you to their level.

A great man shows his greatness; by the way he treats little men - with grace. You can agree to disagree, walk arm-in-arm even if you don't see eye-to eye on every issue.

The first to apologise is the bravest. The first to forgive is the strongest. The first to forget is the happiest. (Unknown)

28. Giving - Generosity

Never measure your generosity by what you give, but rather by what you have left. (Fulton Sheen)

In Charles Dickens' 1843 classic; A Christmas Carol the cold-hearted, tight-fisted, penny-pinching, callous and stingy Ebenezer Scrooge is transformed into a benevolent, generous, magnanimous and charitable soul after his encounter with the three spirits who show him his past, present and future. It's a terrifying experience that leaves him visibly shaken. Not knowing whether it was a dream or real, he was swift in making amends. Scrooge lives out the rest of his days spending his time and money generously for the good of others. By his generosity his life was forever transformed from sad, lonely and miserable to joyful and blessed.[20]

Mother Teresa once said in an interview when asked if it is only the wealthy who give. She replied, 'No, even the poorest of the poor give. The other day a very poor beggar came up to me and said, "Everyone gives to you and I also want to give you twenty paisa" – which is about tuppence. I thought to myself, what do I do? If I take it he won't have anything to eat, but if I don't take it I would hurt him so much. So I took it, and he was so happy because he had given to Mother Teresa of Calcutta to help the poor. Giving cleans the heart and helps you get closer to God. You get so much back in return.'[21]

Giving purges the character from the constricting grip of materialism that destroys lives. (Nicky Gumbel)

Giving destroys the stranglehold of money over our lives and makes God the stronghold of our lives. (Yomi Akinpelu)

Rick Warren shares a story of man who goes with his son to a fast food restaurant and bought him some French fries. On the way home, the fries smelled so good he reached over and took one French fry out of his son's carton and ate it. His son got all upset and said, 'Dad, you can't have that one. These are my fries!' The dad immediately had three thoughts. First, my child has forgotten that I am the source of all fries. I took him to McDonald's, I made the order, I paid for the order, I handed them to him, and I'm driving him back home. The only reason he got any fries was because of me, the Great Fry Giver! Second, my child doesn't realise I could take the fries away in a second if I wanted to. Or, on the other hand, I could buy him an entire truckload of fries if I wanted to, because I have the power to do either. Third, I didn't need his fries. I could easily get my own. I could buy myself a hundred cartons of them if I wanted to. I just wanted him to learn to be unselfish.[38]

Generosity is a beautiful characteristic in people. We love and admire generosity. The lord loves a cheerful giver and so does everybody else. How do you think of God? Do you think of him as a little bit mean or tight-fisted? Or do you think of him as extraordinarily generous? God's generosity is seen in the natural world. For example, there are over 25,000 varieties of orchids. The orchid is just one of 270,000 species of flowers. God does not do things by halves! In our galaxy there are over 100 billion stars like our sun. Our galaxy is one of over 100 billion galaxies. It is thought that for every grain of sand there are a million stars. God is extraordinarily, extravagantly, generous.

John Wesley said, 'When I have money, I get rid of it quickly, lest it find a way into my heart.' Generosity is the way to break the hold of money in our lives. Francis Bacon said, 'Money is like manure. It's not good unless it is spread around.'

Jewish wisdom

If you see someone donating to charity, be assured that his wealth is increasing. Giving money away makes you feel a better person, which makes you come across as a better person. If you feel like a grasshopper, you most certainly appear to be one from the perspective of those around you (ask the ten spies). If you have generosity of spirit to give money away, you also have the courage to seek profit by placing your money at risk.

The internal quality that allows you to give money away is exactly the same quality that allows you to invest money in business to make a profit. Investing or giving might be counterintuitive, but it offers the best chance and opportunity of successfully growing your money. Make money flow by giving, and you will inevitably be creating bonds. With bonds in place, more money flows. Like anything else that flows, money requires pipelines. The process of giving creates channels and conduits that remain open and usable even after they have served their purpose of conveying your money to others. Now that the pipelines exist, they are able to be used for cash-flow in the reverse direction too. Giving away money keeps your investment muscle fully exercised and ready for opportunity.

You have to feel that you deserve good things, or else your subconscious might very well sabotage all your best efforts. If you do not feel you deserve financial success, you have an uphill task. Giving regular gifts to charities, church, the needy and family is an excellent way of persuading your subconscious that you indeed deserve to be wealthy. In this way the subconscious will end its sabotage and even actively assist you in your quest.[22]

When God blesses you, don't just give Him the credit, give Him some cash too.

When God blesses people, some raise their standard of living, other raise their standard of giving. Which category do you fall into? Giving creates a window in the spiritual/intangible realm. The size of the window determines what comes back to you. Giving destroys the hold of greed and the fear of not having enough; giving releases the spirit of abundance into your life and helps you develop an abundance mindset. Life gets better when you share, give and serve. The law of the harvest is that you reap more than you sow. It is what you give that adds value to your life, not what you receive.

A glass that is completely full can take more only if you pour out of it. You grow by pouring out; giving and sharing. Your capacity grows and expands when you share. When you share your knowledge with ten people, they get to hear it once; you get to hear it ten times, and that expands your capacity and increases your depth.

You reap what you sow. Sow generously and you will reap generously. Sow many acts of value over your lifetime, and you will be amazed at the harvest when you are old. Sow sparingly and you will find yourself impoverished when you meet the grim reaper.

He is no fool who gives what he cannot keep to gain that which he cannot lose. (Jim Elliot)

Giving versus Loaning

Over twenty-five years ago I loaned someone hundreds of pounds. It meant a lot to me because it represented almost all I had in life-savings. They promised to pay it back in a couple of months, in about four or five instalments. About a year on, they had not paid even half of it. I was very bitter, but for the sake of my peace of mind and well-being I decided to forgive the debt and move on. What a relief I felt!

Now, when it comes to loaning money I believe that if you can't afford to lose it, you shouldn't lend it. You are better off being generous than putting yourself in a position where someone else has power over your peace and joy. That is why it's better to give than loan money to family members or friends because, if they don't pay you, it can cause a rift and destroy relationships. If you can't afford to lose it, don't loan it! Someone said: the quickest way to lose a friend is to lend them money. What may be partially true is you have the wrong kind of friends!

29. Goals

When you reach for the stars, you may not quite get them, but you won't come up with a handful of mud either. (Leo Burnett)

He arrived in America with nothing but $250 in his pocket, but he had other stuff: a big plan to achieve his goal and a belief that he could grow a business faster than any business in history. Sabeer Bhatia created Hotmail. Microsoft, seeing Hotmail's spectacular growth, eventually bought it for $400 million. Bhatia had an unrelenting conviction he would accomplish his goal - and he did.

The best way to predict the future is to create it. (Abraham Lincoln)

A high-school teacher asked the class to write about what they wanted to do when they grew up. A young boy wrote that he wanted to own a ranch and raise thoroughbred racehorses. His teacher gave him an F and explained that the dream was unrealistic for a boy living in a camper in the back of a pickup truck: he would never be able to make this a reality. When the teacher offered the chance to rewrite his paper for a higher grade, he told him, 'You keep your F; I'm keeping my dream.' That boy was Monty Roberts. Today, Monty's 154-acre ranch in Solvang, California, is home to world-class thoroughbred racehorses.[23]

Give me a stock clerk with a goal, and I'll give you someone who'll make history. On the other hand, give me someone without a goal, and I'll give you a stock clerk. (J. C. Penney)

As you are working on your goals, your goals are working on you. The process of working on your goals makes you grow. The achievement of your goals is not nearly so important as who you become in the process of achieving it. Dreams are the seedlings of reality. Set goals and attempt things so big that if they are accomplished, only God can get the credit. A God-given goal will stretch you. The first part of identifying your dream is in identifying what you love to do and what you are great at doing. Having clearly defined goals simplifies life.

You can analyse the past, but you have to design the future. (Edward De Bono)

A wise man once said: 'Set goals not for what you will obtain, but for what you will become in the process of achieving it.' For example, set a goal to become a millionaire not for the million pounds per se, but for the skills you will develop in the process of achieving it, or just for who you will become in the process of achieving it.

When you get a huge dream, you have to be ready for the window of opportunity to open, because the window isn't always open. However, if you're ready when that window opens and you seize the opportunity, that open window will take you one step closer to the dream. There have been periods in my life when a window of opportunity opened and I walked through it. And possibly others that I missed.

It is said that 50% of the people around you have no idea where they're going. Another 40% will go in any direction they're led. The remaining 10% know where they'd like to go - but fewer than half of them are prepared to pay the price to get there.

Where you are used to is not where you belong. What you believe and dream is where you belong. Success does not drift to people, you have to swim to meet it. Success is peace of mind, which is a direct result of knowing you did your best to become the best that you are capable of being, that you left no stone unturned. The possibility of having a dream come true makes life interesting - so dream big. When you want something, all the universe conspires in helping you achieve it.

People are capable, at anytime in their lives, of doing what they dream of.

How frequently you bring to mind your goals and keep them in front of you has an impact on how quickly and well they manifest. Always keep a written and pictorial form of your goals before you. It must never be off your radar at any time. Out of sight is out of mind. If this happens to your goals, they will lie dormant and unfulfilled. Know this: you're not going to create a desired result if you write your goals down and never look at them again. Success is the result of keeping those images and goals in front of you, focusing on them, praying over them and thanking God for them. The more time spent doing this, the more you're going to create a driving desire to go after and ultimately accomplish your goals. Success-coaches like Terry Savelle encourage you to make a vision board; a picture form of your goals and dreams and keep it before you. Other coaches encourage you write out your list of goals daily; keeping it before your eyes daily. As you keep your goals before your eyes daily, God is going to give you ideas and new ways of doing things that you never thought of before. He will bring into your life people that will help you accomplish your goals - people you never imagined you would meet, people you dreamed about meeting one day. God is looking for dreamers. He wants you to enlarge your thinking. He wants you to think beyond the realm of possibilities. He's unlimited, so stop thinking small. God needs you to open your imagination to believe that the dreams you have in your heart can happen for you. Stretch your faith to believe in something that's totally impossible because He specialises in the impossible.

You've got to have a dream if you want a dream to come true. (Oscar Hammerstein II)

I recently came across the story of Oliver Wendell Holmes and his train-ticket. Holmes was a Supreme Court justice who was very respected, very intelligent but a little bit absent-minded. Apparently, Holmes was on a train one day when the ticket-inspector began walking down the carriage, checking tickets. As Holmes searched for it, the conductor, obviously irritated, said, 'It's okay, your honour; just mail it in. We all know you and trust you.' Holmes replied, I'm not concerned about finding my ticket - I just want to know where I'm going!' Having goals lets you know where you're going in life.

Start the process of achieving your goals today. Start acting the part of where you see yourself. Look your best! Look sharp! Look the part (without paying a fortune) of where you are going and who you want to be, not where you are. Take action towards your goals - take that first step. Do not quit no matter what - be persistent. Take one step at a time. Avoid the nay-sayers, surround yourself with positive people. Welcome feedback and put it to use. No one does it alone - you need others - ask for help and give help.

Obstacles are what we see when we take our eyes off the goal. (Henry James)

A list of goals is important: goals are your vision of the future. You can face your future with either apprehension or anticipation. It will be with apprehension if you don't have it well designed.

People are afraid to pursue their most important dreams because they feel they don't deserve them or that they'll be unable to achieve them. In the process of pursuing your dreams, you will discover things on the way that you never would have seen had you not had the courage to try things that seemed impossible for you to achieve. Before a dream is realised, one must endure tests. So in addition to realising our dreams, master the lessons we've learned as we've moved towards that dream. That's the point at which most people give up. So, how do you go about achieving your goals? Write them down in present tense and first person - as if you have achieved them already. Focus on three to seven goals until they are achieved. Read and speak them out daily. Express gratitude for them daily. Additionally write your goals down daily over thirty days: this will cause them to be ingrained indelibly on your mind. You might even decide to make a life-long habit of writing your goals every morning in your journal.

According to a study on goal-setting, people who write down their goals are more likely to achieve them than those who don't. A group of students were about to graduate, and they were asked to set goals for themselves. Some didn't set goals and some did without writing them down, but a small percentage in the group, wrote down their goals. After many years this same group of students were interviewed and something very astonishing was discovered. Those who set goals and never wrote them were earning twice as much as those who never set any goals, and those who set goals and wrote them down were earning ten times as much as those who set goals but never wrote them down.[24]

A final word on goals: they are not an end in themselves and they do not determine success. To be sure, without them you're on the road to nowhere, but remember, goals give you a sense of direction, but it is your consistent habits that will take you there. You do not rise to the level of your goals: you fall to the level of your habits or systems that take you to the goal.

The tragedy of life lies not in not reaching your goals but in having no goals to reach. (Benjamin Elijah Mays)

30. Gratitude

We pray for the big things and forget to give thanks for the ordinary, small (and yet really not small) gifts. (Dietrich Bonhoeffer)

During the Great Depression, an impoverished old woman who resided in the heart of Appalachia lived in a tiny shack with dirt floors, no heating and no indoor plumbing was asked what she would do if someone gave her some money to help her out. The woman thought for a moment and answered, 'I guess I'd give it to the poor.' Apparently she did not see herself as poor, despite her situation. What a great perspective! Life is a miracle - be grateful for it. Realising there are people around you who have much bigger problems than yours brings gratitude and perspective.

Some people complain that roses have thorns. Instead be thankful that thorns have roses. (Alphonse Karr)

Joy and depression cannot reside in the same space, they cannot co-exist at the same time, they are mutually exclusive. Gratitude changes your focus from what you don't have to what you do have. Gratitude changes your perception. Your perception changes your existence. Steve Harvey says that, to overcome depression, start writing down in detail everything you have to be grateful for; big or small, just write it down, e.g. health, friends, food accommodation. Start thanking God every morning for what you are grateful for. It will surprise you how long you will be writing. Gratitude erases negativity. Also, gratitude changes your focus from what you don't have to what you do have. After you've thanked God for what you're grateful for, then take another piece of paper and write a list of everything you want. According to Steve Harvey, God is going to take the two lists and tie them together and, because you've expressed gratitude for the things on the first list, He's going to begin to transfer the things on the second list to the first list so you can have more things to be grateful for. The more grateful you are, the more He's going to give you more things to be grateful for. He's going to keep on taking more stuff from your want list and putting it on the gratitude list.

More things matter little until they are lost. Give your attention to the really important things. (Ola-Vincent Odulele)

Terry Savelle Foy often says: 'A grateful heart is a magnet for miracles and a positive attitude creates positive results. When you complain, you are magnifying how bad things are and you'll attract more to complain about. The opposite is true as well: When you focus on what's going right in your life, you'll attract more positive results!' If you can't be thankful for what you have, be thankful for what you have escaped! The seeds of discouragement will not grow in a thankful heart. Be aggressively thankful. Don't take things for granted; seize them for gratitude. An old African saying states: If you can think, you will be able to thank. If you think more, you will thank more. Both words think and thank come from the same Latin root. The most highly satisfied life can be found in being thankful. Appreciative words are one of the most powerful forces for good on earth.

By celebrating the small stuff and feeling gratitude for it, things you never noticed before will come into focus. (Jane Trumbull)

Being thankful causes you to attract more to be thankful for. Being disgruntled and complaining causes you to attract more of what you complain about. Your life will begin to change tremendously when you begin to vocalise what you believe God intends to do for you and through you. If you appreciate what you already have, you will find that you have more to appreciate. What you appreciate, appreciates. The more you complain the less you obtain.

There are only two ways to live your life. One is as though nothing is a miracle. The other is as though everything is a miracle. (Albert Einstein)

Miracles are the deliberate acts of God provoked by the desperate faith of men. (Dr David Oyedepo)

Be thankful for what you have; you'll end up having more. If you concentrate on what you don't have, you will never have enough. (Oprah Winfrey)

We've heard it said that happy people are not always grateful but grateful people are almost always happy. Let's think about that. Of all the grateful people we know, how many of them are miserable? Zero. How do we remain grateful in the hustle and bustle of daily life? By being intentional. The most rewarding things in our lives take a great amount of intention. And remaining in a grateful state of mind each day requires intentionality. One of the best ways for our heart to stay in a gratitude posture is to count our blessings. That's right: literally start naming them. To simply stop and count our blessings will lead to an attitude overhaul.

I started out giving thanks for small things, and the more thankful I became, the more my bounty increased. That's because — for sure — what you focus on expands. (Oprah Winfrey)

31. Habits

People do not decide their futures: they decide their habits, and their habits decide their futures. (F. M. Alexander)

In 2002 Terri was in a terrible place: no goals, no vision, no money and on the verge of marital breakdown. She decided that she would do five things daily. Twelve years later she is an author of many books, international speaking engagements, restored marriage, money in the bank, lovely home and much more. According to Terry Savelle Foy, your repetition is your reputation. The secret of your future is hidden in your daily routine so; conquer the covers, win the battle of the bed and practise the habit of mind over mattress. Furthermore, she says, 'If you can change your routine, you can change your whole life.' Terri shares what she calls the 'Rule of Five': it simply refers to choosing and doing five things daily. These five habits will cause you to go from ordinary to extraordinary. All you have to do is find the five things necessary to achieve your own specific life-goals and do them every day. You have to figure out what your five things are: e.g. to pray, read, listen to something inspiring, meditate and think. Some of these are my five daily habits; your five things may differ from mine. Doing these five habits daily is like swinging an axe five times a day to cut down a tree. Eventually the tree will come down depending on how big your tree is. Now all you have to do once you have figured out your five daily habits is: find your tree; find your purpose.

Motivation is what gets you started. Habit is what keeps you going. (Jim Ryun)

Have you ever thought that in order to change your life you need to make big drastic changes? Well, apparently you don't. According to a world-renowned habits expert, James Clear, the real changes in life come from the compound effect of a few small changes. They can be as small as waking up five minutes earlier; or already having your clothes ready the night before; or even to reading a book for ten minutes before going to bed. Be careful not to neglect doing the small things in your life that make the big things happen.[25]

Good habits formed at youth make all the difference. (Aristotle)

Some people say it takes twenty-one to thirty days to develop a habit. Personally I have not developed any habit in such a short period, so naturally I was delighted when I read that researchers at University College, London suggest that it takes an average of sixty-six days for a new habit to become ingrained. The full range was 18 to 254 days, but sixty-six days represented the ideal. Habits can be good or bad. Therefore, over time, you can be developing habits that will enhance your life or set you back. The great value of a habit is that it becomes automatic: practise the good habit long enough and you don't have to think about it anymore, you just do it. Change starts first in the mind. The way you think determines the way you feel, and the way you feel influences the way you act. Thinking determines feelings; feelings determine actions; actions determine habits; habits determine destiny.

Chains of habit are too light to be felt until they are too heavy to be broken. (Warren Buffet)

The foundation for achievement is regularly working at something until it regularly works for you. When you discipline yourself, you're essentially training yourself to act in a specific way. Stay with it long enough and it becomes a habit. Success is about doing the right thing, not about doing everything right. The payoff from developing the right habits are quite remarkable: it simplifies your life, your life gets clearer and less complicated. You don't have to monitor everything; you just have to do the right thing. Developing these good habits is hard only in the beginning: over time, the habit becomes easier and easier to sustain because it's automatic and so requires less effort and energy than in the beginning. The hard stuff becomes a habit, and habit makes the hard stuff easy.

Habits change into character. (Ovid)

Habit is the daily battleground of character. Habits start as fine, weak cobwebs and end up as thick as cables. Because you don't see results fast enough, you think those small good or bad habits don't matter much. Somebody said it can take 300 repetitions of a good habit to replace a bad habit! It takes discipline to change a habit because habits are formed a little bit each day, day by day, every day. Once habits are formed they act like giant cables: almost unbreakable. The adage; old habits die hard, is true.

First we form habits, then they form us. Conquer your bad habits, or they will eventually conquer you. (Anon)

Ultimately, people don't decide their future; they decide their habits, and their habits decide their future. From the time you get up in the morning to the time you go to sleep at night, your habits largely control you: the words you say, the things you do and the ways you react and respond.

What separates successful people from unsuccessful people can be summed up in one word - habits. Aristotle says 95% of everything you do is as a result of habits. 80% of those who win the lottery file for bankruptcy within five years because of habits. Psychologists say that 90% of what we do is as a result of habit, i.e. basically action on autopilot. Bad habits are easy to form but hard to live with. Good habits are hard to form but easy to live with.

The secret to permanently breaking any bad habit is to love something greater than the habit. (Bryant McGill)

So, how do we break bad habits and start new and better ones? Because habits happen instinctively and subconsciously, they can only be broken by long-term disciplined activity. We must unweave every strand of the cable of habit slowly and methodically until the giant cable that once held us bound becomes scattered strands of wire. Consistent application of a new more desirable discipline will help us to overcome a bad habit.

A wise man said, 'What we do on some great occasion will depend on what you are, and what we are is the result of previous years of self-discipline.' In other words, a person's secret to success is found in their daily agenda. A dream becomes a reality as a result of your actions, and your actions are controlled, to a large extent, by your habits.

Small disciplines done consistently lead to big results over time. (Craig Groeschel)

Making and breaking habits consists of tons of daily attainable steps that result in huge change. In other words, small achievements seriously matter. Habits aren't grand destinations you reach in one day — *they're small* steps you take every day. Some of the most important small achievements you can make are often called 'keystone habits'. A keystone is also known as a capstone: it is the term for the wedge-shaped stone that would sit at the top and centre of an arch of bricks or stones. Each stone in the arch pushes its weight toward the keystone, and the triangular shape of the keystone wedge locks all the stones into position so the entire arch is supported. If you remove the keystone, the entire structure falls down. A keystone habit provides support and momentum for other habits in your life.

Here are six keystone habits that can affect your health spiritually, relationally, mentally and even materially. Which ones will you consider adding to your life?[26]

1. Wake up early enough to pray, meditate and plan the day ahead.

2. Read at least twenty minutes daily.

3. Connect meaningfully with your family or friends daily e.g. eat a meal together.

4. Make positive affirmations about yourself every day.

5. Listen to motivational and inspirational audio every day.

6. Exercise at least three-four times a week for at least twenty minutes.

When you cut an orange there might be only five or six seeds inside — which doesn't seem like much — but imagine how many more oranges each of those seeds could produce. Developing a half dozen habits might not seem like much but the secret to your future success can be found in those half dozen habits.

You'll never change your life until you change something you do daily. The secret to your success is found in your daily routine. (John Maxwell)

32. Happiness / joy

The secret to happiness is making someone else happy.

There is a humorous story of a middle-aged woman who had a heart-attack and was rushed to the hospital. On the operating table she had a near-death experience. Seeing the angel Gabriel, she asked whether she would make it. Gabriel told her she had about four more decades to live. After she recovered, reasoning that she had several decades to live, she decided to be happy, enjoy her life to the full and live a little. So at the hospital before returning home she had plastic surgery on her face, a tummy tuck, sucked out some fat and enhanced some curves in the right places; you know, the whole works. She had a hairdresser come in to the hospital to give her a hair-cut and she even changed her hair colour. When she observed herself in the mirror, she was elated with her new look. Feeling a little heady, she made her way home. Unfortunately she was knocked down right outside the hospital by a speeding vehicle and rushed back to the operating theatre. When she arrived at the gates of heaven, she was livid and said:

'I thought you said I had another forty years to live?'

'I didn't recognise you!' the angel replied.

The point of the story? Live a little, be happy, enjoy your life, but don't go overboard. (And don't get distracted, so you don't get knocked out before your time).

Unhappiness is not knowing what we want and killing ourselves to get it. (Don Herold)

Don't postpone your happiness to a later date or when you achieve a certain goal. Don't wait until you have a near-death experience before you begin to enjoy life. Be happy on your way to your ideal. Most people get into what is called the 'when and then' thinking: when this happens, then I'll be happy; when I buy a house, then I'll be happy; when I get married, then I'll be happy; when I have kids, then I'll be happy; when my kids go off to school, then I'll be happy; when I make my first million, then I'll be happy. Don't save your happiness for a special occasion. Every day you're alive is a special occasion. Don't put off, hold back, or save anything that would add laughter and lustre to your life or that of your loved ones.

Happiness is going somewhere you desire wholeheartedly in one direction without regret or reservation.

Refuse to force hilarity into the back seat every time responsibility takes the wheel. If the fun's gone, it's because we didn't want it around - not because it didn't fit. You are as happy as you choose to be. Happiness is a choice! If you're not happy now, you're not going to be happy later. If you go to some of the worst slums in the world you will see two people living right next door to each other. One is miserable, and one is happy. If you visit the most opulent parts of the world the same situation prevails. Why? Happiness has nothing to do with your circumstances. It has everything to do with your attitude. If you're not happy living on what you're living on right now, you're not going to be happy with any more. Because you're always going to want a little bit more. Happiness is a choice. Choose to enjoy what God has given you right now for your enjoyment! When I was squatting with friends, I was happy; when I got a council flat, I was dizzy with joy; when we bought our first house I was delighted; when we bought another house in a nicer neighbourhood, I was elated; and when we move to our mansion, I will still be happy.

Joy is the springboard of answers. Happiness is an inside job. He who laughs will last, but he who doesn't expires fast. Happiness is moving in the right direction, even if you are not at your final destination. Happiness does not come from what you get, from the size of your bank account or from material possessions, happiness comes from what or who you are becoming.

Whoever is happy will make others happy. (Anne Frank)

The writer of *Ecclesiastes* says, 'We should make the most of what God gives, both the bounty and the capacity to enjoy it, accepting what's given and delighting in the work. It's God's gift! God deals out joy in the present, the now' (Ecclesiastes 5:19, MSG). Learn to enjoy this wonderful gift of life in the present. If you do not, life will pass you by and you will never enjoy where you are right now. Don't keep on postponing your enjoyment to the future. If you die today you cannot take your wealth with you. You will have to leave it all, and who knows: those who get to enjoy it may blow it all on things you don't value or approve of. So while you're chasing success and working round the clock, remember to live a little, take a break (perhaps have a Kit Kat) and enjoy the financial and material rewards that come from your labour. Be mindful to share your blessings with others less fortunate than you. This is another fabulous way to double your joy.

You'll be as happy as you make up your mind to be. (Abraham Lincoln)

Happiness comes as a result of satisfaction with our activity. It is contact and connection with people of substance who value us. It is contentment with the tasks of your life, it is activity with purpose. It is life in balance. The money won't make you happy, it's who (or what) you become that determines your happiness. Happiness comes not from pieces of great success but from small advantages hammered out daily. We must be happy with what we've got when we're in pursuit of what we want. You won't be happier than you are now when you reach your goals. Make your mind up to be happy now: every day enjoy the journey on your way to your great goals.

Knowing God is happiness, as atheist-turned-apologist C. S. Lewis explains: 'God cannot give us happiness and peace apart from Himself, because it is not there.' It can only be found in Him – and His Word.

Laughter is good medicine. (Pr 17:22)

Nicky Gumbel, shares a story of someone who found real joy: This young man called Earl had a lot of money. He took all kinds of drugs, including heroin. At the age of thirty he ended up in hospital. Someone came to visit him in hospital and gave him a New Testament. He was thrilled. The paper was very thin and was ideal for rolling joints. He rolled his way through the Gospels of Matthew, Mark and Luke. However when he came to John's Gospel, he started reading. Subsequently he encountered Jesus, just by reading John. He was filled with joy.

The psychologist in charge of his case; a beautiful young woman, one day she said to Earl, 'Look, I have it all – success, beauty and endless qualifications – yet I am not fulfilled. Your life is a mess yet you seem to have something – a peace and a joy. What is it?'

He told her his experience and led her to faith in Jesus Christ. Later they were married and attended theological college in Oxford.[7]

Happenings should not determine your happiness or quality of life, it's what you do with what happens and your perspective that determines the quality of your life.

Smile More

You never are fully dressed until you wear a smile. It's the best face-lift. Each time you smile, you throw a little feel-good party in your brain. The act of smiling activates neural messaging that benefits your health and happiness. The feel-good neurotransmitters — dopamine, endorphins and serotonin — are all released when a smile flashes across your face. This not only relaxes your body, but it can also lower your heart-rate and blood-pressure. You're actually better-looking when you smile. When you smile, people treat you differently. You're viewed as attractive, relaxed and sincere. Did you know that your smile is actually contagious? If you're smiling at someone, it's likely they can't help but smile back. Your face reflects your heart. Some people's faces radiate love and joy. Their smile puts us at ease and cheers us up. Others have a sour expression on their face and can make us feel very uncomfortable.

Your face often reflects your heart. 'A happy heart makes the face cheerful' (Proverbs 15:13 MSG). A wise man once said the life we have lived eventually shows on our face; therefore everybody over forty is responsible for their face! It can be hard to smile if life's tough, but a smile truly does transform a face. So smile more, it's free!

It's one short step from 'why me' to 'woe is me' so don't go there!

Good humour is the health of the soul, sadness is its poison. (Philip Stanhope, 4th Earl of Chesterfield)

I have chosen to be happy because it is good for my health. (Voltaire)

33. Health

It is health that is real wealth and not pieces of gold and silver.
(Mahatma Gandhi)

Someone once said, 'Take care of your body; it's the only place you have to live.' Your body is your earth suit and if you lose it or run it down, you're out of here. Your body is what gives you permission to stay on planet earth. If it packs up, you become 'illegal' on earth. You can't do well if you don't feel well. You can't perform to your peak if you don't have your health. Your health is valuable. Les Brown once said; your body is the only vehicle that will carry you through out this experience called life. Make sure it's well-tuned and well taken care of so it doesn't breakdown before you reach your desired destination.

We often take our health for granted especially when we're young. Wisdom demands that we stop doing that. We need to treat our bodies with respect. The human body is an incredible divine creation. It's priceless and should be treated as such. When we are in poor health everything ceases to matter except getting well again. Don't wait to lose your health before you appreciate it. There are a few general rules to keep our bodies in good health.

He who has health has hope; and he who has hope has everything. (Arabian proverb)

Three things in life – your health, your mission, and the people you love. That's it. (Naval Ravikant)

When the heart is at ease, the body is healthy. (Chinese proverb)

A Healthy Diet

There is a wide range of opinion about what constitutes a healthy diet; so I'm going to keep it really simple. What you absorb into your body must affect how it functions, right? What you eat cannot help but contribute to how you are. 'You are what you eat' is fundamentally a true statement. Food provides your cells with the nutrients that serve as their building blocks and protect your cell's important functions like energy production and immunity. Food is the source of nourishment and energy to support the health of our body. Research shows that eating a healthy diet can help prevent or reduce the severity of various diseases, e.g. asthma, cancer, diabetes, osteoporosis, irritable bowel syndrome, Crohn's disease. Poor nutrition directly leads to degenerative disease and poor health.

The flip-side to this statement is that good nutrition can lead to a longer healthier life. Your physical well-being is to a very large extent dependent upon what goes through your mouth. Regardless of your genetic make-up what you consume day after day is what is assimilated through your digestive system and becomes part of your physical body. If you eat healthy food or junk food it will be absorbed and become integrated into your flesh: literally you become what you eat. No matter the genes you have inherited a healthy diet will benefit your health and quality of life.

Your genetics load the gun, but your lifestyle pulls the trigger. (Mehmet Oz)

In order to understand the impact of our diet on our health it might help to view your bodies as a machine or a car which requires fuel to function optimally. The right kind of fuel ensures the smooth running of our car but the wrong type of fuel will clog up the system and eventually cause it to break down. Naturally our bodies are so much better designed than the best of machines and so we can go for decades on a poor diet, but eventually it will begin to show signs of distress.

In considering a healthy diet, let us keep in mind two key factors: assimilation and elimination. Firstly, aim for wholesome foods that provide good nourishment and essential nutrients to be assimilated into your body. Secondly, endeavour to eat nourishing foods which aid efficient elimination of by-products of digestion. Nourishing foods are wholegrain products, fish, eggs, milk, sweet potatoes etc. Such foods contain essential nutrients and micronutrients. Foods which aid bowel movement, elimination of waste and potentially harmful by-products of digestion such as free radicals include foods rich in fibre and antioxidants e.g. fruits, vegetables, unrefined wholemeal foods and water.

Water: Drink lots of water and keep well-hydrated. After all, our bodies are 60-70% water.

Sleep: Rest is absolutely necessary for good health. Rest is crucial to the health of the body and soul. Sleep is when the body renews, refreshes, replenishes and repairs itself. If you don't want to burn out or get stressed out, my advice is take a break every seven days, i.e. one out of every seven days and get about seven hours of sleep daily for optimal health (average for an adult: some people will need slightly less while some might need more).

Exercise: Brisk walking is one of the most effective, easiest, most accessible forms of exercise. It can be time-saving too because it can be easily incorporated into any lifestyle and it will not cost a penny in gym or club membership if money is an issue. The Bible (1 Tim 4:8) says physical exercise profits little. Forget about the 'little', and concentrate on the 'profit' bit! No matter how little at least there is some profit.

Laughter, fun, happiness: Laughter they say is good medicine. Proverbs 17:22 states that, 'a merry heart doeth good like a medicine.' Research has shown this to be true.

Prayer/communion: Studies have shown that those who pray, read their Bible, sing and attend church are less likely to complain of sickness or visit the doctor.

Avoid stress and negative environments: Never underestimate the effect that a negative environment has on health/stress levels. Many workers testify to poor health and stress as a result of a stressful work environment or unfriendly work colleagues, and the same goes for stressful marriages and homes. High stress or unhappy negative environments can affect you psychologically and reduce your immune system's ability to fight disease adequately. So avoid stress and strife and instead be happy and joyful. A joyful heart will do your health a lot of good.

When we are faced with danger or trouble the basic human instinct is the fight or flight reaction. This reaction causes a release of adrenalin (hormone produced by the adrenal gland; it converts stored sugar into glucose used for energy) needed for the fight or flight. The chemicals released when you are angry or stressed for prolonged periods have a potentially damaging effect on health. If the body is in a continuous state of fight or flight, the body's equilibrium is disrupted and this can be potentially harmful to the body and may produce abnormalities in body function. These include the so-called psychosomatic disorders, i.e. mind/body related disorders.[27]

It's only a small journey to a new direction. The direction for good health starts with an apple a day, or walking the block for twenty minutes. Just commit to a new direction. Just munch on the first apple. That first step gives you self-esteem and if you do it the second day you could become almost delirious, according to Jim Rohn. That's how easy it is to get back on a better track. It is easy to do and the effects are powerful, but beware: it's also easy not to do.

I believe that the greatest gift you can give your family and the world is a healthy you. (Joyce Meyer)

Sickness – nature's vengeance for violating her laws. (Charles Simmons)

The greatest of follies is to sacrifice health for any other kind of happiness. (Arthur Schopenhauer)

34. Imagination

You cannot do it unless you imagine it. (George Lucas, film-maker)

Walt Disney had a dream to build a theme park in Florida. So, he bought the land and drew up the plans, but before the theme park was built he passed away after a bout of sickness. When the park finally opened in 1971, five years after his death, someone said, 'It is too bad that Walt didn't live to see this.' The Disney Creative Director said, 'He did see it.' He saw it in his imagination and what was in his heart came to pass for all to see. All meaningful and lasting change starts first in your imagination and then works its way out.

Nothing shall be withheld that they have imagined. (Genesis 11:6)

A man whose small business was failing had his gas cut off by the gas company because he couldn't pay his bill. He was in the middle of very important experiments, and to have the gas man plunge him into darkness and cause his work to stall made him so mad that at once he began to read up on gas technique and economics. He resolved to try to see whether electricity could be made to replace gas and give the gas company a run for their money. His imagination paid off. That man was Thomas Edison, the founder of General Electrics, also famous for the incandescent light bulb. Problems and adversity are wake-up calls for creativity; they stir up our imagination; they prompt us to engage our minds; to use our God-given abilities, rally our resources and step out in faith.

Talent hits a target no one else can hit; genius hits a target no one else can see. (Arthur Schopenhauer)

People say not to cross a bridge until you come to it, but as someone once said, 'This world is owned by people who have crossed bridges in their imagination before anyone else has.' Not being a person of imagination causes your life to be less than it was intended to be. Everything starts with a dream. Every invention ever made, every building ever built, every painting ever painted, every book ever written, every movie ever filmed: all started with a dream. So imagine big, enlarge the place of your tent, stretch out the curtains of your habitation, spare not, break forward on the left and on the right. Expect great things from God and attempt great things for God.

Imagination is everything. It's the preview to life's coming attractions. (Albert Einstein)

Maybe you already have a dream. Or maybe you once had a dream but the dream got dashed. The good news is, you can dream again. God can stir up your imagination again. What is stirring inside you? Maybe it's the dream to start a new business. Maybe it's the dream to go back to college. Maybe it's the dream of writing a book. Maybe it's the dream of having better health, or the dream of getting married someday. It's important to understand that before you see a dream on the outside, you have to see it on the inside.

Being realistic is the most common path to mediocrity. (Will Smith)

To turn nothing into something, you start with ideas and imagination. Imagination is more powerful than knowledge because knowledge is what is, but imagination is what can be! Imagination should be used not to escape reality but to create the reality you desire. Life reflects what it finds in your imagination. To put it another way, imagination is the pre-view of coming attractions - i.e. what you have been attracting with your thoughts and words.

Think big or you'll get in God's way!

35. Influence

If you think you're too small to have an impact, try going to bed with a mosquito in the room. (Anita Roddick)

For over a decade I worked in a laboratory where mosquitoes were reared for medical research at one of the postgraduate schools of the University of London. I know those blood-sucking bugs too well. Just one mosquito makes a difference in an annoying way, but the principle is the same in the positive. One person can stop a great injustice. One person can be a voice for truth. One person's kindness can save a life. Each person matters.

Hitler, Stalin and Pol Pot are glaring examples of this principle. One human being can use their influence for evil and cause great harm. But the influence does not have to be as great as these tyrants in order to have a bad effect.

Dead flies in perfume make it stink, and a little foolishness decomposes much wisdom. (Ecclesiastes 10:1, MSG)

If even a dead fly can have a bad influence, the least influential human being can have an influence for evil or good. We can all be the fly in the ointment!

The people who influence you are the people who believe in you. (Henry Drummond)

You have to decide whether you want to influence people or simply impress them. Impressing people is superficial but influencing goes deeper. You can impress from a distance but can influence people only when you get close and identify with them. So how can we grow in influence? Here are some of the ways. First, sincerely love people and show it; be warm. Second, be an encourager not a critic; speak gracious words. Avoid gossiping and bad-mouthing others, be careful what you say or even think. Third, find out people's ambitions and interests in life; everyone loves a chance to talk about themselves. Fourth, let people know if they have helped or inspired you; everybody loves to be appreciated. Last, let people know what you have actually achieved in life. This will inspire confidence in you. People are influenced by achievers.

The influence of teachers extends beyond the classroom, well into the future. It is they who shape and enrich the minds of the young, who touch their hearts and souls. It is they who shape a nation's future. (F. Sionil Jose)

Sociologists tell us that even the most introverted individual will influence 10,000 other people during his or her lifetime. We all influence one another in all sorts of ways, from what to have for lunch and what films to watch to more important matters of truth.

Think twice before you speak, because your words and influence will plant the seed of either success or failure in the mind of another. (Napoleon Hill)

The influence of a mother upon the lives of her children cannot be measured. They know and absorb her example and attitudes when it comes to questions of honesty, temperance, kindness, and industry. (Billy Graham)

There are only two ways to influence human behaviour: You can manipulate it or inspire it.

36. Integrity

*Integrity is the glue that holds our way of life together. We must
constantly strive to keep our integrity intact. When wealth is lost, nothing
is lost; when health is lost, something is lost; when character is lost, all is
lost. (Billy Graham)*

When the Titanic set sail in 1912, it was declared to be 'unsinkable'
because it was constructed using a new technology. The ship's hull
was divided into sixteen watertight compartments. Up to four of
these compartments could be damaged or even flooded, and still
the ship would float. Tragically, the Titanic sank on 15 April 1912 at
2.20 am. 1,513 people lost their lives. At the time, it was thought that
five of its watertight compartments had been ruptured in a collision
with an iceberg. However, on 1 September 1985, when the wreck of
the Titanic was found lying upright on the ocean floor, there was no
sign of the long gash previously thought to have been ripped in the
ship's hull. What they discovered was that damage to one
compartment affected all the rest. James Cameron, director of the
movie *Titanic*, describes the Titanic as a 'metaphor of life': 'We are
all living on... [the] Titanic.'[28]

Many people make the Titanic mistake. They think they can divide
their lives into different 'compartments' and that what they do in
one will not affect the rest. However, as Rick Warren explains; The
Titanic was supposed to be unsinkable because it was the first ship
to segment and compartmentalize the hull. Theoretically, if the boat
took on water in a certain area, you could batten down the hatch,
and it wouldn't sink the whole ship. But folks, when it comes to
your life, a hole in the boat is a hole in the boat, and eventually it's
going to sink you. That little area you thought you had under
control will eventually take you down. Rick Warren says, 'A life of
integrity is one that is not divided into compartments.'[29]

The most important persuasion tool you have in your entire arsenal is integrity. (Zig Ziglar)

Integrity in speech

We must endeavour to speak ill of no man and speak all the good we know of everybody. Cultivate the habit of making understatements; never exaggerate. Integrity does not mean being perfect. It means being honest, real and authentic (it is the opposite of hypocrisy). Truth becomes hard if it is not softened by love; love becomes soft if it is not strengthened by truth. Lack of integrity has its own inherent built-in consequences.

Mark Twain once said, 'If you tell the truth, you don't have to remember anything.'

Integrity in relationships

What a person does in his private life is a strong indication of what is going on in his heart. And what could be more private than the sexual relationship you have with your spouse? If a leader is unfaithful to his spouse, he is unfaithful to all who would follow him. This is so because the marriage relationship is the foundation for all other relationships we form in society and it mirrors our character. Marriage is a promise that puts someone else's interests ahead of your own. Leadership, like marriage, is as much a responsibility as it is a privilege and is based on trust earned over time through hard work. If a follower cannot trust you, will they follow you? Integrity starts at home. Learn to be a person of your word and stick with your commitments even when you no longer feel like it.

I was shocked when I read of a campaign by a Canada-based online dating agency offering a dating service for married men and women who wanted to have an affair. Its slogan is, 'Life is short. Have an affair.'

The agency is by no means alone in this market. Another agency executed an extensive advertising campaign specifically on massive billboards next to motorways with the slogan, 'The grass is always greener.' A book recently published in the UK suggests that adultery may be good for the health of marriages. Nothing could be further from the truth. Intimate relationships require faithfulness.

Essentially, agencies like those mentioned are making money feeding on people's weaknesses and helping them to be unfaithful. The reality is that it will ruin the lives of the individuals involved, as well as the lives of their partners, their families and their children. Unfaithfulness has the potential to destroy a marriage, or a future marriage, and to ruin lives. That is why, on a wedding day, the man and woman promise to be faithful to each other as long as they both shall live. As has often been said, 'The grass is not greener on the other side of the fence – it is greener where we water it.' If the grass looks greener, it's probably artificial!

'Confidence...thrives on honesty, on honour, on the sacredness of obligations, on faithful protection and on unselfish performance.' (Franklin D. Roosevelt)

Former US President Eisenhower, Supreme Commander of the Allied Forces in Western Europe during World War II, said, 'The supreme quality for leadership is unquestionably integrity. Without it, no real success is possible, no matter whether it is … on a football field, in an army, or in an office.' Cavett Roberts said it well: 'If my people understand me, I'll get their attention. If my people trust me, I'll get their action.' That's the power of great character.

There is no pillow as soft as a clear conscience. (Glen Campbell)

A dishonest life is full of rot and will be exposed, causing you great embarrassment. It is not a question of 'if' but 'when' you will be exposed. The writer of *Proverbs* exalts the virtue of honesty. Where does honesty rank in your set of values?[30] I am ashamed to admit that I have often struggled with being completely honest in all areas of my life. Maybe you have failings in some area of your life too. Clinical psychologist Dr Henry Cloud writes that 'a person with integrity has the – often rare – ability to pull everything together, to make it all happen no matter how challenging the circumstances.'[31]

Honesty is a very expensive gift, don't expect it from cheap people. (Warren Buffett)

If you lack integrity in your relationships, you can be sure that your sin will find you out. The theory of six degrees of separation says that no one is more than six relationships removed from anyone else. This idea is not just about networking—it speaks to your need to be honest as well. Once you are proved to be dishonest, it is difficult to regain the trust of others; difficult, but not impossible. Confess your lie immediately or take back what was stolen. Don't let it go uncorrected or it will fester and become a 'rotten stench' in your character. Face up to your sin and admit that it is wrong. That is the pathway to healing and restoration. There is nothing so pure and strong as a man with a clear conscience. Determine that honesty will be a hallmark of your life and pay scrupulous attention to maintaining it at all times, no matter what the cost.

Money and success don't change people; they merely amplify what is already there. (Will Smith)

Integrity with money

Jesus spoke about money more than virtually any other subject (including prayer and heaven). Twelve out of his thirty-eight parables are about money or possessions. As Billy Graham put it, 'If a person gets their attitude towards money straight, it will help straighten out almost every other area in their life.' In the rather strange parable of the dishonest manager, who is commended for his shrewdness, Jesus teaches us how to get a right view of money.

Money is a tool. The use of our money on earth can have eternal consequences. Your money can be used to help others with eternal consequences.

Money is a test. Jesus says, 'Whoever can be trusted with very little can also be trusted with much, and whoever is dishonest with very little will also be dishonest with much. So if you have not been trustworthy in handling worldly wealth, who will trust you with true riches?' (Lk 16:11). Be an honest and trustworthy steward of everything God has given you, including your money. The more trustworthy you are with money, the more God will give you 'true riches'.

Money is a threat - Jesus says, 'No one can be a slave to two masters. Either you will hate the one and love the other, or you will be devoted to the one and despise the other. You cannot be a slave to both God and money' (Mt 6:24). As Dietrich Bonhoeffer put it, 'Our hearts have room for only one all-embracing devotion, and we can cleave to only one Lord.'[32]

Money is to be used but not loved. Don't love money and use people. Love people and use money. The threat is that love of money leads to hatred of God. Don't love money, treat it with contempt by giving generously and focusing your love not on money but on God.

Integrity helps you get ahead in business and life without leaving your values behind.

Be a person of integrity; you can learn the easy way, or you can learn from UHK (University of Hard Knocks). Yomi Akinpelu

37. Intentional living

You cannot drift to the top of a mountain. (Jim Rohn)

There was a man who was born in sorrowful circumstances. To rise above the circumstances of his birth was deemed nigh impossible. He was destined to be a nonentity in life. But one day he suddenly 'woke up' and decided to be intentional. He decided he wanted to have more and to be more. He made a simple direct request to God for a change of status. God said yes, and his status was changed forever. That man was called Jabez. In the Bible he prayed this prayer: Lord, I want more than I've got and I'm asking You for it! He got all he asked for (1Chronicles 4:9-10). He was intentional. One crucial way to be intentional is by asking: 'Ask and you shall receive', says the Bible (Mt 7:7).

Intentional living is the art of making our own choices before others' choices make us. (Richie Norton)

John Maxwell says, 'Intentional living is about living your best story. An unintentional life accepts everything and does nothing. An intentional life embraces only the things that will add to the mission of significance. If I wanted to make a difference … wishing for things to change wouldn't make them change. Hoping for improvements wouldn't bring them. Dreaming wouldn't provide all the answers I needed. Vision wouldn't be enough to bring transformation to me or others. Only by managing my thinking and shifting my thoughts from desire to deeds would I be able to bring about positive change. I needed to go from wanting to doing.' In other words, being intentional is the difference maker.[33]

So say goodbye to the status quo and become intentional in every area of your life. Be intentional in speech, character, dressing and work; so much so that you make people around you curious about the positive changes in your life that they want to know what you know. To be intentional in every area of your life, you must go after wisdom and understanding. For instance, knowledge will not just fall upon you, you must go out and acquire it. You must seek to grow mentally or intellectually intentionally, you have to seek it out, it will not come looking for you.

Someone said, 'Tell me what you're committed to, and I'll tell you what you're going to be in fifteen years, because you are becoming whatever you are committed to.' Being intentional about what we commit ourselves to seriously affects our lives. Nothing affects your life more than your commitments. Your commitments shape your life! And if you're not committed to anything, other people are shaping your life; that can't be a good thing for you, because they will shape it according to what they think you should be, not in line with your true worth and value. If others are shaping your life, you're definitely not living with intentionality.

If you have dreams, goals or aspirations, you have to grow to achieve them. Physical growth is automatic, but mental, spiritual and emotional growth must be intentionally pursued to happen. We won't improve or grow in any area unless we are highly intentional about it. No one improves by accident. You cannot coast to the top of a mountain, you have to overcome gravity and put in some effort.

If you are clear about what you want, the world responds with clarity. Some people learn from the school of hard knocks - the lessons are random and difficult - you might become bitter or better as a result. It's less painful and much better to plan your growth intentionally. You decide where you need or want to grow, you choose what you will learn, and you follow through with discipline going at your own pace.

There's an old maxim that those who were seen dancing were thought to be insane by those who could not hear the music. When you are intentional, you will seem a bit strange to the average person because you're swimming against the tide. That is certainly true of those who walk to the beat of another drummer.

One of the key ways to be intentional is in the use of our time. In an extremely busy world like ours, it's easy to be swept along and spend our time doing the things that seem important, only to look back and realise we missed out on the things that matter most. It's easy to choose the things that seem right and are urgent because that's what everyone else is doing rather than the things that we are meant to be doing because they are meaningful. Choosing the meaningful over the urgent will ensure that your life will be peaceful and purposeful and reflects the values and the influence you want to have in life. This requires being reflective and takes planning.

Make it a habit to pause and focus on the present moment, calm your mind and think more clearly. This will help you to begin to choose the significant over the seemingly urgent. This practice of stopping and taking stock of the situation is called mindfulness. Mindfulness is mental training. It is learning to turn off our autopilot, jump off the status quo bandwagon and take control of our thoughts. You have to be highly intentional to do this.

If you intentionally choose what's meaningful over the false urgencies that try to demand your attention, then you can reclaim your time and live with peace rather than regret. Know where you are heading and head there with determination and resolve. To be meaningful is to be significant, relevant, important, consequential, or worthwhile — worthy of your time. We must choose what is meaningful now. In this very moment. What is meaningful today will also be meaningful tomorrow or next year or even decades from now. Meaningful is timeless. It transcends the moment. Intentional living means choosing to spend your time aligned with the natural pace of a spiritually grounded life that prioritises relationships and people and a pace that gives you the margin to invest in what you value.

Be intentional in your decision-making. Take a moment to clarify what is most meaningful to you about a particular decision. This will help you make better, more efficient decisions with less chance of regret. You will have to forego some things and miss out on other things; it's okay to miss out. With the right perspective we can even find joy in missing out when we see our choices as a sign of personal growth. We must put our stake in the ground and decide to be intentional about what will give us the meaning and joy.

Be intentional and make promises to yourself; set goals and keep them. When you do this, you begin to establish an inner integrity and honour that gives you the awareness of self-control and the courage and strength you feel more in control of your life; a by-product of intentional living.

Now for some questions to augment your new intentional life-style. Think about your top goal in life. What will achieving it give you that you don't already have? In other words, what makes it worth spending your time to pursue it? What false urgencies are stealing time from what is most meaningful to you? What do you need to say no to? Do you need to say no to the rat race? How can you invest God's gift of time in more meaningful ways? What are your true priorities, and how does the way you spend your time reflect those priorities?

If you win the rat race, you're still a rat. (Lily Tomlin)

The intentional person is the one who is done with low living, small thinking, smooth knees, colourless dreams, tame visions and dwarfed goals. Their pace is set, their gait is fast, their goal divine and although their road is narrow, the way rough, companions few: yet, their mission is clear. They cannot be bought, compromised, deterred, lured away, turned back or delayed. They will not flinch in the face of sacrifice, hesitate in the presence of adversity, negotiate at the table of the enemy, ponder at the pool of popularity, or meander in the maze of mediocrity.[34]

38. Journaling / writing

As soon as you think it, ink it. (Mark Victor Hansen)

Recently, I was asked to give a talk about how to write a book. I wanted the talk to be thoroughly practical and useful to the audience, so I thought carefully about all the disciplines that had contributed most significantly to my writing career. Many came to mind, but I distilled them down to two indispensable, simple habits: reading and keeping a journal, i.e. writing down my thoughts and discoveries on paper. Journaling is absolutely essential for recording ideas and clarifying your thoughts. Ideas flying around in your head become more concrete and logical as you write them down. It is as if the act of writing helps to pin them down from the nebulous world of imagination into the precise realm of reality.

According to Myles Monroe, writing a book is not to be taken lightly. It is a transmission of light. Where you can never go, your book can get there. People I've never met read my books, my books have gone to places I've never been. Writing is the most powerful contribution you can make not only to your generation but to generations after you're gone. Furthermore, Monroe went on to say that when you write a book, you are doing something very strategically significant: you are leaving ideas that will outlive you. These ideas have the potential to affect generations after you. Writing immortalises you. Myles Monroe likes to say that the cemetery is the richest place on earth, richer than the gold and diamond-mines of South Africa, richer than the oil-wells of the Middle East. In the cemetery are buried books that were never written, dreams that never saw the light of day, ideas and inventions that were never actualised.[35]

Forgotten experiences are worthless. That's why you need a spiritual journal. Learning to write is learning to think. A journal is for collecting good ideas about life, work, business relationships etc.

So take things out of your head and put them on paper. Jim Rohn once said, a life worth living is a life worth recording. Journals are for collecting good ideas. Don't trust it to your memory, put them on paper. It is uncanny: leave that illuminating idea ungarnered, for even ten minutes ... and it's gone! [36]

Capture your ideas by writing them down. Always carry a note book or electronic device to capture your best thoughts and insights. Writing down your thoughts or ideas produces clarity. It also expands and improves your ideas as your brain tries to process and express the thoughts on paper.

According to Brian Tracy studies at Yale, Harvard etc. showed that students who write down their notes perform much better than those who typed their notes. This is because writing forces you to use three abilities: physical ability (the act of writing with your hand and fingers), visual ability (sight) and auditory ability (hearing yourself say it in your head as you write). You use three major parts of your brain simultaneously. Thus like a laser beam from a space station, your subconscious mind accepts it as a command and your super conscious mind begins to work on it round the clock to bring results. Your whole brain is engaged in the writing process. Everything you write down is automatically recorded in your mental hard drive and goes into your subconscious and begins working 24 hours a day to bring results.

Writing helps you think on paper. And people who have learnt to think on paper will eventually discover that they have developed the ability to think on their feet. Writing helps you in carving out the right word and therefore in stretching your vocabulary. You will find one day that you are able, seemingly, to pull words out of the air on those occasions when notes are inappropriate. Moments of overwhelming clarity must be harnessed as they occur by documentation. To delay, even by five minutes, may well put the lid on it; half an hour later will find you scratching your head and wondering what it was that had so gripped you! [36]

The most powerful tool in the world may well be a pen and piece of paper. The saying that springs to mind right now is: The pen is mightier than the sword!

The shortest pencil is better than the longest memory. (Benjamin Franklin)

39. Kindness

It is one of the beautiful compensations of this life that no man can
sincerely try to help another without helping himself.
(Ralph Waldo Emerson)

Two men, both seriously ill, occupied the same hospital room. One man was allowed to sit up in his bed for an hour each afternoon to help drain the fluid from his lungs. His bed was next to the room's only window. The other man had to spend all his time flat on his back. The men talked for hours on end. They spoke of their wives and families, their homes, their jobs, their involvement in the military service, where they had been on vacation. And every afternoon when the man in the bed by the window could sit up, he would pass the time by describing to his room-mate all the things he could see outside the window. The man in the other bed began to live for those one-hour periods where his world would be broadened and enlivened by all the activity and colour of the world outside. The window overlooked a park with a lovely lake. Ducks and swans played on the water while children sailed their model boats. Young lovers walked arm in arm amidst flowers of every colour of the rainbow. Grand old trees graced the landscape, and a fine view of the city skyline could be seen in the distance. As the man by the window described all this in exquisite detail, the man on the other side of the room would close his eyes and imagine the picturesque scene. One warm afternoon, the man by the window described a parade passing by. Although the other man couldn't hear the band, he could see it in his mind's eye as the man by the window portrayed it with descriptive words. Days and weeks passed. One morning, the day nurse arrived to bring water for their baths only to find the lifeless body of the man by the window, who had died peacefully in his sleep. She was saddened and called the hospital attendants to take the body away. As soon as it seemed appropriate, the other man asked whether he could be moved next to the window. The nurse was happy to make the switch, and after making sure he was comfortable, she left him alone. Slowly, painfully, he propped himself up on one elbow to take his first look at the world outside. Finally, he would have the joy of seeing it for himself. He strained to slowly turn to look out the window beside the bed. It faced a blank wall. The man asked the nurse what could have compelled his deceased roommate who had described such wonderful things outside this window. The nurse responded that the man was blind and could not even see the wall. She said, 'Perhaps he just wanted to encourage you.'

As John Wesley said, 'Do all the good you can, by all the means you can, in all the ways you can, in all the places you can, at all the times you can, to all the people you can, as long as ever you can.' Love and kindness are our most valuable possessions. They can be shared without diminishing and, when shared, they multiply.

Be kind, for everyone you meet is fighting a hard battle. (Plato)

Perhaps the best way to grasp the value of kindness is through real-life stories. Here is another well-known story of the showing kindness.

Strangers on a Stormy Night

One stormy night many years ago, an elderly man and his wife entered the lobby of a small hotel in Philadelphia. Trying to get out of the rain, the couple approached the front desk hoping to get some shelter for the night. 'Could you possibly give us a room here?' the husband asked. The clerk, a friendly man with a winning smile, looked at the couple and explained that there were three conventions in town. 'All of our rooms are taken,' the clerk said. 'But I can't send a nice couple like you out into the rain at one o'clock in the morning. Would you perhaps be willing to sleep in my room? It's not exactly a suite, but it will be good enough to make you folks comfortable for the night.' When the couple declined, the young man pressed on. 'Don't worry about me; I'll make out just fine,' the clerk told them. So the couple agreed. As he paid his bill the next morning, the elderly man said to the clerk, 'You are the kind of manager who should be the boss of the best hotel in the United States. Maybe someday I'll build one for you.' The clerk looked at them and smiled. The three of them had a good laugh. As they drove away, the elderly couple agreed that the helpful clerk was indeed exceptional, as finding people who are both friendly and helpful isn't easy. Two years passed. The clerk had almost forgotten the incident when he received a letter from the old man. It recalled that stormy night and enclosed a round-trip ticket to New York, asking the young man to pay them a visit. The old man met him in New York and led him to the corner of Fifth Avenue and 34th Street. He then pointed to a great new building there, a palace of reddish stone, with turrets and watchtowers thrusting up to the sky. 'That,' said the older man, 'is the hotel I have just built for you to manage.' 'You must be joking,' the young man said. 'I can assure you I am not,' said the older man, a sly smile playing around his mouth. The older man's name was William Waldorf Astor, and the magnificent structure was the original Waldorf-Astoria Hotel. The young clerk who became its first manager was George C. Boldt. This young clerk never foresaw the turn of events that would lead him to become the manager of one of the world's most glamorous hotels.

Kindness is love in work clothes. Showing God's love in practical ways, is one of the greatest ways to effect positive change, both in your life and in the lives of people around you. Unexpected kindness is the most powerful, least costly and most underrated agent of human change. When kindness is expressed, healthy relationships are created, community connections are nourished and people are inspired to pass on kindness.

There are times when what is happening in the world requires you to leverage or risk whatever you have—status, resources, access, knowledge, connections, and finances. You must do it heartily. Why? Because people are worth it.[7]

40. Leadership

A leader is one who knows the way, goes the way, and shows the way.
(John Maxwell)

On January 15, 2009, US Airways, Airbus A320-214 Flight 1549 with call sign 'CACTUS 1549' left New York City's LaGuardia Airport (LGA) at around 3.25pm. About 3 minutes into the flight the plane struck a flock of Canada geese. The pilots' view was filled with the large birds. Passengers and crew heard very loud bangs and saw flames from the engines, followed by silence and an odour of fuel.

Realising that both engines had shut down, the pilot in command; 57-year-old Chesley B. Sullenberger, a former fighter pilot took control, and resorted to an emergency but safe gliding/landing of the plane into the Hudson River. About six minutes later the plane landed/ditched in the Hudson River. The captain calmly opened the cockpit door and gave the evacuation order. The crew guided the passengers out of the plane and all of them 155 passengers on board survived, including one on a wheel chair. None of the passengers sustained serious or major injuries.

Later on, when interviewed, they said what kept their sanity during the ordeal was the composure of the captain. The Guild of Air Pilots and Air Navigators awarded the crew a Master's Medal on January 22, 2009. This feat is now popularly referred to as the 'Miracle of the Hudson'. Many lives were saved because the captain maintained his composure. A leader must never lose his/her cool under pressure; the lives of people sometimes depend on him/her.

Sir Winston Churchill has been described as Britain's greatest ever leader. He lived a long heroic life, and he rallied a nation with his inspiring rhetoric. One of the most striking parts of his biography is that he had to resign from the Admiralty during WWI over the failed Dardanelles campaign. He had failed spectacularly, yet he was to learn not to give up. In a speech he made at his old school,

143

Harrow, the whole school assembled to listen to his words of wisdom. The great man arose to speak: 'Young men, never give up, never give up, never give up.' The entire speech lasted for a very short time, but no one present ever forgot his words. He also said, 'Never give in. Never give in. Never, never, never, never – in nothing, great or small, large or petty – never give in, except to convictions of honour and good sense. Never yield to force. Never yield to the apparently overwhelming might of the enemy.'[37]

John C. Maxwell, whose organisations have trained more than 1,000,000 leaders worldwide, points out that leadership is influence. He said that, according to sociologists, even the most isolated individual will influence 10,000 other people during his or her lifetime!

Even by secular standards, Jesus is arguably the most influential leader to have ever lived. He only worked in the public space for three years and in that time gained tens of thousands of followers. 2000 years later, the best-selling book of all time tells the story of His life, and billions of people from every part of the world have committed their entire lives to following Him.

If your actions inspire others to dream more, learn more, do more and become more, you are a leader.

Leadership is key in every level and section of society. Leaders don't seek followers. They passionately follow their purpose, and followers are naturally attracted to people of purpose and passion. Parents are leaders in the home. Teachers are leaders in schools. We need good leadership in the church, marketplace, judiciary, government, media, arts and so on. To lead others, you must first learn to lead yourself well. Your organisation or family will grow and succeed only to the level of your leadership. Leadership is about serving the people you lead so that they will go further and do better than you. The people who influence us are the people who believe in us.

Great leaders all have one thing in common. They know that acquiring and keeping good people is a leader's most important task,' writes John Maxwell in his book, 'Developing the Leaders Around You.' He urges his readers, 'Find the best people you can, then develop them into the best leaders they can be.'[55]

As a leader, you must clarify your motives by asking yourself some questions: is leading people something I want to do because I want to be in charge or boss others around, or is it innately a part of who I am? Lead as if people's lives depend on your leadership, because they do. Pour your life into others. Lead from your truest self. Be authentic, and your leadership will be life giving and energising. Wanting everyone to be happy and making tough decisions are incompatible tasks. Good leadership is disappointing people at a rate they can stand.

As a leader, you must choose whether you want to impress people or influence people. You can impress from a distance but can influence them only when you get close and identify with them. The most essential attribute of a leader is not perfection but credibility. You build credibility not by pretending to be perfect but by being honest. As you relate to others as a leader, don't tell your team members they are wrong - show respect for their opinion (be diplomatic) but be quick to admit it, if you're wrong. Begin with praise and honest appreciation. Call attention to people's mistakes indirectly. Talk about your own mistakes before criticising the other person. Ask questions instead of giving direct orders. Let the other person save face. Praise the slightest improvement and praise every improvement - be lavish with praise. Give the other person a reputation to live up to. Use encouragement. Make the fault easy to correct. Make the other person happy about doing the things you suggest.

Sometimes there are tricks of the trade that others are willing to pass on to save a little time and energy along the way. But when it comes to leading others, there aren't any shortcuts. As a leader, you have to make tough decisions and stand your ground, whatever the outcome, for the greater good of all.

Become the kind of leader that people would follow voluntarily, even if you had no title or position. (Brian Tracy)

Leading your children

When it comes to providing leadership to our children, discipline is a vital ingredient in the recipe of parenting. We all need to learn to bend to authority. There are no short cuts to this, and we must not go with the flow of society. The masses say that discipline of our children will break their spirit, but the wise leader knows this is not the case. Discipline will make your child into the adult you want them to be. It is not always easy to say no to those under our authority, especially if we care about them. But their short-term gratification is not worth the long-term disappointment of a ruined life and a hardened heart. No matter what we teach our children, they insist on behaving just as we do. We teach what we know, but we reproduce what we are. Your children may sometimes doubt what you say, but they will always believe what you do.

Without discipline, you condition your child to a life of heartache. When they're stopped by the police for speeding or penalised by the bank for defaulting on a loan, throwing a tantrum won't get them off the hook. Please think of their future! God disciplines His children; are we wiser than He is? (cf. Hebrews 12:11). A youngster's heart is filled with foolishness, but physical discipline will drive it far away (Proverbs 22:15). Rebellion is part of children's DNA, and it is your job to drive it out.

As leaders, we must learn to manage pressures, stress and challenges well, otherwise we will be limited. Pressures and stress are all parts of life. There is no such thing as a stress-free life. You cannot get rid of stress, you can only become better at handling it. When you approach stress in the right way, it can motivate you towards your dreams and goals.

Another important quality of good leadership is taking action on information that leads to transformation. This means a discipline to start, confrontation, the courage to stop, a person to empower, a system to create, a relationship to initiate, a risk you need to take. Leaders always take the initiative. Take action now, remember, if you always wait until you're ready, you'll always be late.

It has been said, 'If you want to know if you're a leader, turn around and see if anyone is following.' At first take, that makes some sense. Leaders should have followers, but we must understand that sometimes this may not be necessarily true: there might be points in your leadership journey when having followers is not what matters most. A lot of celebrities or politicians have followers, but not all of them are truly leaders. Jesus had a lot of followers when he was providing food and performing miracles, but, at the most crucial point in his leadership journey, he lost his followers; all deserted him. The people who have the biggest 'position' usually have the most followers. So whoever holds the more powerful position can easily maintain the larger following regardless of their actual leadership. Therefore people seek greater power and position so they can claim greater leadership. The fact is that when we do the things that really matter in this world we could find ourselves standing alone with no followers. At times, great leadership comes at the price of being in a lonely place.

Many chase leadership for greater esteem, larger titles and bigger pay cheques: they miss the point. Leadership is not simply about people following you. Leadership is about the lives you impact, and it's also about your following God. It's not about who is behind you when you turn around, but it's about who's ahead of you. If God is leading you, inevitably you will touch the lives he has assigned to you. Jesus set the example of leadership throughout his life all the way to the cross.

One of the greatest things about being a leader is that it gives you the opportunity to amplify your impact in the world. It enables you to produce bigger results faster than you could have done on your own. It also allows you to transform the people you lead at the same time. Leadership is an awesome privilege and responsibility; not to be taken lightly.

41. Money

Money is a terrific servant, but it is a terrible master. (Rick Warren)

Money is the most effective way ever invented for men and women to quantify and measure their creative energy; a most convenient measure of our time, dignity, skills, health, experience and persistence.

Let me open by stating the obvious: money is very important. Nevertheless money is not the most important thing in life. It would be naïve to say that money is simply a commodity of exchange and nothing more. Money is emotional, tangible, and useful. Money is indispensable. It is the currency of stuff, but it is also the currency of life. Money represents your life energy; it determines where you live, what you drive, where your children grow up, and where they go to school. Money dictates how you spend your time and where you spend it. Money puts a roof over your head. It protects you from hunger and nakedness. Money has probably the greatest potential to ruin a marriage or relationship. It is said that money issues cause a breakdown of 50% of marriages before the seventh anniversary. Money provides the basics of life; money answers all things and is therefore important. Money, however, has its limits; it cannot bring healing, it cannot fill an empty soul, it cannot buy happiness, deep and lasting fulfilment or genuine friendship. Money cannot heal a broken heart.

The lessons money teaches us are not only financial, they are spiritual. Money exposes the differences in our personalities, the ways we were brought up, our values and goals. The way we think about money and what we do with it reflects what we believe about it. A lot of people believe that, if they win the lottery, all their problems will disappear. This is not necessarily so: financial problems are rarely about money alone but is often the symptom of a poor value-system, mixed up with issues of self-worth, fear and power.

Money is a legal tender: it has no inherent value of its own, it is only valuable for what it can be exchanged for, or, to put it another way, its value lies in what it can be exchanged for. Money is not power, pleasure, freedom, happiness, security or choices. Rather it is a completely neutral commodity for which we trade our lives, energy, knowledge skills or abilities. Money cannot make us happy: it has no inherent power to do so. However, what we do with money can produce happiness, pleasure, freedom etc. How we use money is therefore what is important. Money bestows options, and options can have a genuinely positive effect on our happiness and quality of life.

Money will not make you happy, but money can give you the freedom you need to do the things that make you happy. What is it that gives you joy in life, playing golf, helping the poor, travelling the world, singing, spending time with your kids? If you have enough money and you don't have to worry about it, then you can devote your time to what it is that truly makes you happy.

Money is a medium for which we choose to exchange our life energy. This should affect our perspective on money and what you spend it on. Many people view money as a necessity for survival rather than something that provides the freedom to concentrate on the things that are really important to us in life. Money gives you a voice. Your money represents your life. When you mismanage your finances or spend foolishly, you need to understand that what you have just bought is not purchased only with your money but with your time which you traded for the money. In effect you swapped a certain portion of your allotted days on earth for that piece of junk that now clutters your home. When you realise that everything you buy is purchased with a portion of your life it will certainly make you more careful with the use of money. Money is not for spending: it is for management and multiplying, then spending.

The way to get money out of the way is to have plenty! (Yomi Akinpelu)

Money can be a hard topic for many Christians to discuss openly and honestly. But it shouldn't be. If Jesus thought it was important enough to talk about, then we should too! Unfortunately, a lot of 'religious' people are offended when you even try to discuss the subject. They think money is evil! Money is not the problem. It's the love of money that can get us into trouble! The extreme love of money tempts people to do bad things and draws them away from God. The money itself is neither good nor bad. We could use it to do something illegal, or we could choose to use our money to:

Buy food for starving orphans

Fund shelters for the homeless after an earthquake

Send doctors and medicine to Central America

Rescue children out of sex-trafficking

Dig wells and start churches in India

Fund research for preventable diseases

We just have to make sure that we develop a right relationship with money. We can do a lot of good for a lot of people once we get out of debt and learn how to manage our finances wisely.[7]

Making money is not shameful, it is not greed, it is not sinful. Making money is largely the consequence of a mutually beneficial interaction with other human beings. If you did not rob, steal or defraud anyone to obtain your money, then you could have obtained that money in only one way: you pleased someone else - a client, customer, employer, parent etc. Having money is not shameful: it is a certificate of good performance granted to you by a grateful fellow citizen.

Money is an abstract numbering system. It is a means of distilling the essence of a person's usefulness to his or her fellow human beings. It sums up a person's creativity, knowledge, experience, diligence and ability to defer gratification. It also takes into account the circle of contacts the person has built. It is virtually impossible to profit without doing something of greater value for other people.

When God gives you lots of money, don't just give Him the credit, give Him an offering too.

A wise man once said: 'If you don't learn to manage money, you will never have enough money to manage.' Money is looking for a good place or home to dwell, i.e. with a good manger. It really matters what you do with your money.

What do all people have in common? One thing is the desire for money and dependence on it. This vice affects the rich as well as the poor. The rich are burdened by how to keep wealth and the poor are haunted by how to get wealth. To both groups, money can be a curse that plagues them all their lives and affects the way they see things. How do we balance our spiritual lives with the needs of the material world? Don't let your love of money blind you to what is truly important or valuable.

Money is the acid-test of your faithfulness. God uses it more than any other thing in your life to test your faith. Why? Because it's the thing we have the hardest time with.

God rewards us when we manage our money wisely: 'Well done, good and faithful servant! You have been faithful with a few things; I will put you in charge of many things. Come and share your master's happiness!' (Matthew 25:21). God (and life) will compensate you for managing your money well. Good money management will bring affirmation, promotion, and celebration.

Jesus said, 'No one can serve two masters. Either you will hate the one and love the other, or you will be devoted to the one and despise the other. You cannot serve both God and money' (Matthew 6:24).

Notice he doesn't say you should not serve God and money. He says you can't. It's impossible. Nobody can serve two masters. So you're going to have to decide what will be number one in your life, God or money.

When it masters you, you're always under stress. You're always worried. You're always uptight about it. When you are the master of your money; when it is your servant, it serves you. When money works for you instead of you working for your money, then you have peace.[38]

Money is a test and a trust: Jesus said if you're not trustworthy about worldly wealth who will trust you with true riches. How I manage my money determines how much God can trust me with spiritual blessings.

When God is your master, money serves you, but if money is your master, you become its slave.

151

42. Motivation

Motivation likes to ride a vehicle already in motion! (Yomi Akinpelu)

In 1907, a university turned down a PhD dissertation from a young physics student. Yet the student went on to change the scientific world forever. Who was he? Albert Einstein.

When a sixteen-year-old student got his report card from his rhetoric teacher in school, the note attached to it said: 'A conspicuous lack of success. He refused to let it demoralise him. Who was he? Winston Churchill; one of the greatest orators known in history.

The same story could be told for Steve Harvey, Les Brown and many more. They were scorned and rejected at the onset of their careers but never allowed this to put them down. They had to encourage themselves and stayed motivated otherwise we would never have heard of them today. Successful people all have one thing in common: they are self-motivated, they have a burning desire to succeed and do not allow setbacks to derail them. Successful people are self-motivated and disciplined to achieve there dreams. Motivation gets you started and self-discipline and the force of habit keeps you going and growing; and the more you go, the more motivated you become. Because motivation likes to jump on an already moving bandwagon. If you keep going through the force of habit, motivation will also bring along his siblings, mum, dad and even some members of its extended family.

Wouldn't it be wonderful to get someone to motivate us every morning and anytime we were feeling low? However the truth is that that's not how life works. You have to develop your own inbuilt self-motivation mechanism or machine and then you have to fuel it with self-discipline. My own self-motivation mechanisms include daily reading, praying, listening to excellent motivational talks by success coaches and mentors, inspiring music, success stories etc.

People often ask how successful people stay motivated month-in-month-out, year-in-year-out. The answer is: they don't.

Zig Ziglar put it aptly. 'People often say that motivation doesn't last. Well, neither does bathing - that's why we recommend it daily.' Never wait to feel motivated before you do what you should do; do it now, the motivation will come later.

This might sound like a contradiction, but don't count on motivation. Motivation is not going to strike you like lightning, don't wait for it, don't expect it to come suddenly...wham! and sweep you off your feet and carry you on puffy clouds of ease to do that task. Guess what? It's not coming! Even if it does, it does not stay for long. That is why people attend seminars and conferences; get all fired up and motivated but after about a week or two nothing comes out of it. The whole idea of motivation is a trap. Motivation is not something that someone else e.g. a coach, teacher, parent, spouse etc. can force or bestow on you. Forget motivation and just do it. Do it without motivation and then - guess what? After you get going and start doing the task or project, that's when the motivation comes and makes it easy for you to keep doing it! Motivation is like happiness and love. It's a by-product. When you're actively engaged in doing something, it sneaks up and zaps you when you least expect it. You're most likely to act yourself into feeling than feel yourself into action, so act now.

While writing this book, there were times I was motivated and there were times I wasn't at all motivated. The times I was mostly motivated was when I got on with the task and the more progress I made, the more motivated I became. It is true motivation loves a vehicle already in motion.

Motivational quotes

Push yourself, because no one else is going to do it for you. (SUCCESS.com)

Make it happen, shock everyone.

Will it be easy? Nope. Will it be worth it? Absolutely.

Success can be a slow process but quitting isn't going to speed it up.

People who wonder whether the glass is half empty or half full are missing the point. The glass is REFILLABLE.

I never dreamed about success. I worked for it. (Estee Lauder)

The only place where success comes before work is in the dictionary. (Vidal Sassoon)

43. Opportunity

Opportunity is a proud goddess who wastes no time with those who are unprepared. (George S. Clason, The Richest Man in Babylon)

Two men went fishing. One was an experienced fisherman, the other wasn't. Every time the experienced fisherman caught a big fish, he put it in his ice chest to keep it fresh. Whenever the inexperienced fisherman caught a big fish, he threw it back. The experienced fisherman watched this go on all day and finally got tired of seeing this man waste good fish. 'Why do you keep throwing back all the big fish you catch?' he asked. The inexperienced fisherman replied, 'I have only a small frying pan.' We laugh at that fisherman who couldn't figure out that all he needed was a bigger frying pan or cut the fish into smaller steaks; yet sometimes, like that fisherman, we shrink back or throw away big opportunities and dreams, because we just can't think beyond our small frying pan.

Studies have shown that people who are immigrants in the United States are three to four times more likely to become millionaires than those born in America. Why is that? It's because the belief that America is a land of opportunity, a place where dreams come true, has been ingrained in their minds. As a result, they go to the United States with the singular focus of finding opportunities that will bring success. And they find it.[23]

When you knock on the door of opportunity, do not be surprised that it is Work who answers. (Brendon Burchard [39])

Occasionally opportunity will drop in your lap, but only if you have your lap where opportunities drop. Opportunities multiply as they are seized. They die if neglected. When an opportunity appears, it's usually too late to prepare. Opportunity passes by the unprepared. Opportunity doesn't always knock: sometimes it stands by, waiting to be recognised! We're surrounded by overwhelming opportunities. There are opportunities lying latent everywhere, waiting for the perceptive eye to discover them. Opportunities are like stars: they are constantly shining, but we usually don't see them until the darkness pervades. The door of opportunity will not open unless you push. We get only those things for which we hunt or strive and for which we are willing to make sacrifices. Nothing ventured, nothing gained. We either venture or vegetate, said a wise man. Security and opportunity are total strangers.

Wherever there is danger, there lurks opportunity; wherever there is opportunity, there lurks danger. The two are inseparable. They go together. (Earl Nightingale)

This year's breakthrough was last year's impossibility.

Shoot for the moon, even if you miss it, at least you will land among the stars! (Norman Vincent Peale)

A wise man said: 'What is impossible? The impossible is what nobody can do until somebody does!' Those who do not dare will not get their share! Those who do not go into the beehive will not get the honey! Every impossible situation, properly viewed, is an opportunity for great achievement.

Opportunity is missed by most people because it is dressed in overalls and looks like work. (Thomas Edison)

When we see a door of opportunity, there is nothing wrong with turning the door's handle to see whether it will open, but a lot of heartache can follow if we break down a door that is locked. People have experienced hard knocks in life and learned bitter lessons when they have done this. Engineering your own success also places a burden on you to sustain that which you have created. If a door of opportunity is shut in your face, trust that another, better suited one, will be opened. God never closes one door without opening another one. When God allows you to go through a door; it is He who keeps the door open as long as you continue to do your part diligently; you can rest in that partnership.

Difficulties always present opportunities. The next time you find yourself in the midst of a bad experience, remind yourself that you are on the cusp of an opportunity, so start hunting for it. Something will always turn up and, if nothing seems to show up, at least there will be an opportunity to change and grow. Problems, difficulties and challenges are the carriages in which opportunity rides. Problems and opportunities are not strange bedfellows.

To succeed, jump as quickly at opportunities as you do at conclusions. (Benjamin Franklin)

44. Pain

Turn your wounds into wisdom. (Oprah Winfrey)

Rick Warren, author of the best-selling *The Purpose-Driven Life,* said, 'Your most effective ministry will come from your deepest hurts.' Your mess becomes your message, your misery becomes your ministry. God can use your pain to develop your character: empathy, humility etc.

Out of pain and problems have come the sweetest songs, and the most gripping stories. (Billy Graham)

Sometimes it is during suffering that we learn to pray our most authentic heartfelt, honest-to-God prayers. When we're in pain, we don't have time or energy for superficial prayers. God is like a jeweller, and we are like jewels: shaped, chiselled and polished by the hammer of adversity. Someone said that, if the hammer does not do the job, God will use a sledgehammer. If we are really stubborn, He will use a jackhammer. He will use whatever it takes. But be assured that everything that happens to a child of God is Father-filtered and He intends it for our good, hard as it may seem. Every pain is a character-building opportunity. The more painful it is, the greater the potential to build spiritual muscle and moral fibre.

According to John Maxwell, every problem introduces a person to himself. Whenever we encounter a painful experience, we get to know ourselves a little better. Pain prompts us to face who we are and where we are. What we do with that experience defines who we become.

Expecting the world to treat you fairly just because you're a good person is a little like expecting the bull not to charge at you because you're a vegetarian. (Dennis Wholey)

Life difficulties do not allow us to stay the same. They move us! The question is, in which direction will we be moved: forward or backward? better or bitter? Painful experiences teach you to let your discomfort be a catalyst for your development. Growth is the best possible outcome for any painful experience. Facing difficulties is inevitable; learning from them is optional! No struggle, no progress; no pain, no gain. Difficulties always present opportunities to learn and grow. The secret to endurance is to remember that your pain is temporary - it's not going to last for ever, it's going to come to an end.

The Latin word for passion means pain. In our fight for change, we must realise that a certain degree of pain is involved. If you want to change your life you must fight for it! Pain is a powerful agent of change. Physical and emotional pain have a way of changing our brains. It's why getting burnt changes how we think about fire. It's how a difficult diagnosis changes a lifestyle, often creating passionate advocates in the fight for a cure and cause. When we experience physical pain our thinking changes. Really painful experiences often lead to powerful passion.

The trial and crucifixion of Jesus are called the 'Passion'. They were followed by the resurrection. Painful experiences often lead to powerful passion and change. Jesus' death and resurrection have the ultimate power to change our thinking and consequently change our behaviour. When we embrace what Jesus accomplished for us through His death and pain, our lives are transformed forever.

We must all suffer from one of two pains: the pain of discipline or the pain of regret. The difference is, discipline weighs ounces while regret weighs tons. (Jim Rohn)

45. Passion

If a man has not found what he will die for, he isn't fit to live.
(Martin Luther King Jnr.)

On October 21, 1993, members of the Hutu tribe in Burundi invaded a high school and captured more than a hundred pupils and teachers of the Tutsi tribe during the Burundian Civil War. Those not immediately killed were beaten and burned alive. After over nine hours buried beneath burning bodies, Gilbert managed to escape and outrun his captors to the safety of a nearby hospital. He was the lone survivor. Gilbert's one passion is running; this passion saved his life. He travelled to Texas and there he kept honing his skills and competing. He obtained a track scholarship from Abilene Christian University and earned the All-American honours six times. After graduation he moved to Austin, where he is the most popular running coach in the city. To help drill for water in Burundi he later co-founded the Gazelle Foundation, whose main fundraiser is 'Run for the Water', a sponsored run through the streets of Austin. Do you see passion running through his life? (Pun intended).[14]

Passion is what drives us crazy, what makes us do extraordinary things, to discover, to challenge ourselves. Passion is and should always be the heart of courage. (Midori Komatsu)

Passion for something leads to disproportionate time doing or engaged with it. That time eventually translates to skill (or knowledge) and, when skill improves, results improve. Better results generally lead to more enjoyment and more passion and more time invested. It is a virtuous cycle all the way to extraordinary results.

Passion gives you purpose and energy. Passion is energy, with which you can get a lot done. Passion helps us put everything we've got into everything we do. You can succeed at almost anything for which you have limitless enthusiasm. What makes us happy in life is not comfort or luxury - it's passion.

A wise man (John Mason) said, 'You're not truly free until you've been made captive by your mission in life.'

A wise woman once said, 'I would rather die than live with no passion for God. For me life is not worth living if I lose my passion for God.' That is awesome! Her life mission is to ignite passion and love for God in others and be a living testimony of the fact that a passion for God makes giants of men.

What generates passion and zeal in you is a clue to your destiny. What you love is a hint to something you contain. You will be remembered in life only for your passions. John Mason also said, 'One individual with passion is greater than the passive force of ninety-nine who only have an interest.' Everyone loves something. We are shaped and motivated by what we love - it is our passion. Don't ignore your passion. If you do, you ignore a part of the potential God has put inside you. A passionate conviction will help you achieve what you desire in your life. A person of passion always stands out. Passion is a confidence-booster.

When you discover your mission, you feel its demand. It will fill you with enthusiasm and a burning desire to get to work on it. (W. Clement Stone)

Successful people have a passion to succeed and an almost obsessive attention to detail. You shine in life when your personality comes to serve your passion. Passion makes us happy and enthusiastic. It improves your personality and others' opinion of you. Enthusiasm is infectious: don't be afraid to show your enthusiasm, it is encouraging to other like-minded people. It might irritate the nay-sayers but will encourage the visionaries. It's your vision that fuels your passion. Passion is spiritual energy; without it you're as limp as a wet noodle and as bland as salt-less food. Even if you miss - keep at it, don't give up. If you give up, you'll miss God's plan and purpose for sure. Don't let your instinct for self-preservation rob you of the only chance you may ever get at life.

The proof of passion is pursuit. (Mike Murdock)

Passion is expressed by the investment of time. If you have a passion for something, you will have a portion in it. There is a direct relationship between finding your passion and reaching your potential. You won't fulfil your potential doing work you hate! Passion gives you an advantage over others. Passion gives you energy, it motivates you and helps you to be excellent. Nothing is work unless you'd rather be doing something else. To be successful you need to do what you're good at. When what motivates you lines up with what satisfies you, it's a powerful combination. You must discover your uniqueness, then discipline yourself to develop it.

Once you have discovered your passion begin to do something every day that will take you closer to your goal. Continue to do it every day. When you start doing what you should do, your behaviour and conduct start to attract like-minded people. The law of magnetism says: 'Who you are is who you attract.' And who you find attractive is who you are! This is true in leadership, but also in every other aspect of life. It is true that birds of a feather flock together. It puts you in a position to begin to build a community of like-minded people. Remember that you cannot get where you want to go on your own. You will need the help of others to guide you on your way. Prepare yourself as well as you possibly can and, when opportunities present themselves, take them even if you feel you are not totally ready. Nobody ever got ready by waiting. You get ready by starting. Nothing else compares to doing what you were created to do: it will be more demanding and difficult than you expect, but it will be better and more impactful than you can ever imagine.[40] Learn to put everything you've got into everything you have to do. Go with all you've got in a definite direction and, if it's the wrong direction, you'll find out more quickly. What fuels your passion? Learn how to harness your strength, focus your power, and replenish your energy. You must be mindful of what makes you feel most fully alive.

Nothing will steal our strength as much as living lives we do not love. The way we generate the force that drives us forward in life is through our desires, values, passions, hopes, dreams and aspirations, and ultimately the greatest force that propels us into our destiny is doing what we love. If getting up in the morning is a struggle and you find yourself lacking the energy to engage life fully, you can be certain that you are not living the life you were created to live. Your energy flows out of your passions. Your passions must flow out of love. It is that love that gives you ultimate joy, and joy gives you bountiful strength.

Negative emotions can also generate passion. And although they do cause you to be passionate, they lead you not to create but rather to destroy. You must find the why in the race you are running. Choose the right people to run with. Remember that your associates fuel your passion and will shape your identity and your identity will shape your future. The future will be created by those with the courage to create it. A better world will happen only if we find the strength and energy to give our lives to it. Although our passion and energy come from God, ultimately what we do with that passion and energy is up to us. You can discover your passion by asking a few questions like these: what ignites my passions? what moments in my life do I feel most invigorated? do I see in the people currently around me the ability to fit into my dream?

The worst bankruptcy in the world is the man who has lost his passion. (H. W. Arnold-Forbes)

46. Patience

He that can have patience can have what he will. (Benjamin Franklin)

You must've heard the saying, 'Patience is a virtue'. Patience is the king of virtues. The story of John DeLorean; an American engineer, inventor and executive in the U.S. automobile industry, illustrates it. He was founder of the DeLorean Motor Company. DeLorean rose to success in the auto industry with his development of the Pontiac GTO and then later his own car-make named after himself. DeLorean lost it all: his family, his business and, yes, even his car, because he went too far too fast in his pursuit of success. Patience was not a virtue in his fast-paced life and in the auto-industry in which the young and ambitious DeLorean circulated - and it may not be in the circles in which you travel, either. Impatience was a major factor in bringing about his downfall. John Zachary DeLorean became a follower of Christ when he hit the speed-bumps of life and became a new person. It is fair to say that John learned the truth of Proverbs 6:1-5 late in life, after he had almost given himself away to his debtors and strangers while travelling down the fast track searching for fame and success.

According to the online dictionary, patience is the capacity to accept or tolerate delay, problems, or suffering without becoming annoyed or anxious. Patience is necessary for achieving anything in life. It is maintaining discipline for a while without losing the hope towards our results. This discipline teaches us many things. It injects a never-give-up kind of attitude which will lift our spirits. Patience is when you're supposed to be mad but you choose to understand. Patience is not passive waiting, it's a form of action and a powerful one at that.

Adopt the pace of nature; her secret is patience. (Ralph W. Emerson)

The Bible tells us that there are seasons in life. It says in Ecclesiastes 3:1 that 'there is a time for everything, and a season for every

164

activity under the heavens.' Therefore between the then and the now or the now and the what's-coming-next, there is always a delay. This is irritating for most people, to plant and not reap immediately, to make an investment and not receive rewards instantly or create a plan and not have it instantly come to fruition. You must realise that the vision is for an appointed time, it may tarry: but wait! It will not come behind the appointed time.

Two things define us: Our patience when we have nothing and our attitude when we have everything. (George Bernard Shaw)

The day you plant your seed is not the day you'll eat the fruit, and, even when the fruit comes, it ripens slowly. Would you rather eat a vine-ripened tomato or one that has been picked green and then gassed to turn it red? There's no comparison between a vine-ripened tomato, which was allowed to grow slowly, and a tomato that was picked prematurely. If you pick too soon, you miss the flavour.

When it comes to money management, you always reap in a different season from that in which you sow. And by the way, not all fruit ripens at the same time. When you have a peach tree, they're not all ripe at once. They come in little by little; you pick a few a day. When you give in the offering on Sunday, you might not get a windfall tomorrow. It's going to come in over time. You're going to have to wait to reap in a different season. But while you're waiting, God is working. When you're waiting for the fulfilment of the efforts or energy that you've put into something, you may think nothing's happening. But it's happening! While that seed is hidden in the ground, it is slowly germinating. And when that seed bursts out of the soil, the little shoot will stick up out of the ground, and then you will see that it's working. That's the beginning of a harvest season. It will continue growing and growing. But until then, you need to trust that God is working even though it seems you can't see any fruit from your labour.

Plants take time to grow. There's no such thing as instant maturity. No farmer goes out, plants the seed in the ground, comes back an hour later, digs it up, and expects it to have grown. You've just got to let it be. Leave it covered and let God grow it in his time.

Galatians 6:9 says, 'Let's not get tired of doing what is good. At just the right time we will reap a harvest of blessing if we don't give up' (NLT).[58] It is never too late to throw the gears of your life into reverse if you sense you're going down the wrong road. Be honest with yourself and ask God to help you develop the patience you need to wait on Him and not create your own success. Patiently wait on God for your success and He will give you results greater than you could engineer on your own.

47. Persistence

Giving up is the ultimate tragedy. (Robert Donovan)

Can you see anything?' his assistant asked as Carter's eyes adjusted to the semi-darkness. Carter could see well enough, but he had difficulty speaking because of the dazzling array of treasure spread out before him.

For more than two thousand years, tourists, grave-robbers and archaeologists had searched for the burial places of Egypt's pharaohs. Armed with only a few scraps of evidence, British archaeologist Howard Carter's searched for many years and his efforts seemed doomed to failure. But Carter pressed on and finally unlocked an ancient Egyptian tomb. No one in the modern world had ever seen anything like it. The king's embalmed body lay within a nest of three coffins, the inner one of solid gold. On the king's head was a magnificent golden portrait mask, and numerous pieces of jewellery lay on the body and in its wrappings. Other rooms were crammed with statues, a chariot, weapons, chests, vases, daggers, jewels and a throne. It was the priceless tomb and treasure of King Tutankhamun, who reigned from 1352 to 1343 BC. It was on 26 November 1922 that Carter made this discovery. He made the world's most exciting archaeological discovery because he did not give up searching. He stuck with it, persevered, pressed on until he broke through. [7]

In the struggle between the stone and water, in time, the water wins. (Japanese proverb)

The leadership of Winston Churchill, Abraham Lincoln, and Teddy Roosevelt always inspires me because they knew how to overcome great obstacles through steady persistence. These men were heroes. I like them because they inspire me to be persistent in the face of adversity. They never gave up!

Paralyse resistance with persistence. (Woody Hayes)

Don't give up. Successful people are people who have conquered the temptation to give up. The nose of the bulldog is slanted backwards so he can continue to breathe without letting go. Consider the postage stamp. Its effectiveness is in sticking to one thing until it reaches its destination. Most people fail due to lack of staying power. We need to develop stick-to-it-ness.

Fall down seven times, get up eight times. (Japanese maxim)

I recall a story about a salesman. He looked out of the window of a restaurant at the blinding snowstorm. He asked the waiter, ' Do you think the roads will be clear enough in the morning to travel?' The waiter replied, 'Depends on if you're on salary or commission.'

How many things apparently impossible have nevertheless been performed by resolute men who had no alternative but death.! (Napoleon)

Refuse to give up; work to obtain all the knowledge you can about what you want to achieve. Fix your mind on your purpose, persist! Keep searching, no matter how many times you meet with disappointment. Refuse to be influenced by the fact that someone else tried the same thing and failed. Stay sold on the idea that somewhere a solution to the problem exists and you will find it. Focus more on what you are doing daily and succeed at it and that will affect who you will be in future. Little by little does not mean slow. Our greatest weakness lies in giving up. The most certain way to succeed is always to persist and try just one more time.

A river cuts through rock not because of its power but because of its persistence. (James M. Watkins)

Heroism is endurance for one moment more. (George F. Kennan)

Endurance is one of the most difficult disciplines, but it is to the one who endures that the final victory comes. (Gautama Buddha)

It does not matter how slowly you go as long as you do not stop. (Confucius)

48. Perspective

Be careful how you interpret the world; it is like that. (Erich Heller)

In a *Peanuts* cartoon, Snoopy (the dog) looks in on Thanksgiving Day and sees the family sitting around the table enjoying a dinner of delicious turkey and all the trimmings while he's outside eating dog food. 'How about that?' he thinks. 'Everybody's eating turkey today, but because I'm just a dog I get dog food.' Then suddenly his perspective changes. 'Of course, things could be worse: I could have been born a turkey!'

We don't see things as they are: we see things as we are. (Anaïs Nin)

When you see a Goliath-sized problem, what do you think? It's too big I can't overcome this? or, It's so big, I can't miss, I'll take this out! Your perspective will determine your outcome. Whenever challenges come, praise God and rejoice because it is an opportunity to develop your problem-solving muscles (spiritual and physical) and, when you have bigger muscles, God commits into your hands bigger projects, blessings, responsibilities, visions and accomplishments. Therefore challenging times signal promotion time. Your perspective will determine your outcome.

Your circumstances don't determine the quality of your life: how you think about them does. Two labourers working at a building site were asked about their work. One said: I'm working for a lousy £15 per hour in scorching heat. The other said: I'm building a magnificent edifice for the worship of the King of Kings. Identical circumstances, different perspectives. So how do you change your emotional response when you feel powerless over people and circumstances? By changing your perspective!

The way you see your life shapes your life. It's the view of life that you hold, consciously or unconsciously that shapes your life. It determines your expectations, your values, your relationships, your goals and your priorities. When we see a thing, we will see it filtered through our own perceptions. So none of us really sees things objectively. Each person sees it with their own beliefs, preconceptions, interpretation, and attitude.

When we change the way we look at things, the things we look at change.
(Wayne Dyer)

Angel story

Two travelling angels stopped to spend the night in the home of a wealthy family. The family was rude and refused to let the angels stay in the mansion's guestroom. Instead the angels were given a space in the cold basement. As they made their bed on the hard floor, the older angel saw a hole in the wall and repaired it. When the younger angel asked why, the older angel replied, 'Things aren't always what they seem.' The next night the pair came to rest at the house of a very poor but very hospitable farmer and his wife. After sharing what little food they had, the couple let the angels sleep in their bed where they could have a good night's rest. When the sun came up the next morning the angels found the farmer and his wife in tears. Their only cow, whose milk had been their sole income, lay dead in the field. The younger angel was infuriated and asked the older angel, 'How could you have let this happen? The first man had everything, yet you helped him. The second family had little but was willing to share everything, and you let their cow die.' 'Things aren't always what they seem,' the older angel replied. 'When we stayed in the basement of the mansion, I noticed there was gold stored in that hole in the wall. Since the owner was so obsessed with greed and unwilling to share his good fortune, I sealed the wall so he wouldn't find it. Then last night as we slept in the farmer's bed, the angel of death came for his wife. I gave him the cow instead. Things aren't always what they seem.'

You've probably heard the saying, 'I grumbled because I had no shoes, then I met a man who had no feet' (Helen Keller). How big or how difficult our problem appear to be is often a matter of perspective. A lot of the difficulties and problems we face are pretty insignificant in the larger scheme of things. When I lost a very dear friend this year, I was reminded of just how petty a lot of my 'problems' really are.

49. Personal finance management

If your outgo exceeds your inflow then your up-keep will become your downfall. (Jim Rohn)

If you want to be financially strong, you need to start writing down what you spend until you know where it's all going. This is the principle of sound financial management. You've got to keep track of where all your money is going! This is Personal Finance 101 - the bare bones of sound financial management.

Plan carefully and you will have plenty. (Pr 21:5).

This passage seems to imply that, if you don't have plenty, it's because you're not planning carefully (in most cases). And consequently you don't have anybody to blame but yourself, ouch! You may say, 'But I had this emergency!' Everybody has emergencies. People get laid off all the time, everybody has unexpected expenses. The difference between the people who make it through and those who don't is how they planned for those emergencies. If you don't expect them, of course you're going to be wrecked by them. Ignorance of your true financial condition, plus availability of easy credit leads to financial disaster. If you are constantly scratching your head at the end of the month wondering where all your money went, or why you always seem to have more month left at the end of your money, here are four things you need to get to grips with:

what you own

what you owe

what you earn

where it's going.

There are several ways to budget, and you need to figure out which one is best for you. You need to get online, get into your bank, get to your accountant's office, get into your books — whatever it takes to get on track and understand your money so that it works for you and not against you.

Proverbs 23:5 says, 'Your money can be gone in a flash, as if it had grown wings and flown away like an eagle'. That's a pretty descriptive picture. If you don't know where your money is going, it's just going to fly away like an eagle. You've got to keep good records so you know where your money is going. Interestingly the U.S. dollar has an eagle on every dollar bill. So every time you look at that bill, let it be a reminder that it's going to fly away to an unknown destination unless you give it a specific assignment.

A budget is telling your money where to go, instead of wondering where it went. (John Maxwell)

Budget

An essential part of personal finance management is a budget. A budget is simply a document that tells every single penny of your money where it is to go every month. Budgets can be boring and restraining, but they are the foundation of financial well-being, no matter your salary or financial situation. Budgeting is how you tell your money where to go and what to do e.g. paying bills, eliminating debt, saving for a purchase or project, rather than spending freely and then wondering where all your money went at the end of the month. It takes discipline and a concerted effort to create and stick to a budget. But the benefits are well worth it. There are many different kinds of budgets. Do your research and find the one that works the best for you.

Credit Cards

Credit cards when used properly, can be a valuable financial tool. They can help you build credit or repair a poor credit score. This is especially important if you are gearing up for a big purchase, such as buying a house. But to do this, you have to use credit cards correctly. For example, say you have a recurring bill set up to be paid via your credit card each month. Set aside that money in a separate current or savings account, then have it automatically routed to your credit-card bill each month. That way, even though you'll be accruing a balance each month, you'll also be paying it off in full when due. It is very important that you don't use your credit cards for any unexpected spends, or anything that you simply can't afford that month.

Pay Yourself First

This can seem like an impossible piece of advice, especially if you are living on a strict budget, but it's immensely important. Simply put: paying yourself first means that every single month/week, depending on when you receive your pay, you set aside money to save. Do this before paying any bills or before any discretionary spends. You can tuck these funds away in your nest egg, your rainy-day fund or your retirement account. You can also pay yourself first to cover larger spends, like paying for home-repairs or sending your child to summer-camp. Allocating these funds to a larger goal the moment they hit your account will prevent you from spending that money unnecessarily or on things you don't need.

Invest Wisely

Whether it's building a small stock-portfolio, owning your own home or religiously contributing to your pension-fund, learning how to invest properly is a bedrock of financial health and future wealth owing to the miracle of compound interest and time.

50. Personal growth and self-development

Dreams often come one size too big so that we can grow into them.
(John Maxwell)

John Maxwell, in his book *The Fifteen Laws of Growth*, talks about how his investment of $799 in a personal growth plan allowed him to reap a harvest beyond his wildest dreams. He's written over 100 books. Spoken to thousands of people. Impacted millions of lives. Why can't that be you? With the right plan and action, it can. You just need to take the first step.

The major key to my better future is me. (Jim Rohn)

You don't achieve beyond your level of development. Unless you are in a plane you cannot overcome the law of gravity. Unless you're growing and learning you're deteriorating or declining. You can greatly alter the course of your life. You can change, you can always change, you're not a tree so you're not stuck. If a tree used up all the nourishment around it, it would die because it's stuck. But human beings can change location; they can move east, north, west or south.

A great breakthrough in your life comes when you realise that you can learn anything you need to know in order to accomplish any goal you set for yourself.

Income doesn't exceed personal development. You can't give what you don't have. You don't achieve beyond your level of development. According to Jim Rohn, if someone hands you a million pounds, best you grow quickly so you get to keep the money. Otherwise sure enough it will disappear. Somebody once said, 'If you took all the money in the world and divided it up equally among everybody, it would soon end up in the same pockets.' Incredible! Success is something you attract, not something you pursue. Success is looking for a good place to stay, so instead of going after it, work on yourself through personal development.

The biggest room in the world is room for improvement. (Helmut Schmidt)

The major question to ask on the job is not, what am I getting? but, what am I becoming? am I growing? You will do much better in the market-place if you go to work primarily on yourself. To earn an above-average income, you need to become an above-average person. To be a success in life learn to work harder on yourself than you do on the job. You don't *achieve* goals: you *grow into* them.

The cost of growth is always less than the cost of stagnation, just like the pain of regret is greater than the pain of self-discipline. Personal growth leads to success in all areas of life. Grow into the person you have the potential to be. Make personal growth your daily habit. The dream and destination are not the most important things. The most important thing is the growth you experience along the way - i.e. the person you become in the process of achieving your dream. You also discover there is no finishing line.

Andy Stanley said, 'You will never maximize your potential in any area without coaching. It is impossible.'

One of the easiest ways to grow is to learn from mentors. The quickest way to get to where you want to go is by finding someone who's already doing what you want to do. It's so important that you connect with someone who's two to ten steps ahead of you!

A coach remains something or someone, who carries a valued person from where they are to where they want to be. So if you had a coach, you knew you would end up at your desired destination. According to Terry Savelle and John Maxwell, you will never maximize your potential in any area without coaching.

Terry Savelle Foy said, 'When I hit my own rock bottom in 2002, I heard someone say, "God will change your circumstances, but He'll change you first."' And that's when she started taking steps to get out of the rut she was in and saw God truly transform her entire life!

We see further when we stand on the shoulder of giants. (Priscian)

Too many people suffer from destination disease. They reach a certain level and want to just coast on what they already know. (Joel Osteen)

Whether you are nine or ninety, you should constantly be learning, improving your skills and staying curious. Growth has to be intentional. Are you reading books? Listening to audios? Have you enrolled in a course lately? Who are your mentors? I want to encourage you to never stop learning new things! (Terri Savelle)

Your number-one job is to grow yourself into the best of yourself. The maximum development and utilisation of your giftings, passion and resources. Personal development is self-administered. There will be no one standing over your shoulder telling you what to do and how to do it. You alone can give yourself the order or command to get going to grow and develop yourself. Only you can bring about the change you desire. 'If it must be, then it's up to me,' must be your theme song. If you neglect to do what you must do to grow yourself, you will have to live with yourself and the regret and if you choose to do whatever it takes you will live with the rewards and the respect and esteem, admiration you will get from friends and family.

It's possible to change without growing, but it's impossible to grow without changing.

Without change there is no growth. Value and prioritise yourself, choose excellence, fail your way to success by learning from those failures, empower yourself and live out loud.

After you have done new things consistently for a while, you begin to feel yourself becoming a different person. One consequence of becoming a different person is that you won't be vulnerable to trends and fads. Acquiring more money will require that you learn not only new facts but also new intuitions and new ways of responding to situations. Seeing oneself as having become an entirely new and different person is essential to any major growth step. If you really grow then you will really change. You must learn, understand and then practise. Practise, practise, practise! This will help you become proficient in technique and skill but also enable you to become a different, changed, grown-up, better person. By doing different things - integrating new behaviour and habits in daily life - eventually you will become a new person.[41]

A substantial and meaningful increase in the amount of money you own changes you. You become a slightly different person and people notice the change. If extra money makes a new person of you, then being a new person is a step on the road to having more money. Therefore to acquire more money, you need to work on far more than learning new skills. You have to work on changing yourself. It may not be easy, but it can be done, and it works. We achieve our full potential by growth - no other way. To be able to maximize and fulfil our potential we must grow and we must be highly intentional about it, because it will not just happen or fall on us like ripe cherries. Growth does not just happen - it must be made to happen. You cannot change your life until you change something you do every day.

People are anxious to improve their circumstances but are unwilling to improve themselves. They therefore remain bound.' (James Allen, As a man thinketh)

Attend Automobile University

Listen to audio messages, talks and podcasts while driving, showering, eating, cooking, exercising etc. While you are doing mundane jobs or tasks; go to 'automobile university'. Mary Kay said, 'I never drive in my car without listening to a faith-building message.' The knowledge and understanding gained just listening daily to a topic of interest for a year can be the equivalent of what you learn in a college degree! You will begin to grow, and growth compounds and accelerates if you remain intentional about it. So start now!

I have spent time with Nelson Mandela, Oprah Winfery, Joyce Meyer, Barak Obama, Michelle Obama, Richard Branson, John Maxwell, Myles Monroe, Bill Gates, Warren Buffet, but I've never met any of them. I hang out with them regularly as I listen to them on audio books, CDs and YouTube. I even carry them around in my car as I attend automobile university. The most successful people attend this university. A habit Terry Savelle Foy calls 'push-play'. Listen to audio books and messages: it is one of the key habits that will change your life. It will build your faith, motivate and inspire you, bring direction and insight.

A coach is your fiercest critic, but also your best friend.

Focus on self-development (how to serve others), not self-fulfilment (how it serves me). Keep growing to keep giving - if you want to keep having something of quality and substance to give, you have to keep growing and developing. If you stop learning you stop growing; you lose your spark, passion, sharpness, vibrancy, enthusiasm, your edge and innovative spirit.

The greatest gift you can give to someone is your own personal development. (Jim Rohn)

Growing and developing yourself enables you to be able to grow others and contribute to their lives. Be growth-focused, not goal-focused, because if you grow you will accomplish the goals. Difficulties always present opportunities to learn and grow. Find and pursue the opportunity and enjoy the growth. Always treat and see difficulties as growth opportunities. Whether you choose to grow or not, you will experience pain - the pain of self-discipline or the pain of regret. Choose right: the pain of self-discipline is mild compared with that of regret!

The only job security we have is our individual commitment to personal development. There are no short cuts to anywhere worth going. Instant gratification and personal growth are incompatible. Immediate gratification is almost always the enemy of growth. If you delay gratification you grow. When your capacity grows, what once caused you distress no longer does. Growing and developing your potential or capacity is an ongoing journey that yields a fulfilling life.

There is no future in any job. The future lies in the man who holds the job. (George W. Crane)

Growth always increases your capacity because the potential that exists within us is limitless and largely untapped. When you think of limits, you create them. The way to increase your capacity internally is to change the way you approach personal growth. Acquiring more information isn't enough, we must change how we think and we must change our actions.

Man's mind, once stretched by a new idea, never regains its original dimensions. (Oliver Wendell Holmes)

51. Planning / preparation / organisation

Planning is bringing the future into the present so that you can do something about it now. (Alan Lakein)

A university student sent this email to his mum at the end of term: 'Dropped out of uni, coming home tomorrow. Prepare dad.' The email he got back said:

'Dad prepared. Prepare yourself!'

A student asked his master: 'You talk about peace but teach me to fight?' His master said: 'It is better to be a warrior in a garden than a gardener in a war.' The moral is: be prepared. If you fail to plan, you plan to fail.

Jim Rohn has said, 'You can't get rid of January or winter by tearing it off the calendar!'[42] You've got to learn to prepare for it and handle it. If you don't prepare or plan your life, chaos will reign, things will fall apart, the centre will not hold and anarchy will be on the loose in your world (to borrow the words of author Chinua Achebe).

Life is mostly about preparation. School is preparation for life. Studying is preparation for the examination. We go the direction we face, and we face the direction we design. Direction determines destination. You cannot change destination, but today you can change your direction. A tiny change of direction today will make a massive difference in five years' time. It would not take much to change direction today: a few decisions in discipline, eating healthily, maybe just an apple a day, a little bit of exercise, spending a little time in prayer and meditation, learning, setting goals, taking action, saving a little, avoiding debt. All these little changes in direction today can massively affect where you arrive at in five to seven years' time. It's only a small journey to a new direction.

Psychologists have correctly observed that when one is truly ready for a thing, it puts in its appearance.

Time and change cannot be stopped but they can be controlled by planning. Strategic planning is a crucial key to success.[43] A good plan is a road map: it shows the best way to get to a desired destination. We plan for failure by not planning for success. We plan for poverty by not having a plan to be rich.

I will not allow somebody else's lack of a plan become my emergency. (Oluwole Omiyale)

Planning is the best way to conserve energy and preserve waste of time and resources. Planning is a step by step approach to accomplishing a set goal or task. It is a process of action or a set of activities designed to accomplish a dream. The greatest protection against wasted time is planning. A plan shows time how you are going to spend it, just as your budget tells your money how it is going to be sent on your errands.

Productivity is never an accident. It is always the result of a commitment to excellence, intelligent planning and focused effort. (Paul Meyer)

Even the biggest tasks can be broken down into small pieces that are manageable. Your life's goals can be broken into bite-sized chunks that are not so difficult to achieve. First, you need to decide what you want to accomplish and work back from there to where you are now. When you've decided on that, then seek out someone who is doing what you want to do and learn from them. When you do this, one thing will lead to another, and doors will begin to open for you.

Preparation is planning ahead. Preparation causes you to be at ease, it prevents pressure. When I'm well prepared for a task, like an exam or giving a talk, speech or training, I feel minimal stress but great excitement. Good organisation and good preparation diminish stress. Therefore whatever it is you are hoping for and expecting, it is important to be prepared for it. How can you say one day I will do this or that but do nothing to prepare or put yourself in the position to be able to receive it? Be ready for tomorrow by doing all you must do today. Being organised gives you a sense of power. The number one time-waster for most people is looking for things they have lost or misplaced. I read that when a dove returns to its nest, it won't land if the nest is out of order. If a simple dove is concerned about order so should you be!

Doing first things first and prioritising the most important things help us live a more productive life. You might have seen the illustration about putting golf balls into a jar, then putting small pebbles in the jars, then sand into the jar, then water into the jar. All these could only fit into the jar because of the order in which the objects were placed in. If you put the sand or water into the jar first, nothing else will fit in. In the same way we need to put first things first, God, family, health, career, goals, aspirations, leisure etc. all in the right order.

We all need systems for maximum efficiency in our daily lives. A system is a set of principles or procedures according to which something is done. Our system is our *modus operandi*, the way we do things. We all have systems, deliberately created or created by default. Perhaps you're thinking, 'I don't really have systems,' or, 'I just go with the flow; I don't really need systems.' The fact is, you have systems. Your system might be to start the day with meditation or prayer, or it might be checking your phone or switching on the T.V. to watch the breaking news in the morning on your way out to work, handling emergencies, or prioritising your schedule. Whichever way you do it, that's a system. You have systems by intent or by default, but either way you have them. And the systems you have are a result of what you've created or of what you've tolerated. So, if you want a better outcome, start by creating a better system.

In the first chapter of the Bible, the world was formless, and God said, 'Let there be light.' Then He went on to separate day from night, earth from sky, land from water, birds from fish, and so on. You might notice God handles specific systems together and doesn't move on until He thinks it's good. Finally, God created humans and gave them directions for caring for it all— including a system of resting once a week. Isn't that awesome! Your body consists of a system of organs. Your life is full of systems. Healthy systems never happen by accident. They were created on purpose. What system do you need to create to get the results you want? Always ask yourself what you can do to make yourself ready. Always be ready, because opportunity will come. Prepare by saving, prepare by reading, prepare yourself for fortune.

Life does not waste success on the unprepared. Prepare yourself always - then you will deserve success. Life gives you not what you want but what you deserve. Opportunity passes the unprepared by.

According to the Bible God is a meticulous planner. For example He scheduled a banquet called 'the marriage supper of the Lamb' - two thousand years in advance (Revelation 19:9)! He instructed Noah to build an ark with a specific type of wood (gopher) and dimensions 450 feet long, 75 feet wide, 45 feet high (Genesis 6:15). He gave Moses the specific colours (blue, purple, scarlet) and fabrics (linen) and design (embroidered cherubim) that He wanted used in constructing and furnishing the tabernacle (Exodus 26:1). Look at how precisely He orders the seasons and positions stars. Can you imagine such a God having no plan for you (His living temple), and your finances the product of your work life? He certainly does and He says so (Jeremiah 29:11).

Learning to prioritise can help us with planning and organising our lives better because, if the first thing isn't first, everything else is out of order. The greatest priority in a person's life should be their relationship with God. The wisdom of *Proverbs* (Proverbs 3) indicates that, if God is at the top, every other aspect of life will fall into place. I have put this promise to the test in my own life and can vouch for its reliability. God always keeps His word. We will fail, but He never fails. Only a few things matter - say no to more things, so you can be more effective and successful in the few things that matter.

Order is knowing that what you do, i.e. your input, will lead to a predictable outcome. Planning brings order into our lives.

Henry Ford once said, 'Before everything else, getting ready is the secret of success.'

52. Positive thinking

A pessimist sees the difficulty in every opportunity; an optimist sees the opportunity in every difficulty. (Winston Churchill)

Norman Vincent Peale shares the story of some American sailors who years ago were visiting a port in China and came across a tattoo-parlour. One of the tattoos displayed on the window caught their attention. It read: 'Born to lose.' They were shocked, so they asked the Chinese man if anyone ever got this negative tattoo. The man answered in broken English, 'Before tattoo on body, tattoo on mind.'

If you have good thoughts they will shine out of your face like sunbeams and you will always look lovely. (Roald Dahl)

Poet Frederick Langbridge wrote, 'Two men looked out through prison bars; one saw mud, the other saw stars.' Both men were in identical circumstances, but their outlooks were entirely different. One looked for beauty and found it; the other focused on ugliness and found it. Your circumstances in life will produce certain emotions. So how do you change your emotional response when you feel trapped by your situation and circumstances? By changing your perspective, changing how you see and changing how you think about them. True change always begins in your mind. As you think in your heart, so you are. The way you think inevitably controls your feelings. To change your feelings, you must go to the source and deal with the thing that produced them - how you think. Thoughts produce feelings, not the other way around. The way you think determines the way you feel and the way you feel influences the way you act. Thinking determines feelings; feelings determine actions; actions determine habits; habits determine destiny.

Your attitude is more important than the tragedy. Your viewpoint is stronger than any calamity. Your mind-set is bigger than the details of the catastrophe. When you choose to be positive about the situation you've been handed, you set a course to turn the situation round or bring out the opportunity from the adversity. No one has more control over your attitude today than you do. And as you choose a hope-filled forward-thinking can-do attitude, you begin to walk in greater victory and success no matter what the situation is.

When bad things happen to you, focus on what you can learn from it. If you focus on the bad, you're doomed to repeat it. (Mel Robbins)

There was a lady who, after going through a trying time, complained to her friend that the whole world was against her. The friend retorted, 'No, that can't be true, the whole world doesn't even know you yet!' The actions that become springboards to success are informed by positive thinking. On the journey to achieving big success, you get bigger. This is because big requires growth and a positive mind-set. Your thinking, your skills, your relationships, your sense of what is possible and what it takes all grow on the journey to success. As you think positive, and think big, you experience big and you become big.

A strong positive self-image is one of the best possible preparations for success in life. When you think positively about yourself and your self-talk is constantly positive it is going to affect every area of your life because your thoughts deeply affect your life and the direction in which you are going. The negative, pessimistic person is half-defeated before even beginning! Proverbs 23:7 says: as a man thinks so he is. In other words, as a man thinks continually so he is becoming.

Negative thoughts lead to negative words, when we speak negative words they affect us negatively because the words we speak out of our mouth affect our entire being. Your subconscious mind picks up your words, treats them as true valid statements, then sets about trying to fulfil them. Your words create an atmosphere for good or trouble, and you are going to have to live in that environment created by your words. There is a miracle in your mouth. If you want to change your world, start by changing your words. When you change your words to positive, your thoughts start to go in the same direction and then your life starts going in the same direction.

A gland in the body called the hypothalamus gland responds to thought and to the environment of your life and it plays an important role in many psychosomatic illnesses. The hypothalamus gland can be described as the link between your body and soul/spirit or the connection between your thoughts and body. The hypothalamus acts as the body's watchman. It has sensors that detect changes in the blood. It is informed of emotions through tracts that connect it with the emotional centres of the brain. When a stress situation arises, the hypothalamus is stimulated to react through various pathways of the body and produces alarm reactions. These alarm reactions produce increase in the levels of blood-sugar and oxygen to organs that are most needed to ward off danger, e.g. brain, skeletal muscles and heart. The point of the biology lecture is this: negative thinking such as fear, stress and anxiety affect our bodies negatively.

Faith and positive thinking, based on God's word, are vital keys to maintaining a positive mindset. A positive mind affects one's life, well-being and health. Medical science attests to this mind/body connection.[27]

I am an optimist. It does not seem too much use being anything else. (Churchill)

53. Prayer and meditation

When I pray coincidences happen; when I don't, they don't. (William Temple, one-time archbishop of Canterbury)

Prayer is alien to our proud human nature. To people in the fast lane, determined to make it on their own, prayer is an embarrassing interruption.[44]

Max Lucado has rightly said, 'When we work, we work; but when we pray, God works.' The most powerful energy anyone can generate is prayer energy. Get into the habit of dealing with God about everything. When you feel swept off your feet by life's issues, get on your knees.

Saint John Chrysostom (349–407) wrote, 'Prayer … is the root, the fountain, the mother of a thousand blessings … The potency of prayer has subdued the strength of fire, it has bridled the rage of lions … extinguished wars, appeased the elements, expelled demons, burst the chains of death, expanded the gates of heaven, assuaged diseases … rescued cities from destruction … and arrested the progress of the thunderbolt.' [45]

Watchman Nee wrote, 'Our prayers lay the track down which God's power can come. Like a mighty locomotive, his power is irresistible, but it cannot reach us without rails.'

Oswald Chambers said, 'Unless in the first waking moments of the day you learn to fling the door wide back and let God in, you will walk on a wrong level all day; but swing the door wide open and pray to your Father in secret and every public thing will be stamped with the presence of God.' Prayer is spiritual nutrition. Just as the body needs physical food, so the soul needs spiritual food. Prayer changes us. However, the Bible goes much further than this. Prayer is powerful; it has the power to change circumstances, other people and even the course of history.

Prayer is the slender nerve that moves the muscles of omnipotence. (Charles Haddon Spurgeon)

Many Hebrew terms are used to describe prayer in the Bible. One of the Hebrew words for prayer used in the Bible is 'tefillah'; it is one of many, but the most common in the Bible. The Hebrew root means 'to think, entreat, judge, intercede', and the reflexive means 'to judge oneself', and 'to pray'. So to the Jews of the Bible, prayer was not a time when they simply asked God for things; it was a time when they scrutinised themselves and their relationship with God. They used prayer as a way to evaluate every aspect of their lives and their relationship with God. God's Spirit helps us to pray aright and effectively (Romans 8:26-27). The Hebrew word for God's Spirit is 'ruach', which means 'wind'. Sailors can't control the wind — they can only respond to it. They can only adjust the sails to make the most of what they are given. So a person who has learned to rely and follow the direction of God's Spirit in prayer can adjust their lives to make the most of every situation He leads them into, just like a sailing boat. Another kind of boat is the motor-boat. Motor-boats do not need the wind because they are powered by their own engine, and so the captain can set its course and direction as desired, no matter which way the wind is blowing. In theory this sort of control may appear good, but motor-boats need fuel to run and can experience a breakdown at any time. We all have a choice: to follow God's will or our own. To be a sailing boat or a motor-boat. Make prayer your daily habit. Prayer is the great stress-reliever.

Jesus rose up a great while before dawn, while it was still dark, went out of the house and went to pray in a quiet place. (Mark 1:35)

Spiritual Hunger

The revivalist John G. Lake said that the most powerful prayer any Christian can pray is, 'God, make me hungry for you.' I agree with him. We are all a product of our spiritual appetite and none of us is greater than our prayer life. There is a healthy restlessness that each of us should embrace – the restlessness that longs for heaven, for a deeper knowledge of God's presence; the restlessness that marks us out as nothing more than pilgrims, passing through this temporary place and heading for our true destination. Stay hungry for God!

John Piper said, 'If you don't feel strong desires for the manifestation of the glory of God, it is not because you have drunk deeply and are satisfied. It is because you have nibbled so long at the table of the world. Your soul is stuffed with small things, and there is no room for the great.'

'The greatest enemy of hunger for God is not poison but apple pie. It is not the banquet of the wicked that dulls our appetite for heaven, but endless nibbling at the table of the world. It is not the X-rated video, but the prime-time dribble of triviality we drink in every night.[46]

All humans have a spiritual appetite as part of their makeup. This yearning for spiritual fulfilment is a constant in daily life. My question is: where is your hunger being satisfied? If you are not hungry for the presence and glory of God, then you can be sure you are hungry for something else. People pursue many things in order to satisfy this hunger: fame, fortune, success, affirmation of others, beauty, relationships etc. Only one thing can truly satisfy and that is God Himself. The more hungry for God we are, the more alive we are and the more alive we feel.

Prayer is a window to opportunity, a doorway to miracles, a channel for blessings, and a path to dreams coming true. It's so much more than a cold call! (Brian Houston)

Sometimes we think we are too busy to pray. That is a mistake, for praying is a saving of time. (Charles Spurgeon)

Facts about prayer

It is impossible to be prayerful and pessimistic.

Amazing things happen when we start praying.

Prayer time is not wasted time.

When you take one step toward God in prayer, He will take many more steps towards you (a giant step).

Prayer is not a means of getting things, it is a means of getting more of God into your life.

Prayer cannot be answered until you have prayed.

Nothing significant happens until you pray fervently. God rewards our desperation.

The great tragedy of life is not unanswered prayer, but unoffered prayer.

Frequency on your knees in prayer will keep you in right standing with God.

Prayer is not overcoming God's reluctance but taking hold of God's willingness.

Prayerlessness is a unilateral declaration of independence from God.

The closer you live to God, the smaller everything appears.

In prayer we learn to change. You cannot truly pray and stay the same. Prayer is one of the most life-changing experiences we will ever know. (Unknown)

Prayerlessness is our declaration of independence from God. (Chris Inman)

Great one-line prayers:

I want to be in your will, not in your way!

God, make me hungry for you.

I will not let you go unless you bless me.

Lord, enlarge my territory.

Men may spurn our appeals, reject our message, oppose our arguments, despise our persons, but they are helpless against our prayers. (Sidlow Baxter)

Meditation

The eighteenth-century philosopher and critic of Christianity, Voltaire, said, 'Within a hundred years the Bible will be obsolete and will have gone out of circulation altogether.' A hundred years later the Bible was more popular than ever. His own house in Paris was converted into a Bible factory, churning out Bibles by the hour![7]

Biblical meditation is one of the greatest weapons for prayer and a most effective way to live a victorious life. As we ponder, picture, and personalise God's Word, we begin looking at life through His lens, viewing the world from His perspective. We begin to see God in the true light: He is good, faithful, willing and able to do exceedingly abundantly above what we can ask, think or imagine.

We practise biblical meditation by writing, speaking, memorising and devoting ourselves to whatever passage of Scripture we're reading or studying, based on the premise that God's Word is flawless, faultless, and unfailing. Meditation helps and heals the mind while shoring up the soul. It lessens anxiety, reduces stress and generates peace. As we meditate, God guides and changes our thoughts, helps us to process whatever issues we are facing, to appreciate His greatness and to furnish us for what He has planned for us, just as He did for the heroes of Scripture.

By meditation, we view our circumstances differently. We see our world from another angle. And because His thoughts are becoming our thoughts as we develop the mind of Christ, we are then able to relax, to trust, to quiet ourselves and to discover peace and confidence.

Systematically studying the Word of God is the best way to meditate, not simply picking random verses. God whispers words of wisdom and guidance into our hearts as we meditate on Scripture. He keeps us from the shipwrecks of life as we let His Word dwell in us richly. He enables us to set our minds on things above, not on earthly things.

Immanuel Kant said, 'The Bible is an inexhaustible fountain of all truths. The existence of the Bible is the greatest blessing which humanity ever experienced.' It is full of inexhaustible treasure for you to read and digest, and through which you can encounter God.

What will become of your life is determined by the Word of God in your life. (David Oyedepo Jnr.)

54. Procrastination

A wise person does at once what a fool does at last. Both do the same thing; only at different times. (Lord Acton)

On March 24, 1975 Chuck Wepner, a relatively unknown 30-1 underdog prize-fighter, went fifteen rounds with heavyweight boxing champion Muhammad Ali. In the ninth round, Wepner knocked Ali to the ground, causing shock waves to everyone watching the fight as well as the champ. Though Muhammad Ali went on to win the fight and retain his title, Wepner came within seconds of defeating his formidable opponent. While this is an extraordinary story, the real inspiration is what was happening to someone watching this fight a thousand miles away. A struggling actor named Sylvester Stallone saw the fight on TV. He had been contemplating the idea of writing a screenplay about a down-and-out fighter getting a title but had thought it too unrealistic for a movie studio to buy the story. But after seeing this fight, the actor knew he had to write his story. He started writing that very night. Three days later, Stallone had completed the script for the movie *Rocky*. This story went on to win three Oscars, including one for best picture. It also launched Stallone's multimillion-dollar movie career. Had Stallone decided to wait until the next day, he might have lost some of his inspiration, because the fight wasn't fresh in his mind.[47] Perhaps the script would not have been so compelling and powerful. But he didn't wait. His entire destiny changed as a result of acting promptly on an idea. Act when the emotion is hot!

I need to deal with the problem of procrastination now, but I'll get to it some day. The days of the week don't go Sunday, Monday, Tuesday, Wednesday, Thursday, Friday, someday, Terri Savelle humorously says! Someday is *not* a day of the week! Take action now! Every day comes bearing its own gifts ---untie the ribbons by taking action.

Tomorrow is the only day that appeals to a lazy man.

We've heard the adage, procrastination is the thief of time. It is not only a thief of time, it is also the thief of peace and progress. Never leave till tomorrow what you can do now and today. Tackle any difficulty now - the longer you wait, the weightier it becomes! When you do what you know you should do, when you should do it, then you get to do what you want to do, when you want to do it. Start now! 'No Waiting'!

Mark Twain famously said that if the first thing you do each morning is to eat a live frog, you can go through the day with the satisfaction of knowing that that is probably the worst thing that is going to happen to you all day long. Also if you have to eat a frog, it does not pay to look at it for too long, just eat it and get it over with! Furthermore if you have two frogs to eat, eat the ugliest frog first! What he is trying to say is this: a key to daily success is to do the hardest or significant thing first. Your "frog" is your principal and most important task, the one you are most likely to procrastinate on if you don't do something about it. It is also the one task that can have the greatest positive impact on your life and results at the moment. Until you've eaten your frog everything else is a distraction.

For most, the thought of working hard is something we are committed to doing some day, but right now it's not a priority. We think that when we get that dream job, that leadership position, that amount of money, then we will work hard, read the Bible more and be generous. However, being the person God has called you to be in the future starts with you right now. Stop pressing the snooze button on your life; if you wait for tomorrow, tomorrow may never come. God wants to start working in and through your life starting now.

Rather than wait for tomorrow, we must start working ourselves today; we must develop ourselves and grow. There are things you can do, starting today, that the future version of yourself will thank you for.

You can start right now. In your journal, write down what type of business person, leader, husband, wife, parent, minister, employee you want to be in the future. Now ask yourself: if I continue in the way I am going, will I eventually become that person? Ask yourself what needs to change and what daily disciplines you need to introduce in order to become the person you are meant to be. What small step can you take this very moment that will take you a step closer to the vision of your future self? Do that one thing now, take that step now, don't put it off a moment longer! Don't use your age as an excuse to keep hitting the snooze button on your life.

Sometimes we get the erroneous idea that it's easier to put something off until the next day. In most cases, postponing a task makes it more difficult. You put yourself under more pressure because the deadline becomes tighter. In addition you may now have people breathing down your neck because your procrastination affects them. You will miss great opportunities in life if you wait too long. The bottom line is this: when you put things off, you risk paying a costly price. If you have a tendency to procrastinate, then tackle just one task you keep putting off. Everyone has the tendency to put off unpleasant tasks like weeding the garden or tackling a really difficult subject or confronting a problematic colleague. Putting these tasks off will make them worse. So tackle just one of them at a time and get it out of the way. I know it's more easily said than done, but do just one of them. Get it out of the way and you will feel free and experience great relief.

Many spend too much time dreaming of what's coming in the future, never realising that a little of the future arrives every day.

55. Purpose

No Individual has any right to come into the world and go out of it
without leaving behind him distinct and legitimate reasons for having
passed through it. (George Washington Carver)

She was born into poverty in 1954 in Mississippi, to a teenage single
mother, Vernita Lee, a housemaid. Until the age of six, she lived
with her grandmother, who was reportedly so poor that she was
sent to school wearing dresses made of potato sacks. Her childhood
was marred by more than poverty. She became pregnant at
fourteen, as a result of sexual abuse, but her son was born
prematurely and died shortly after birth. Due to her grandmother's
values, she had religion and God instilled in her at a very young
age. Her grandmother taught her to read and write before the age of
three. Grandma's dream was that her little granddaughter would
become a school-teacher. This girl, however, knew she was born for
much more; so much more. She would recite poems during church
and verses from the Bible. Soon, the church and the entire
neighbourhood knew she had a gift and was nicknamed 'The Little
Speaker'. At school, she flourished, excelling particularly in speech
and drama, and won a full scholarship to Tennessee State
University. Just before leaving for college, aged 17, she won the
Miss Black Tennessee beauty pageant and was hired by a local radio
station, WVOL, to read the news part-time while still at high school.
And at nineteen, she dropped out of her degree when she was
offered a job as the youngest, and the first black, female news-
anchor at Nashville's WLAC-TV. Though she was hired by WJZ-TV
to co-anchor the evening news, her emotional style did not go down
well on a straight news programme, so she was fired and
transferred to an ailing daytime chat programme, 'People Are
Talking', in 1978. Immediately after the first show, she knew this
was what she wanted to do for the rest of her life. According to

Oprah, it was one of the moments of perfect alignment. She had found her purpose and calling. In 1984, she relocated to Chicago to take over a morning chat-show. Its name was quickly changed from 'AM Chicago' to 'The Oprah Winfrey Show'. It was syndicated nationally, quickly becoming the No1 talk-show in the US. Oprah Winfrey is worth $2.7 billion today, is a philanthropist and is thought by many to be the most influential woman in the world today.

There are two great days in a person's life: the day they were born and the day they found out why. Successful people have found out why. (John Maxwell)

Having a powerful why will provide you with the necessary how. Have you found a worthwhile purpose in your life? The height of your accomplishments will equal the depth of your conviction. Success has been defined as the progressive realisation of a worthwhile predetermined goal. Establish a handful of worthy goals in your life and give yourself fully to accomplishing them. In establishing your life purposes, start with your relationship with God, your family, and your work. These top three areas of your life need the most urgent attention.

He who has a why to live for can bear almost any how. (Friedrich Nietzsche)

Those who follow the crowd usually get lost in it. A sure key to failure is to try to please everyone. Without a purpose, life is motion without meaning, activity without direction and events without reason. Without a clear purpose you have no foundation on which you base decisions, allocate time and use resources. You will tend to make choices based on circumstances, pressures and the mood at that moment. People who don't know their purpose try to do too much - and that causes stress, fatigue and conflict. It is impossible to do everything people want you to do - you have just enough time to do God's will. If you truly can't get it all done, then it means you are doing more than God intended or you are not using your time wisely. A purpose-driven life leads to a simpler life and peace of mind.

Your purpose in life is to find your purpose and give your whole heart and soul to it. (Buddha)

Purpose always produces passion. Nothing energises like a clear purpose. Meaningless work is what makes you tired, wears you out and saps strength and joy. Where I want to be must be in direct proportion to what I am doing with where I am now! If your life is not lived on purpose, it will be spent on the sidelines looking on at the game being played by others. You've got to get up in the morning with determination and purpose if you're going to go to bed with satisfaction.

If you're not doing something with your life, it doesn't matter how long it is! (John Maxwell)

The will of God

Some people are always waiting, doing nothing and they excuse their inaction with the excuse that they are waiting to find out the will of God for their lives. The best way to find God's unknown will is to do the known will of God. You will find God's special plan and purpose for your life while walking on the well-worn path. God will show you the next step to take while you're being the kind of employee that employers dream of. Begin to weave and God will give you the thread. By living what we know, God is preparing us to live what we don't know yet. Doing God's will leads to discovering God's will. The place where you are doing your ordinary work faithfully is the place where God will unveil your extraordinary work. Moses was tending his father-in-law's sheep in the desert when he got a burning bush experience. Don't look for the burning bush experience, tend the sheep faithfully and God will speak to you in a way that will set your heart aflame with His purpose.

Walk on road, hm? Walk left side, safe. Walk right side, safe. Walk middle, sooner or later – Squish! (Mr Miyagi in 'Karate Kid')

God's gift to us is our potential; our gift back to Him is what we do with our potential. The greatest insult to our Creator is to be a slacker or to be lazy. Find your purpose and give thanks to God by pursuing that purpose and giving your very best; be the best you you can ever be. If you're unsure what your purpose is, God sometimes leads us through our natural gifts and abilities. A gift is something we can do easily, something that comes naturally; something you derive pleasure from doing; something people commend you for. Do what you're good at, it's God's gift to you. No matter what our talents, we derive great pleasure from doing what we are naturally good at doing. If we do what we are good at doing, we sense God's grace on our efforts. We will know we are operating in our gifts and that doing so honours God and ministers life to others.

The more tuned in you are to your purpose, and the more dedicated you are to growing towards it, the better your chances of reaching your potential, expanding your possibilities and doing something significant.

Life is like a ten-speed bike. Most of us have gears we never use. (Charles Schulz)

Talent is a little like an inheritance you receive from your parents: it is necessary but is not enough. If you fail to use your gift, you lose it; use it and God will increase it. Whatever gifts you have can be enlarged, developed and improved through practice, study, feedback. Don't settle for a half-developed gift. Stretch yourself and learn all you can. Concentrate on doing the very best work you won't be ashamed of.

The successful person has the habit of doing the things that failures don't like to do. The successful person doesn't like doing them either, but his dislike is subordinated to his purpose. (E.M. Gray)

56. Questions

It is not the answer that enlightens, but the question. (Eugene Ionesco)

A famous educator once said: 'One of the biggest things you get out of a college education is a questioning attitude, a habit of demanding, weighing evidence ... a scientific approach. One of the best ways to get men to think is to ask them questions. Pertinent questions. In fact in most cases, it is the only way to get them to think. Asking questions brings more clarity.'

There are no right answers to wrong questions. (Ursula K. Le Guin)

Learning is not about consumption, it's about creation. Asking questions and answering them is the best form of learning. We learn by doing, the brain works by *pulling* in information, not by *pushing* it in. Learning is not a spectator sport. Memory is not something you have, it's something you do.

In school, we're rewarded for having the answer, not for asking a good question. (Richard Saul Wurman)

The Socratic method of teaching through questions is still embraced by educators from the heights of Harvard Law School to the local kindergarten class. Research shows that asking questions improves learning and performance by as much as 150%.

Sometimes questions are more important than answers. (Nancy Willard)

Questions can be very useful in many settings. People in general don't like taking orders or even instruction. Therefore give suggestions or couch your instructions gently or wisely as a question.

Good questions are at the heart of reflection. Successful people ask better questions and as a result get better answers. The challenge is that the right question isn't always so obvious. If your questions are focused, they will stimulate creative thinking because there is something about a well-worded question that often penetrates to the heart of the matter, outwits the average mindset, circumvents the status quo, triggers new ideas and insights and sparks focused action. If you ask high quality questions, they will help you create a high-quality life.

I find intelligence is better spotted when analysing the questions asked than the answers given. (Sir Isaac Newton)

Asking good questions is the key to being a good conversationalist. It was said of President J. F. Kennedy that he made you think he had nothing else to do except ask you questions and listen, with extraordinary concentration, to your answer.

French philosopher Claude Lévi-Strauss once said: 'Scientists are not people who give the right answers: they are those who ask the right questions.' Write out the questions and answers you discover, because you will find that what you think after you write the answer is different from what you thought before you wrote it. Writing helps you discover what you truly know, think and believe.

Judge a man by his questions rather than by his answers. (Voltaire)

Ask more questions, listen more, speak less - don't be a know-it-all! Make 'why' your favourite word but be careful not to turn your conversations into the Spanish inquisition. Any time a person is answering more than asking, you can be sure they've slowed down in their growth and have lost the fire for personal growth. The more questions you ask, the more the results you get, and the better questions you ask the better results you get. A major stimulant to creative thinking is focused questions.

Asking the right questions takes as much skill as giving the right answers. (Robert Half)

Life's most important answers can be found in asking the right questions. (John Mason)

Don't ask leading questions, don't ask limiting questions, don't ask questions that assume a certain answer. Don't ask questions that already include an answer in the question; or leave no room for a variety of options. You already know what you know. Great questions are designed to find out what the other person knows. So stay quiet and listen. You never know what you'll learn when you ask the right way.

Wrong question: Can you think of a good reason not to discipline this child?

Right question: What do you think is the best way to deal with this child's situation?

Anyone who knows all the answers is not asking the right questions. (Confucius)

Learn something new every day and evaluate and reflect on it at the end of the day. For example, an average person asks, 'can I do this?' A growing person asks, ' How can I do this?' Ask why - explore - evaluate discoveries -- repeat. Be curious and ask questions. I think it was John Maxwell who said: 'Whenever I learn something new I ask myself these questions: Where can I use this? When can I use this? Who needs to know this?'

He who asks a question is a fool for five minutes; he who does not ask a question remains a fool forever. (Chinese proverb)

A prudent question is one half of wisdom. (Sir Francis Bacon)

57. Relationships / Association

Friendship is the crown of life and school of virtue. Friendship multiplies joy and divides sorrow. (C. S. Lewis, The Four Loves)

I read the story of a young man. He was the son of a company director who managed his father's company. He was always speaking harshly to employees. This came to a head one day when the father caught him berating one of the employees. The father calmly called him into his office, and sitting at his executive desk said, 'As your boss I will not tolerate your speaking to other employees in that way. You're fired!' Then he walked over to his son with his eyes full of love and said, 'Son, I heard you lost your job today, how can I help you get back into gainful employment?'[54]

He lost his job because he did not value the people who worked for his father's company, he did not realise that the success of the organisation rises or falls on the quality of the leaders and their relationship with their employees. He was a fool.

Your net worth is equal to your network. (Unknown)

You are the sum of the average of your five closest associates. It is better to be alone than in the wrong company. We become like those with whom we associate. The company you keep influences your conduct and character, and those two things decide your future. Did you know it's been reported that 99% of your success is due to your reference group? In fact, Harvard did an eighty-year study proving that your physical health is determined more by your relationships than by the food you eat, exercise program you're on or the genes you've inherited[55]. You're going to conform to the environment you put yourself in. Therefore, if you want to upgrade your life, you have to upgrade your peer group. You have to connect with the right friends. You may find this shocking and eye-opening, but the right friendship group is vital to your success and dreams. Spend time with successful people or their books or messages or podcasts - associate with successful people. Associate with great people and you will be great.

Friendship is precious, not only in the shade but in the sunshine of life, and, thanks to a benevolent arrangement, the greater part of life is sunshine. (Thomas Jefferson)

I can do things you cannot; you can do things I cannot; together we can do great things. (Mother Teresa)

There's an old Zambian proverb that says, 'When you run alone, you run fast. But when you run together, you run far.' Be the kind of friend you like to have. Don't criticise, condemn or complain. Give honest and sincere appreciation. Be genuinely interested in other people. Smile. Call people by name: a person's name is the sweetest and most important sound (so remember it). Be a good listener. Encourage others to talk about themselves. Talk in terms of the other person's interests. Make the other person feel important - and do it sincerely. Try to see things from others' point of view.

People are lonely because they build walls instead of bridges. (Joseph F. Newton)

It has been said people don't care about how much you know until they know how much you care. Make friends for the sheer joy of forming and maintaining human relationships, not just for financial benefit. Learn how to relate to strangers with sincere warmth and interest that turns them into friends. Build the relationship with no thought of what you can get from them; leave that side of things to God - He always brings amazing benefit out of this, directly and indirectly. We all need people who will defend us, stand up for us, protect us, help us stay on track, and warn us. We all need this, because we all have blind spots.

A person standing alone can be attacked and defeated, but two can stand back-to-back and conquer. Three are even better, for a triple braided cord is not easily broken. (Ecclesiastes 4:12 NLT, second edition)[58]

Treat a man as he is, and he will remain as he is. Treat a man as he could be, and he will become what he should be. (Ralph Waldo Emerson)

Love doesn't make the world go round. Love is what makes the ride worthwhile. (Elizabeth Browning)

It's Contagious

Cold and flu viruses aren't the only things that are contagious: attitudes are also. Bad company corrupts good character. Researchers call it 'emotional contagion'. It is the phenomenon of having one person's emotions and related behaviours directly trigger similar emotions and behaviours in other people. It affects every aspect of life in the same way a rotten apple corrupts the whole barrel or one rotten egg in an omelette renders the whole omelette inedible. A wise man said, 'One negative employee can pollute an entire squad and create a toxic work environment. Complaining can act like a cancer and spread through an entire organisation, sabotaging the morale and performance of teams with great talent and potential. You can be a germ and attack your organisation's immune system, or you can act like a dose of vitamin C and strengthen it ... your emotions impact the world around you.'

Assumptions are the termites of relationships. (Henry Winkler)

The worst distance between two people is misunderstanding. (Neetesh Dixit)

Are your associates dead-weight or parachute? Associating with the wrong people can drown you. Jonah was on a boat of innocent travellers but his disobedience was going to drown a shipload of people. Wrong associations can cause you or your business, ministry or reputation to go down. Don't be afraid to dissociate from people who may be dragging you down spiritually or financially. Don't allow sentiment to keep them on your boat. Cast them out gently but firmly. Your carrying along the wrong people can hinder them and you from finding your purpose in life. They can be family or friends or associates.

The kind of person you are is reflected in the friends you pick. 'Show me your friends and I will tell you who you are' is indeed a true saying. Have you heard the saying, "Show me your friends and I'll show you your future?" Your friends are influencing who you are today and who you will be tomorrow. You are being sharpened, and you are sharpening others. Proverbs 27:17 says, "As iron sharpens iron, so a friend sharpens a friend." 1 Corinthians 15:33 (NLT) says, "Don't be fooled by those who say such things, for "bad company corrupts good character."

Friendships, good and bad, indicate the direction you're going in. So if your life is unproductive or stagnant, look at the people you've surrounded yourself with. Misery loves company, so steer clear of negative thinkers. It's better to travel alone than spend your life hanging around with people who drag you down. Author John Mason writes: 'The less you associate with some people, the more your life will improve.' The right friends and associations bring out the original you. These are the kind of people that, after you've been with them, you find yourself full of vision and faith; you feel as if you can do more and be more. Your friends will either stretch or shrink your vision; they will either cheer you on or choke you.

As you grow in life, your associations will change. Some friends won't want to grow with you; they'll want to stay where they are. Love them but leave them and move on. As Edwin Louis Cole said, 'When you let someone else create your world for you ... they always make it too small.' Wise is the person who fortifies their life with right relationships.

You're born an original, don't die a copy! (John Mason)

Solomon, one of the wisest men who ever lived, wrote: 'Walk with the wise and become wise ... ' (Pr 13:20). In other words, wisdom is contagious. Do life with the wise and, over time, you'll become wise. It happens automatically. And there's a second part: ' ... for a companion of fools suffers harm.' When you hang out with a fool, you get caught up in the consequences of their bad decisions. You catch the shrapnel. Your reputation is ruined like his. You get fired like them.

If you're always at the head of the class you're in the wrong class. (John Maxwell)

The people you habitually associate with are your reference growth and these people determine as much as 95% of your success or failure in life. You cannot take the growth journey alone - not if you want to reach your potential. The most significant factor in a person's environment is people. Significant growth will not occur in your life if you are not continually challenged in your environment.

Joyce Meyer points out, 'God always puts us around someone who is like sandpaper to smooth off our rough edges ... a testing that takes place before we get promoted. If you want to lead you must first serve in circumstances that may not be ideal and learn to behave wisely. This prepares us to be greatly used by God.' You may be one relationship away from changing the course of your destiny. When it comes to spending time with others, don't just respond to the people who ask. Initiate time with people who stretch you, push you and even confuse you. We often judge what we don't understand. Don't just meet people of your age, in your field or with similar experience. Are you stuck? Find someone a few steps ahead of you. If you're thirty, meet a forty-year-old and ask them how they think differently now from when they were thirty. Come prepared to listen a lot, ask great questions and follow good examples. Don't just copy what others do but learn how they think.

In the Journey of Life, We Need Each Other!

You were never meant to walk through life alone. This has nothing to do with whether you're single or married. Marriage does not solve the issue; community does. You may enjoy your own company best, but you need others to walk with you through life. This is because it's safer (and it is not just safer: it also provides support and counsel). It's supportive. Life is not a fifty-yard dash: it's a marathon! The only way you're going to finish the race well and not burn out is by having other people involved in your life through meaningful relationships. It's smarter: you learn more by walking with others than you do by yourself. When you're with others you can use them as a sounding board for your ideas. The ideas that look like the best thing since sliced bread may not be actually all that when aired out to others. Others are actually able to see the blind spots you have missed. When you walk alone, you don't have anybody to tell you you've veered off course or help redirect you on to the right path. You've got to have the right people in your life to help you grow and go in the right direction. Life is about relationships. Relationships double the fun and halve the trouble. What's the point of good news if you have no one to share it with?

Keep away from people who belittle your ambitions. Small people always do that, but the really great make you feel that you, too, can become great. (Mark Twain)

Friendship

Friendship is a rare and precious gift. I lost a dear friend this year: Abel Oluwole Omiyale; he was my brother from another mother; the pain was palpable. However, I will forever be grateful for his friendship, the privilege of knowing him, the laughter, the good-natured banter, the wonderful rapport we shared for the few short years I'd known him. He was a real gentleman and a great leader; a leader of leaders who enlarged my vision and made me feel that I, too, could become great. It was a divine relationship. You recognise divine relationships because, when your friend speaks, something within you resonates or jumps for joy. Their presence invigorates you. They are always 'taking the words out of your mouth', they say what you were about to say. That's because you're filled with the same Spirit.

Friendship can be so good. It can be a source of incredible pleasure, encouragement and comfort. Friendship is a priceless gift of God. Our friendships affect us beyond what we think. To a large extent, we tend to become like our friends over the years. We tend to adopt their values, their attitudes, their convictions and their interests. For good or ill, we will become like our friends. 'Whoever walks with the wise becomes wise, but the companion of fools will suffer harm' (Pr 13:20).

If friendship is so life-impacting it is vital that we choose our friends carefully. Seek friends with godly wisdom, friends who understand what really matters in life. Make friends with people who know God and walk with God. One day, you will become like the friends you choose.

We often have blind spots that harm us. Sometimes we even become prideful and get too big for our breeches; at times we begin to wander from God. If you have real friends, they will confront you and challenge you and call you to order, even if this hurts and is uncomfortable, because your welfare is more important than their comfort. The Bible says: 'Better are the wounds of a friend than the kisses of an enemy' (Pr 27:6).

Your friend will rejoice with you when something wonderful happens to you, and, if you are discouraged, worried or down in the dumps and need someone who will just listen, a real friend will be available. This kind of friend, a loyal friend, a friend who loves at all times, is an incredible gift of God.

The question now is not: Do I have friends like this? The question is rather: Am I a friend like this? There are people in your life who you think are friends, but, when you really need them, they will let you down. Or drag you down with their less than godly character and worldview. Be very careful of the friends you choose. They have a dramatic impact on how you interpret life and everything you do. The same is true of business associates, partners, your spouse, and anyone else you let into your life. If you choose foolish people to share your world with, you will end up a fool as well.

Your proximity to certain kind of people affect you. Research has shown that your life is greatly affected by those in your proximity - where you live, those you work with and those with whom you closely associate all affect you positively or otherwise.

Finally, if you haven't yet initiated a friendship with Jesus, you may be one relationship away from changing the course of your destiny.

Great things happen whenever we stop seeing ourselves as God's gift to others and begin seeing others as God's gifts to us. (James Vuocolo)

58. Responsibility

The major key to my better future is me. (Jim Rohn)

Do what you should do, when you should do it, whether you feel like it or not. (Thomas Huxley)

Brian Tracy tells a story about his encounter with an older gentleman he met when he attended a conference in Washington. The man was looking for a place to sit during lunch, so Brian immediately arose and invited the older gentleman to join him. He was hesitant, but Brian insisted. As they chatted over lunch, it turned out that the name of the older gentleman was Kop Kopmeyer. Brian immediately knew who he was. He was a legend in the field of success and achievement. Kop Kopmeyer had written four large books, each of which contained 250 success principles that he had derived from more than fifty years of research and study. Brian had read all four books from cover to cover, more than once. After they chatted for a while, Brian asked him the question that many people in this situation would ask: 'Of all the one thousand success principles that you have discovered, which do you think is the most important?' He smiled at Brian with a twinkle in his eye, as if he had been asked this question many times, and replied, without hesitating, 'The most important success principle of all was stated by Thomas Huxley many years ago. "Do what you should do, when you should do it, whether you feel like it or not."'

In other words, take responsibility. You are 100% responsible for the outcome of your life.

Kop then went on to say, 'There are 999 other success principles that I have found in my reading and experience, but, without self-discipline, none of them work.' Brian also asked for the fastest way to succeed - to which Mr Kopmeyer responded, 'You have to learn from other people, because you'll never live long enough to learn it all yourself.'

We all desire a great life. Some of us think it is our entitlement, but we don't always think of what we need to do to bring it to pass. Jim Rohn, American's foremost business philosopher, said, 'You must take personal responsibility. You cannot change the circumstances, the seasons or the wind, but you can change yourself.' Only one person is responsible for the quality of life you live and that person is YOU. [48]

Responsibility is responding appropriately to the ability you have been born with. Doing what you should do at the right time irrespective of your feelings. Your life is not a coincidence: It is a reflection of you! If you would like to know who is responsible for the majority of your troubles - take a look in the mirror! Your life in the future depends on many things, but mostly on you.

Doctors won't make you healthy. Nutritionists won't make you slim. Teachers won't make you smart. Gurus won't make you calm. Mentors won't make you rich. Trainers won't make you fit. Ultimately, you have to take responsibility. Save yourself. (Naval Ravikant)

Years are made up of months, months of weeks and weeks of days. Every day of your life, take responsibility. To seize the day, you must own the day. The first step toward owning our day is to take responsibility. Your day is your responsibility. My day is my responsibility. What we each do with our day is up to us. At the end of your day, you cannot look at your husband, your wife, your kids, your parents, your teacher or your friends and say, 'Why did I waste my day?' The day is yours. Take responsibility for yourself.

You are not a victim. Many of your life circumstances may have been difficult. Times may be hard. Sometimes, you do not have control over those circumstances, yet you must master them, or you will spend your whole life being controlled by your past experiences. Now, sometimes you find yourself in hard times and difficult circumstances, and, when you take a good look, you know it's your own choices that put you there. Many times, this is the case. Did you make the decision that landed you where you are today? Perhaps you did. Take responsibility for that decision and move forward.

If you want to be successful, the first thing you have to do is fully realise that you are the one, and the only one, responsible for yourself. You choose. Remember - your choices will make or break you. Do you want to have a successful day? Start by making the choice to look for the good. Choose to think of how to win instead of reasons you could lose. Choose to focus on greatness. The easiest thing to do is to look for what is wrong. That's the lazy way. Instead, choose to be great. It is your choice – own it.

A sign of wisdom and maturity is when we come to terms with the realisation that your decisions have brought you to where you are today: you are responsible. When we grow through changes, we become active. We take control of our attitude and emotions. We become agents of positive change in our own lives. You are responsible for your life, and your ultimate success depends on the choices you make. You are responsible for your choice to do nothing, keep quiet or speak up, do something or do nothing, and you will have to live with the consequence of your actions or passivity! So take responsibility.

You can't hire someone else to do your push-ups. (Jim Rohn)

You only have one life to live, and no one is responsible for it but you. What if you allowed the seemingly impossible to become possible? What if every day you made choices that caused you to live differently? If you allow fear to stop you, you're responsible. If you live a life of mediocrity, you're responsible. If you pursue an amazing dream and achieve greatness, you, my friend, are responsible. You will have to live with you all the days of your life. So live courageously, dream wildly, don't just do something, be responsible—become someone! You cannot change what you do not take responsibility for. When you blame someone else, you become dependent on that individual to solve your problem and change your circumstance. After all, if it is that person's fault, then he or she is the only one who has the power to change your condition.

There is an unexpected relationship between blame and fear. When you blame others for your failure, you become powerless to change the world around you. You begin to live your life filled with fear, paralysed by uncertainty and embittered by a sense of victimisation. Fear may cause you to abdicate responsibility, but the abdication of responsibility will most certainly cause you to live in fear. Take personal responsibility for your life; life is a do-it-yourself project.

59. Risk

Life is inherently risky. There is only one big risk you should avoid at all costs, and that is the risk of doing nothing. (Denis Waitley)

Vivian was in her mid-forties. She ran a small business, but it wasn't doing very well at all. She was not even making enough for her basic needs. However, she had a tidy sum in savings which she had accumulated owing to a frugal lifestyle from her previous employment; it was just enough for a deposit on a rental property. It was a risk because it represented most of her life-savings; she also had a few thousands in stocks and shares. She had researched quite a bit about investing in property; the risks and rewards. She reckoned if she didn't invest the money she would soon begin to spend it on her living expenses. That thought was totally abhorrent to her, so she invested the money in a rental property. Soon after the investment, property prices sky-rocketed and within a couple of years the property appreciated and she was able to pull out her initial investment and invest in another property and then another and another. Her cash flow also improved substantially as a result of rental income. It was a risky move, but it paid off. If she had delayed at that particular time the window of opportunity could have closed.

When you take risks you learn that there will be times when you succeed and there will be times when you fail, and both are equally important. (Ellen DeGeneres)

Life is risky; you're not going to get out alive, says Jim Rohn. To be sure change is risky, but we only experience positive change in our lives when we take risks. Whether you're a teenager in college, well into your career or in retirement, now is the right time to take a risk. Take risks when you're growing and when you're declining. No one ever accomplished anything great by playing it safe.

I'm not telling you to take a risk on the wrong things. Don't put healthy relationships at risk, don't put your health at risk, and don't blow up what's working well. But what theory do you have? What hunch are you sitting on? What deeply held motivation do you have? Take a risk in faith. To try is to risk failure. But risks must be taken, because the greatest hazard in life is to risk nothing. If we are too cautious we will never achieve anything. 'Whoever watches the wind will not plant; whoever looks at the clouds will not reap' (Ecclesiastes 11:4).

Go out on a limb, that's where the fruit is. (President Jimmy Carter)

If you want to be who you've always been, do what you've always done. If you want to change who you are, change what you do. In other words, to change the fruit in your life, you might have to go out on a limb.

Do you need to start writing a book, ask someone on a date, launch a product, start a ministry, start going to church, start a podcast, or something else? Based on what God's leading you to do, what risk do you need to take? Unless you take a risk (small or great) nothing much will change.

The biggest risk is not taking any risk ... In a world that's changing really quickly, the only strategy that is guaranteed to fail is not taking risks. (Mark Zuckerberg)

If you don't play you can't win. (Judith McNaught)

The future belongs to the risk-takers, not the comfort-seekers. (Brian Tracy)

If you are not willing to risk the unusual, you will have to settle for the ordinary. (Jim Rohn)

60. Savings

Do not save what is left after spending, but spend what is left after saving.
(Warren Buffet)

The story of Vivian in the previous chapter is a real-life story. It shows the difference having savings or not having any substantial savings can make. Vivian chose to run her business instead of working 9-5 for an employer because she wanted to be able to give quality time to her children and family. Even though her small business struggled, the tidy sum she had accumulated over a decade of her work life was ultimately what gave her the breakthrough she desired. Her savings saved her from drowning. Without the savings she would not have been able to take advantage of the opportunity in a timely manner. Interestingly Vivian even managed to save a little amount monthly from her struggling business after she came across the phrase, *'I found the road to wealth when I decided that a part of all I earned was mine to keep'* in the book *The Richest Man in Babylon.*

I have allocated a separate chapter to savings instead of including it in the chapter about money because I think it is such an important topic. You see, saving is not a luxury but a necessity. Having some savings can help you give up working for someone else and start your own business.

There are two main reasons why you need to save: for expected expenses (new tyres, holiday, house deposit, new car, wedding, university fees etc.) and for unexpected expenses (legal fees, job loss, broken-down boiler or washing-machine etc.).

There are two ways to pay for most foreseeable and unforeseeable expenses: either with money which you can get from your savings or an emergency fund (a kind of savings) which you have set aside for the purpose, plus any interest accrued, or with money borrowed from a bank, credit card, 'loan shark' plus the high interest these institutions might choose to charge you (i.e. the price of not having your own savings). It is easy to save by setting up a standing order or direct debit which automatically takes money straight out from where your income is paid into a different savings account. Because you don't see this money you are not likely to miss it much.

I have had an opportunity to study how my clients got rich. A few got lucky, but most just stopped spending every penny they had. (Michael Stolper)

The Guaranteed Rewards of Saving

Why save? why do you need to manage your money prudently? why can't you just spend it all and take each day as it comes? 'Eat and drink for tomorrow we die' as some might say. Is it so you can flaunt your wealth or is it so you can roll in a pile of cash? The answer is obviously no. The real reason for saving is for freedom (don't worry, I will explain). Good financial management can give you the freedom to do what you want to do with your life. That may be to quit your job and start a new career if need be. It may be to become a stay-at-home mum (or dad) to take care of your young children if that is what you really desire. The habit of saving, together with sound financial management, can give you the freedom to pursue a dream, or even transform a hobby into a million-dollar or million-pound business. Life can be exciting and wonderful when you have the freedom to pursue your dreams, while at the same time making a ton of money (or no money) from what you enjoy. Not having to worry about the bailiffs knocking down your door, your house being repossessed or the credit-card companies draining your meagre resources through exorbitant interest charges is what I call freedom. This is possible if you save and manage your finances judiciously.

Money is not primarily for spending, it is for managing first, *then* for spending. If you manage your money efficiently, you can have the freedom to choose the way you want your life to go without being at the mercy of a pay-cheque, a dead-end job or an overbearing boss. Spending all the money you earn today without planning to save, invest and build for the future is like eating uncooked food: it may fill your stomach but will offer no real lasting satisfaction. Eating the ingredients for a chocolate cake (egg, sugar, flour, cocoa powder, butter), for example, may get rid of immediate hunger but it is sure to leave you gutted afterwards. Imagine the scrumptious cake you could have made from those ingredients. The same is applicable to your money: when you spend every penny you earn, you squandered your savings, investment and a potential return on both. True, the money you earn might not be much, and you might think I can't do much with this so I'll just spend it, I'll start saving when I earn more. (Don't fall for that line.) If you can't save when you earn little you are unlikely to do so if you have more. Those who build great wealth have started with very little and built this up over the years.

When next you are tempted to spend all your earnings or get into more debt, remember that what you are actually doing is trading that designer wear or fancy gizmo (which will be obsolete or out of fashion in a few months) for your freedom, your dreams and your future wealth. The instant gratification you get from spending money on a shiny car or the latest gadget can never be compared with the joy and pleasure of seeing your savings or investments grow. The peace of mind that comes with it is priceless. The guaranteed reward you get for saving is the money you've saved plus interest and a measure of freedom.

Saving also gives you a choice and a certain level of control over your life. If you haven't started, take control of your life and start saving today. One of the easiest ways to save is to determine how much you can save after all your necessary monthly expenses have been deducted, i.e. rent, mortgage, bills, food, transport etc (not entertainment or leisure). Whatever figure you come up with must be included in your monthly budget as a necessary monthly expense. Then set up a standing order or automatic debit instruction for this amount of money to be moved from your current account to a savings account without instant access. Of course I don't expect you to save if you are in debt because any interest you get from your savings will be nothing compared to that which you will pay on your debt. So pay off those debts first. Then, when you have finished, divert all that credit-card payment into your savings, for your own future and freedom.

One who takes advice about his savings from one who is inexperienced in such matters will pay with his savings. (The Richest Man in Babylon)

61. Self-discipline / Self-Control

Discipline is the soul of an army. It makes small numbers formidable; procures success to the weak and esteem to all. (George Washington)

The Sirens were three mysterious women who, according to Homer's *Odyssey*, lived on an island. Whenever a ship passed by, they would stand on the cliffs and sing. Their beautiful song would tempt sailors closer and closer, until eventually they were shipwrecked on the rocks below. Odysseus was curious to hear the Sirens' song but was well aware of the dangers. He ordered his men to tie him to the mast as they approached the island and then to plug their own ears with beeswax. When Odysseus heard the Siren call, he demanded to be untied, but his shipmates bound him more tightly, releasing him only when the danger had passed. The story explores the powerful pull we all feel at times to flirt with choices that take us off the right course. The point of this story is that self-discipline is what ties you to your purpose and stops you from making a shipwreck of your life and destiny.

When he was diagnosed with ADHD as a child, his kindergarten teacher told his mother, Michael can't sit still. He can't be quiet, he's not gifted. Your son will never be able to focus on anything. Yet Michael Fred Phelps II is the most successful and most decorated Olympian of all time, with a total of 28 medals. Phelps also holds the all-time records for Olympic gold medals, Olympic gold medals in individual events and Olympic medals in individual events. Today, his mother reports, Michael's ability to focus amazes me. His coach since the age of eleven, Bob Bowman, calls it his strongest attribute. How did it happen? He trained daily 365 days a year from the age of fourteen. He spent up to six hours in water daily. He channelled all his energy into one discipline.

I have found 999 keys to success, but without self-discipline none of them works! (Kop Kopmeyer)

Discipline is a constant human awareness of a need for action and a conscious act by us to implement that action. If our awareness and action happen at the same time, then we begin a valued sequence of disciplined activity. If there is considerable time that passes between our time of awareness and action, then that is called procrastination. This is an almost exact opposite of discipline. We are always presented with these two choices: do it now or do it later. A choice between a disciplined existence which leads to achievement and contentment or procrastination leading an easy life in which the future will bear the fruit of regret and bare branches of mediocrity. A do-what-you-can attitude or do-what-you-must attitude. Procrastination says, Do it tomorrow instead of today. Discipline says, Get it done today and do it now, to the best of your ability, and then do it every day always, until finally the worthy deed becomes an instinctive habit that leads to achievement. The rewards for a disciplined life are immeasurable, though they are often delayed till sometime in the future; but be assured they will come. The reward for lack of discipline is immediate - like a fun day at the beach - but the reward for discipline can be like owning the beach. Choose fortune over pleasure, choose a disciplined life.

Success is tons of discipline. (Al Tomsik)

Our world seems to be designed to give fewer rewards to easy things and more rewards to the things that are not so easy and require discipline. You cannot succeed beyond your discipline. You must run on a schedule.

Keep doing what you are doing in a disciplined way and it will grow. It will grow, it will keep growing. Just be disciplined. Intelligence is overrated. Discipline can help you achieve beyond those of high intelligence who won't put in the effort. A wise man said if you will do for eighteen months what others won't do, you will do for the rest of your life what others can't do.

Our ambition should be to rule ourselves, the true kingdom for each one of us; and true progress is to know more and be more and do more. (Oscar Wilde)

Self-discipline is the ability to make yourself do what you should do, at the time you should do it, in the way you should do it with consistency and without anyone breathing down your neck. Commitment to do what we should in a consistent way is discipline. Discipline is the difference-maker - the bridge between what we do and what we are capable of doing. Successful people are highly self-disciplined; they guide and encourage themselves to do the work they ought to do. That's what takes average to good and good to great.

With self-discipline almost everything is possible. (Theodore Roosevelt)

Discipline is the bridge between goals and accomplishment. There is little that can withstand a man who can conquer himself, said a wise man. Discipline is the bridge between thought and accomplishment; between inspiration and achievement; between necessity and productivity. It is like a set of magic keys that unlocks all the doors of wealth, self-worth, happiness, culture, high self-esteem, sophistication, satisfaction etc. It helps you feel better about yourself, and that good feeling, that surging feeling of self-worth is almost as good as accomplishing the discipline. Though discipline does not change your destination immediately, it helps you change direction immediately. Discipline attracts opportunity. Opportunity is always looking for ambition, preparation and skill in action. Discipline taps the unlimited power of commitment. Discipline is the unique step of intelligent thought and activity that puts a lid on temper, encourages success and deters failure, enhances health and curbs sickness.

It's not the mountain we conquer but ourselves. (Edmund Hillary)

A Chinese sage named Lao Tze once said, 'Those who dominate others are great, but those who dominate themselves are greater still.' For such people, nothing is impossible. They can succeed at anything they choose. When the competition gets tough, when the pressure gets really heavy, only those with discipline can avoid making mistakes. Winning is easy. All you have to do is train your mind, develop enough discipline to control your thoughts and emotions, so that you can always bring out the best in yourself and avoid those moments of doubt and fear.

Master your time, money, speech, emotions etc. We waste our lives through a lack of self-discipline. Without accountability we can easily become lazy, and this can have disastrous consequences (Pr 6:6–11). We can learn self-discipline from the ant. Nobody tells it what to do. It has no commander, no overseer, no manager, supervisor or ruler, yet it works extremely hard. It stores its provisions in summer and gathers its food at harvest, saves up, invests, lives frugally and is industrious. If you don't have self-discipline as the ant does, you will suddenly find yourself in the workhouse or in the pits!

I've never met a person that was not successful who didn't have a great amount of self-discipline. (John Maxwell)

In this world, we either discipline ourselves, or we are disciplined by the world. I prefer to discipline myself. When life disciplines you, it's more painful and can be embarrassing. So better discipline yourself than let others do it. You will learn discipline one way or the other: either by doing it yourself or attending the UHK (The University of Hard Knocks). Discipline and motivation are two sides of the same coin. If you have the motivation you need, discipline is no problem. If you lack motivation, discipline is always a problem. But you can't wait for motivation to begin you have to begin with self-discipline and then let motivation catch up.

Once you learn to quit, it becomes a habit. (Vince Lombardi).

You have to give yourself more and bigger whys so you can keep wanting to put in the effort to grow. Discipline is the bridge between goals and accomplishments (and that bridge must be crossed every day). Over time, that daily crossing becomes a habit. Self-discipline means you are taking responsibility for your life. It means that you know you're the boss of you.

The difference between what we do and what we are capable of doing would suffice to solve most of the world's problems. (Gandhi)

Discipline is the commitment to do what we should in a consistent way. Once you have a burning yes inside you about what's truly important, it's very easy to say no to the unimportant. (Stephen R. Covey)

Successful people are those who work almost all the time on high-value tasks. (Brian Tracy)

Why is there a difference between what we do and what we are capable of doing? What would make up the difference and close the gap? It's not talent, it's not more time: it's *discipline*. Successful people are highly self-disciplined, they guide and encourage themselves to do the work they ought to do, not just the things they want to do. That's what takes them from average to good and good to great. We grow when we do the things we know we should do even when we don't feel like it. Every time we do what we don't feel like doing and we do it well, we develop and strengthen our discipline muscles. Our lives improve only when we take chances and risks. Take action before you feel like it!

Discipline is commitment to do what we should in a consistent way, to do what you should do, when you should do it, whether you feel like it or not. Discipline is the difference-maker - the bridge between what we do and what we are capable of doing.

62. Service

Everybody can be great because everybody can serve. (Martin Luther King Jnr)

Everyone loves great customer service. I once patronised a business. The service was good, but then a problem developed purely by chance. It meant I had to request the service again in a short space of time. I asked for a discount on the service. They refused and charged me the full price again. Years later, when I needed that same service again, I used another business. The director of the former business chased me for weeks to get my business, but I refused to use their services again. They were short-sighted. They lost my custom because when there was a problem they did not resolve it to my satisfaction. Don't be in business to make a quick buck: think long-term and offer tons of value and you will find that your customers keep coming back. It is more costly to make a new customer than to keep an old one. If you treat your customers right, you will keep getting repeat business with lots of recommendations, referrals and free advertising from them. More profit is made from repeat business than from chasing new customers. It is in your enlightened self-interest to give more than your customers pay for.

No one is useless in this world who lightens the burden of someone else! (Benjamin Franklin)

Never forget a customer. Never let a customer forget you by doing more than you are paid to do. The man who does more than he is paid for will soon be paid for more than he does. If you become valuable to the world, the world pays you for being you. When you do more than you are paid for, the extra work is seed that brings more than you are paid. Consistently doing more than you are paid for brings wealth because that extra is a seed that will bring about much. So if your job does not pay you enough, here is the solution: do more than you are paid for; much more. The extra work you are doing will be the seed that will germinate to bring about a harvest of more income. This applies to business and other areas too. If you don't have enough customers, over-deliver with your current customers and you will eventually reap a harvest of more customers.

If you're tempted to think that you don't have much to offer, remember the boy with the five loaves and two fish. Remember that God will multiply your gift to serve His purposes. All you have to do is offer what you have and let Him use you more deeply and powerfully than you can imagine. You don't have to be a superstar believer with a big audience to be used by the Lord. God takes what we offer to Him in faith and uses it to bless others and grow His kingdom – even the little things that seemingly don't amount to much. God is a multiplier. What you do makes a difference. Your prayer, acts of kindness and words of encouragement matter. God receives your gifts of treasure and service and uses them to minister to others and point people to Himself.

A wise man, Albert Schweizer said: 'I don't know what your destiny will be, but one thing I know: the ones among you who will be really happy are those who have sought and found how to serve.' Help solve other people's problems.

Money comes as a result of giving value. If value is going from you, money will be coming to you. Even if you are not getting anything from those you serve, God will ensure that you get money because God is the one watching over the process. When you do more than you're paid for, you are making an investment in your future. When you do more than you're paid for your income will rise to meet your output i.e. will rise to catch up with the value you give out. If you want to make a fortune from your work, give fortunes of service; loads more than you're paid for. Life does not give you what you need: it gives you what you deserve based on what you've sowed!

We serve God by serving others. We miss many occasions for serving because we lack sensitivity and spontaneity. Great opportunities to serve never last long, they pass quickly, sometimes never to return. You may get only one chance to serve that person, so take advantage of the moment. Do what you can to help people;

less-than-perfect service is always better than best intentions. No task is beneath you when you have a servant's heart. Serve in ordinary ways and God will give you extraordinary tasks. You must find a way to serve and be a blessing to others because the way to the throne-room is through the servants' quarters.

Even if no one acknowledges you, find ways to serve others. Nothing you do for God is wasted effort. A lot of our service is self-serving; so be careful of eye-service. Always being in the spotlight can blind you, so focus on what you can do for others to make them shine. This is what will truly give you glowing satisfaction. Your work doesn't succeed by what you do; your work succeeds by whom you empower. Build people and together you'll build something great.

You can get everything in life you want if you help enough people get what they want. (Zig Ziglar)

63. Significance

Success is when I add value to myself. Significance is when I add value to others. (John Maxwell)

Three of the titans who built America were Cornelius Vanderbilt (a shipping- and railroad-tycoon, self-made multi-millionaire and one of the wealthiest Americans of the 19th century), Andrew Carnegie (who amassed a fortune in the steel industry; he later sold his company to J. P. Morgan for hundreds of millions of dollars) and John D. Rockefeller (an American business magnate, widely considered the wealthiest American of all time, and the richest person in modern history). In addition to being one of the wealthiest men in America, these men were philanthropists. After attending Vanderbilt's funeral, Carnegie and Rockefeller spent the rest of their lives seeing how much money they could give away to do good. Carnegie gave away the bulk of his money, devoted the remainder of his life to large-scale philanthropy, with special emphasis on local libraries, education, scientific research etc. Rockefeller donated more than half a billion dollars to various educational, religious and scientific causes.

After you achieve great wealth you can go higher: simply give it all away. Change levels from wealth to significance: this is what it means to really live. Make the millions and use it to make the life of millions better.

Alfred Nobel (1833–1896) was a Swedish businessman, chemist, engineer and inventor. He is best known for the Nobel Peace Prize. Nobel held 355 different patents, dynamite being the most famous. He was a weapons manufacturer. In 1888, Alfred's brother Ludvig died. A French newspaper erroneously published Alfred's obituary. It condemned him for profiting from the sales of arms, stating: 'The merchant of death is dead … Dr Alfred Nobel, who became rich by finding ways to kill more people faster than ever before, died yesterday.' After reading his premature obituary, Alfred was devastated by the foretaste of how he would be remembered. His last will and testament set aside the bulk of his estate to establish the Nobel prizes. He gave the equivalent of US$ 250m to fund such prizes.

What a rare opportunity! Alfred Nobel had the opportunity to evaluate his life near its end and live long enough to change that evil legacy. What will your legacy be? What will people say or write about you when you're gone? How can you make a real difference in the lives of others, beginning from today? How can your life bring blessing to other people? How can you change the world for the better?

Bill and Melinda Gates established the Bill & Melinda Gates Foundation, the largest private charitable foundation in the world, which has a focus on global health and poverty. It gives billions away to worthy causes. Other philanthropists include Warren Buffett, Oprah Winfrey, Mark Zuckerberg. These men and women have changed the lives of multitudes through their charitable work and giving. They have moved beyond wealth to significance.

You can really make a significant contribution in the world by helping to eradicate global problems which include extreme poverty (as a result of which thousands of children die each day), preventable diseases (millions die of diseases for which we have a relatively easy cure), the need for universal primary education (almost one billion people are unable to read) and the need for worldwide water sanitation (which could be funded by the amount of money that Europeans spend on ice-cream every year).

64. Simplicity

Simplicity boils down to two steps: identify the essential; eliminate the rest. (Leo Babauta)

I read the story of a businessman who travelled to the Far East. One day he got talking to one of the local fishermen and encouraged the fisherman to think big; fish on a bigger scale, make more money, purchase a bigger fishing boat, employ some of the other fisher men, buy a bigger fishing vessel and export fish to other countries. The fisherman asked why he should go to such lengths. The businessman said, 'So you can become rich.' The fisherman said, 'And what do I do with all that money?' The businessman said, 'You retire to a small village with your wife, take life easy; go fishing down the lake, watch the sunrise over the coast in the morning and dance with your wife as the sun sets in the evening.' The fisherman replied, 'But I do all that already.'

Simplicity is the condition of being plain or uncomplicated in form or design. Simplicity is the quality of being easy to understand. Simplicity is being unpretentious, straightforward and clear. Living a life of simplicity is good for the soul. There is a form of quiet grandeur in simplicity, be it in speech, lifestyle or dressing. Simple living is one of those traits that makes a person amicable and liked by all. Simple living is peaceful living. You can be wealthy and live simply. Not having to bother or be overly concerned by all the trappings of wealth and the high life is good for the soul. Simplicity is purity, natural elegance.

God is complex in the sense that we cannot unravel Him, but He is infinitely simple at the same time.

Simplicity is consciously choosing what and what not to care about. (David Srere - Tedtalk on simplicity)

Simplicity is the ultimate sophistication. (Unknown author)

Drawing attention to yourself may be good for business, but the simple life is good for your soul. Humans innately desire simplicity; that is why people make money, then quit the rat race and move to the countryside or some rural area to live more simply. Many dream of taking their feet off the pedal; leaving the fast lane and settling down into a more peaceful existence. A person is wealthy who is satisfied with his or her portion.

My greatest skill has been to want little. (Henry David Thoreau)

One of the ways you can begin to live a simpler life is to declutter your home, car, wardrobe, desk etc. This will help free your mind from excess baggage and aid in simple living. Wisdom simplifies. Wisdom clarifies. Wisdom untangles. Wisdom unshackles. Wisdom illuminates.

Underneath all the glamour and facade, humans are all the same — just clay fashioned into housing for a living soul. Everyone is searching for meaning and purpose in life and shares the same basic human needs. You should neither intimidate others nor be intimidated by the external trappings of success. Attend to the basics — your spirit, soul and body. Cultivate the simple pleasures and have a realistic appraisal of yourself.

Maintain a state-of-life balance; spirituality, wisdom, wealth, power and esteem. Instead of promising yourself something great for the future, take constant little slices of retreats each and every day of your life. This is simplicity and it will give you shalom - wholeness.

Whatever is done without ostentation and without the people being witnesses of it is, in my opinion, most praiseworthy. (Marcus Tullius Cicero)

65. Solitude and Silence

God hides things by putting them near us. (Ralph Waldo Emerson)

To be effective in all areas of our lives, we must carve out some space and time to be alone and quiet so we can become attentive to what is happening within us and around us. We need to calm our busy thoughts and experience stillness if we are to grow as individuals. The need to practise silence and stillness is not an escapist route from reality or the rigours of life. Rather, it is the journey of discovery to a greater and more effective engagement with life.

Some people speak out of experience, some people out of experience do not speak.

Listen to silence. It has so much to say. (Djalâl ad-Dîn Rûmî)

When we practise stillness and reflection in solitude, we begin to live a better life intentionally; we avoid repeating the frequency of previous mistakes. We live with a far deeper consciousness of God with us through the day. Jesus regularly withdrew into the solitude, silence and stillness of the desert, and when he emerged he was more effective in his ministry. Make a habit of practising silence and stillness daily even if it is for a few minutes. Retreat into tranquillity in order to be renewed, refreshed and recharged. Be patient with yourself as you seek to do this—it seldom happens easily.

Isaiah 26:3 says: 'God will keep in perfect peace whose mind is stayed on Him.' 'Perfect peace' makes me think of a beautiful, calm summer's day, sitting by a deserted lake with not a care in the world and no temptations, no problems and no difficulties to cope with. Hmmm, such bliss!

Blessed is the man, who, having nothing to say, abstains from giving wordy evidence of the fact. (George Eliot)

Silence

Silence can never be misquoted. Silence is sometimes the best answer to certain questions. You can never regret saying something you did not say. Ignorance is always eager to speak. The best time to hold your tongue is when you feel you must say something. You are unlikely to be hurt by something you didn't say. Silence is the ultimate weapon of power; sometimes you have to be quiet to be heard. Silence speaks when words can't. The mere fact that you know the answer does not mean that you should give it. I am always so impressed by the restraint in words shown by the truly wise.

Wise men speak because they have something to say; Fools because they have to say something. (Plato)

The Bible has a lot to say about keeping quiet. For example, 'Even a fool is thought to be wise if he holds his tongue. Keep your mouth closed and you'll stay out of trouble' (Pr 21:23 The Living Bible). The Bible also says: 'In the multitude of words, sin is not absent' (Pr 10:19)!

Silence is a friend who will never betray you. Be a good listener; your ears will never get you in trouble. (Frank Tyger)

Over-talking is one of the worst social ills. Quiet gives you bandwidth to hear the divine whispers of wisdom that are drowned out by the noise of false urgencies.

Reflection turns experience into insight. (John Maxwell)

When you follow effective action with quiet reflection, from that reflection will come even more effective action. When repeated over time, this will lead to a cycle of effectiveness and success. According to John Maxwell, learning to pause allows growth to catch up with you. Reflection (pondering, thinking, contemplation) turns experience into insight. People say: experience is the best teacher; not so. It is *evaluated* experience that is the best teacher, not mere experience. Everyone needs a time and a place to pause and think.

Stopping to reflect is one of the most valuable activities you can do to grow it's more important and valuable than motivation and encouragement. Pausing with intention expands and enriches thinking. Pausing allows the lessons learnt from experience to sink into our hearts and then bring about discretion and clearer direction. An absence of reflective thinking is what makes people make the same mistakes over and over without making a change or becoming wiser as a result of that experience. Ten minutes of thought is worth more than an hour of talk. When you take time to pause and incubate, you get illumination. When you take time to stop and reflect, you learn more from your experiences. When you reflect, you are able to put things into perspective, you gain new appreciation for things you didn't notice before. Few people have a clear perspective in the heat of the moment. So we must always take time to pause and think things through before we act. If we don't habitually pause to reflect we would be unable to deal with issues that keep tripping us up and we will keep making the same mistakes over and over.

At the end of every day you should play back the tape of your performance. The results should applaud you or prod you. (Jim Rohn)

Corrie ten Boom once said that if the devil can't make you sin, he'll make you busy. This is because sin and busyness have the exact same effect—they cut off our connection to God, to other people, and even to our own soul. It is only in solitude that you can connect with your real self or innermost being and bring treasures from deep within you on to the surface. Many of us are just too busy to live emotionally healthy and spiritually rich and vibrant lives. There is a healthy kind of busyness where your life is full with things that matter, not wasted on empty leisure or trivial pursuits.

There's nothing wrong with having a lot to do; the problem arises when you have too much to do and have to rush through life and run roughshod over others. This undermines your sanity and tranquility and erodes your sense of shalom (wholeness, peace and well-being).

66. Success

The elevator to success is out of order, but the stairs are always open. (Zig Ziglar)

Brian didn't graduate from high school and, after working for a few years as a labourer, he realised he had limited skills and consequently a limited future. Through hard work and discipline he became a success in sales, marketing, investing, real estate development etc. Today, Brian Tracy is one of America's leading authorities on development of human potential. He speaks to over 250,000 people a year and is also a best-selling author who has written twenty-five books.

Most people think success comes from getting a lucky break or having enormous talent, but many successful people achieve their accomplishments in a simpler way: focus, smart work, persistence and self-discipline.

According to Brian, self-discipline is the key to success. It is the magic quality that opens all doors for you and makes everything else possible. With self-discipline, the average person can succeed as far and as fast as their talents and intelligence can take them. But without discipline, a person with talent, every blessing of background, education and opportunity will seldom rise above mediocrity.

Brian states that, if you study successful people and do what they do, you will be successful. If you study unsuccessful people and avoid doing what they do, you will not be a failure. Successful people do what they hate in order to get what they want or to achieve their goals. Do the things you hate to do first: study, exercise, sales-call etc. In other words, 'Eat that frog' (Brian Tracy). Another businessman (Mark DeMoss) said: 'To be successful you should give God the first hour of every day and the first day out of every week and the first dime of every dollar.'

Much ink has been spilled about the subject of success. I will now build upon what many sages have discovered. Success begins with a state of mind. It's a mentality. When success is a dominating thought, the forces and elements which make for success are attracted towards you. Success-coaches call this the 'law of attraction'. The right people, the right circumstances, the right connections, the 'divine' ideas that make for success also begin to drop into your mind. In like manner those whose dominating thought is fear and failure attract the same. This is why success-coaches advise that you write your vision down and read it every day. When you write the vision down and read it daily, all day long and every day, you'll be running towards it and running into it!

Success is all about creating a domino effect in your life. Toppling dominoes is pretty straightforward. You line them up and tip over the first one. So every day, line up your priorities, find the lead domino, and whack away at it until it falls. Extraordinary success is sequential, not simultaneous. You do the right thing and then you do the next right thing. Over time it adds up and the compound effect or geometric potential of success is unleashed. Success builds on success, and as this happens, over and over, you move towards greater success.[14]

Nobody ever stumbled upon success and says, 'Wait, how did I get here?' (John Maxwell)

Here is the formula for success: a few simple disciplines practised every day – and that's it! Make sure you don't go looking for the exotic answers to success. Success is a very basic process, it doesn't fall out of the sky, it doesn't have any mysteries nor does it fall into the realm of the miraculous. Rather, success is merely a natural result that comes from the consistent operation of the practical fundamentals. To be successful you don't have to do extraordinary things, just do ordinary things extraordinarily well. Success is the sum of small efforts repeated daily. It is an inner ideal followed persistently with courage; having a dream and resolving to follow through until achievement of the desire.

Successful people do consistently what other people occasionally. (Craig Groeschel)

However beautiful the strategy, you should occasionally look at the results. (Sir Winston Churchill)

Success is not perfection, so keep moving on! Focus on results not activities. Success is positive reinforcement. Success is a result of continued action filled with continual adjustments. The greatest enemy of my progress is my last success, so I go forward to achieve more. You can either have excuses or progress - you can't have both!

Success comes as a result of a few simple well-designed disciplines or good habits practised and repeated every day. If success comes as a result of doing a few simple disciplines daily, why are many not successful and why doesn't everybody just do it? The answer, according to Jim Rohn, is that the things that are easy to do are also easy not to do. A few errors in judgement, bad habits repeated consistently over a couple of years result in failure. Why do we repeat errors in judgement or bad habits? It's because failure doesn't fall on us at the end of the first day. Horrible consequences don't show up at the end of the first week or first month and so it's easy to drift a little off course. It's so subtle, you keep drifting a little off course and all of a sudden things spin out of control, slam you in the face and knock you down. To succeed you must not neglect to do the easy things which are also easy not to do. Neglect is the reason for failure, neglecting to do the good habits that bring success, e.g. waking early in the morning, avoiding debt, eating healthily, reading, exercising.

The longest way to success is a short-cut. (Myles Munroe)

Success is a daily thing, not a destination thing. Success is a daily journey. When you go to college, for example, the day you get your diploma or degree is not the day you succeeded. That day is only a recognition of your daily successes throughout the three- or four-year course. Success is every day deciding to study, taking the test, writing the essay, doing the research, attending the lectures (no matter how boring ... yawn), refusing to drop out, goof off or jump ship. There are no short-cuts to success. Success consists of getting up just one time more than you fall down.

The secret to success is to start from scratch - and keep on scratching. (John Mason)

Activity versus success

A wise man pointed out that the most active animal on a farmyard is a chicken that has just had its head cut off. Merely generating a lot of activity is not necessarily a sign of success. Busyness is not equal to productivity. While it is true that you will never accomplish anything without doing something, it is also true that too much busyness can actually blur our ability to think strategically and use our resources to maximise our efficiency.

Learning how to say no is crucial to success. You must be thoughtful about the tasks you undertake and use your skills and gifts effectively to accomplish what only you may be able to do while letting others do what they can do. Accept only responsibilities and tasks that are in line with your vision, skills and passion. Leading yourself effectively can mean reducing the busyness and being strategic in activity. This is not to say you should not take on tasks that will stretch you - in fact you must take on these - but you should avoid being a round peg in a square hole and you must resist the temptation of being all things to all men.

To succeed it is essential to pursue work compatible with your gift. Learn everything possible about your chosen field. Use criticism to your advantage, make it work for you. Recognise that God is your true employer and let this make you do more than what's expected; always give more value than expected. Focus on your true objective and breathe life into your effort through strategic planning.

Success in business means getting on with people. If you are to succeed in business, it won't be because people think you are smart; it will be because people like you.

Our greatest weakness lies in giving up. The most certain way to succeed is always to try just one more time. (Thomas Edison)

Passing Over Opportunities Repeatedly = **POOR**

Keep Educating Yourself = **KEY** (to success)

Success is a discovery of purpose and the fulfilment of that purpose. Success is purpose fulfilled. Success is not outbidding or outshining others. Success is measured by what you have done compared with what you should have done. It is also measured through pleasure:

be happy along the way, pat yourself on the back, enjoy the process. Success is a combination of two things: an inner ideal pursued persistently with courage and outer change associated with that inner ideal.

You don't put your valuables within easy reach of children. Life puts valuable things on the higher shelves so you can reach it by the books you stand upon. Success is not what you achieve, it's what you attract by the person you have become; the person you become through reading, learning, self-development and personal growth. Books are a great go-to resource for success. Short of having a conversation with someone who has accomplished what you hope to achieve, books and published works (and the internet too) offer the most in terms of documented research and role-models for success. You're not the first person to desire success, so you'd be wise to study what others have learned first and then build your actions and plans on the back of their lessons. In other words, stand on the shoulders of giants and see further down the road to success. The discoveries and experiences of others are the best places to start on your journey to success.

It's all right to climb the ladder of success; just make sure it's leaning against the right wall! (Yomi Akinpelu)

235

67. Thoughts

As a person thinks in their heart, so they are. (Proverbs 23:7)

Oliver Hill, born on October 26, 1883, in Pound, Virginia, USA, was an American journalist, salesman and best-selling author. He tells the story of how he purchased a fine dictionary, sought out the word 'impossible' and promptly clipped it out of his new dictionary. He suggested that it would not be an unwise thing for his readers to do the same too. Oliver Napoleon Hill is known best for his book *Think and Grow Rich,* which is among the ten best-selling self-help books of all time.

A grandfather once told his grandson a tale about life. 'A fight is going on inside me' he said. 'It is a fight between two wolves. One is evil: angry, jealous, greedy and full of pride. The other is good: joyful, humble, patient, kind and full of compassion. The same fight goes on inside you and inside every other person, too.' The grandson pondered on what he had just heard, and asked: 'Which wolf will win?' The grandfather simply replied: 'The one you feed.'

What you feed your mind with is what will determine the course your life will take. Feed on great thoughts and your life will go in that direction, dwell on defeating negative thoughts and your life will go in that direction. As you think, so you become.

True change always begins in the mind. The way you think inevitably reflects the way you live. So to become the best version of yourself, think great thoughts! One of the ways you can do that is by feeding your mind on great books. While reading great books, e.g. the Bible, your mind is being bathed and soaked in the high-quality thoughts of the author. This will generate superior thoughts in you and consequently good feelings and those feelings will affect your actions. On the other hand, if you give in to 'stinking thinking', your mood dips, you lose energy, your outlook on life becomes bleak.

Wise thinking leads to right living; stupid thinking leads to wrong living (Ecclesiastes 10:2).

Solomon, the wisest king, writes: 'Guard your heart ... for it determines the course of your life' (Pr 4:23 NLT).[58] We cannot perform outwardly in a way that is inconsistent with how we think inwardly. You cannot be what you believe you aren't. But you can change your thinking and consequently your life. Your brain is like a supercomputer and yourself-talk is the program that determines how it will run. Your mind is always eavesdropping on your self-talk. So if you tell yourself you're not good enough, that's what it will produce, because that is what you programmed into your supercomputer. Monitor your self-talk.

More gold has been mined from the brains of men than has ever been mined from the earth. (Napoleon Hill)

Albert Einstein is known to have said, 'Insanity is doing the same thing over and over again and expecting different results.' In order to maximize your success and accomplish your dream, you will need to do something different. In order to do something different, you will first need to think different. By changing your thoughts and beliefs you will be able to change your life. And the thinking that guides your intelligence is much more important than how intelligent you are. Research shows that thoughts cause the release of hormones that bind DNA turning genes 'on' or 'off' (Pitzer College, Claremont, California). In other words your thoughts can tweak your genetic expression.

Discipline your thoughts

Martin Luther once said, 'You cannot stop a bird from flying over your head but you can sure stop it from making a nest in your hair.' Contrary thoughts and doubts aren't really yours until you allow them to move in and rearrange the furniture. Left unchecked to amble through your mind, a thought can attach itself to your mind and grow until it's like a tumour growing inside you. The Apostle Paul warns, 'Take captive every thought ... make it obedient' (2 Corinthians 10:5). Don't give wrong thoughts an inch or they'll take a mile. Evict them like the unlawful squatters they are, before they weaken your commitment to all that is good, godly and virtuous and leave you in a place of regret. Every day stand guard at the door of your mind. Life drifts in the direction of thoughts, therefore be careful where your mind wanders because your words and actions will follow it!

When your thoughts are going in the wrong direction, talk to your thoughts as if you were addressing an undisciplined child or army. You're the general, you, not your thoughts, are in command, so take the thought captive. If you let your thoughts control you, you'll head straight for disaster, as surely as a general who lets seventeen of his men issue all the orders they want will lose the battle. Imagine the confusion! That's why so many people live in a state of inner chaos and have no idea what to do with their lives. *You* are in charge, *you* should be giving the orders, telling your thoughts what to do. You have to be vigilant: if you detect any undesirable thought, pounce on it and send it packing, get rid of it!

What you become is a direct result of what your mind dwells on. Ralph Waldo Emerson said, 'Life consists of what a man {or woman} is thinking about all day.' John Locke said, 'The actions of men (or women) are the greatest interpreters of their thoughts.'

Watch out for amusement

Excessive amusement can distract or prevent thinking or deep pondering. The word amuse is made up of 'muse', which means to think and ponder, and a- in front of a word usually implies the opposite (as in symmetrical and asymmetrical). So, while musing is your reflective state of mind, 'a-muse' is your non-thinking state. Long periods of screen time means long periods of a non-reflective state. Television and screens in general dull your imaginative powers, whereas reading and listening to the spoken word develop these vital powers. So be wary of things that constantly distract from serious thinking.

If we constantly eat junk food for a long enough period, we aren't going to be as physically healthy as we could or should be. The same is true with what we feed our mind. As the saying goes: 'Sow a thought, reap a deed. Sow a deed, reap a habit. Sow a habit, reap a character. Sow a character, reap a destiny' (Ralph Waldo Emerson). If you want to live a fulfilled life you have to fill your mind correctly.

Success comes to those who are success-conscious, i.e. people who are thinking about succeeding all the time. I heard it said once, if you put a pumpkin in a jug when it's the size a walnut, it will never get bigger than the jug. I believe that can happen to a person's thinking. Don't let it happen to you. People fail to achieve because of how they think, not because of education or connections or birth circumstances or pedigree. Your thinking determines your success because your thinking controls your actions. If you change your thinking you change your life.

White-hot desire is what transmutes thoughts into material possessions.

You cannot directly choose your circumstances in life, but you can choose your thoughts carefully and these will eventually shape your circumstances in life. A particular train of thought persisted in will surely bring, and cannot fail to produce, results in your character and circumstances. You cannot travel inside you and remain still in stagnation. You cannot imagine greatness within you and be mediocre in life.

All achievements, of whatsoever nature, begin as a state of mind; and that state of mind is the one and only thing over which a person has complete unchallenged right of control. It is highly significant that God has provided humankind with total control over nothing except the power over their own thoughts (the one thing they need to shape their lives) and the privilege of fitting them to any pattern of their choice.

You are today where your thoughts have brought you. You will be tomorrow where your thoughts take you. (James Allen)

68. Time

Don't be fooled by the calendar. There are only as many days in the year as you make use of. (Charles Richards)

In 1973, a group of seminary students unknowingly participated in a grand study called the "Good Samaritan Experiment." These students were recruited and divided into two groups to see what factors influenced whether they would help a stranger in distress. Some were told they were going to prepare a talk about seminary jobs; the others, that they were going to give a talk about the Parable of the Good Samaritan, a Biblical story about helping people in need. Within each group, some were told they were late and had to hurry to their destination, while others were told they could take their time. What the students didn't know was that researchers had planted a man along the way - slumped on the ground coughing apparently in distress.

At the end of the study, fewer than half the students stopped to help the distressed stranger. The deciding factor wasn't the task, it was the **time**. 90% of students who were rushed failed to stop and render aid to the stranger. Some actually stepped over him in their hurry to get to where they were supposed to go. It didn't seem to matter that half of them were on their way to deliver a talk on helping others. The point of this story is this: when we are pressed for time we sometimes do stupid things, we don't always think straight and we are prone to make the wrong decisions. When we are in a rush and haven't planned our time, we commit unbelievable blunders on the highway of life; like stepping over people who need our help because we're in a rush to give a talk about helping others!

One of the very worst uses of time is to do something very well that need not to be done at all. (Brian Tracy)

The billionaire and beggar; the young and old, the wise and foolish, all have me in equal quantity. What am I? I am TIME. Time is the one resource that is assigned in a completely egalitarian way. There is absolutely no discrimination. Time is an asset of equality; all humans are given the same amount every day. It is what it is applied to that makes a difference in the outcome of life. Time is a common commodity worldwide; time is the great leveller. Every living person has the same number of hours to use in every day. Wealthy people are not given more time, neither are the poor given less. Busy people are not given a special bonus added on to the hours of the day. The clock plays no favourites. We all have an equal measure of time in every day. Where we differ from one another is in how well we use time. Let us avoid wasting it and maximise our productivity in those allotted hours. However, what is important is not whether you are busy but whether you're making progress.

To kill time is not murder, it's suicide. (Myles Monroe / William James)

Time is a gift given to us by God to fulfil an assignment and complete a specific task and purpose. You are simply a product of how you have used and managed your time and how you have managed the changes that have happened to you. What you become ten years from today will be a product of and totally dependent on how you use your time and manage the changes that will come your way. How you spend your time is more important than how you spend your money. You can always get more money but you can never get any time you have lost back.

Time is not stoppable but it is controllable and can be managed for increased productivity. A new year is the opportunity to review worthwhile goals, redefine priorities and life-vision. How you use the time you have been given will determine the outcome and quality of your life. Time is powerful, whatever you use it for or invest it in is what you will become. Time is life. Wasting time wastes your life. The secret to success in life according to Myles Monroe is the effective management of time and change. The principal key to management of time and change is planning. Planning and self-discipline are the most important principles of success in life. The only thing that can control or regulate time is planning. Without a plan, time and change will ruin your life. You cannot save time but you can control and regulate its use maximally. Life is about development of our potential and wise use of our resources (time, money, energy etc.).[43]

If you want your children to turn out well, spend twice as much time with them and half as much money. (Abigail Van Buren)

The best time to shape your today is when it is called tomorrow. This is because tomorrow is still in a fluid form and can be shaped today. The future arrives an hour at a time. Gain control of your time, and you will gain control of your life. What you plant today is the only guaranteed harvest tomorrow. A year from now you will wish you had started today. Time can be spent or invested. Time well-invested brings a harvest but spent unwisely can never be recovered and is lost forever. What you have and what you become is all down to how you use your time.

The wise man does at once what the fool does finally. *(Niccolò Machiavelli)*

Time is life. It can be a blessing or a curse depending on how you use it. Life is measured and qualified by time. Life is the passing of time. Time stops only when you die. When you die you step out of time into eternity. Time is an interruption of eternity. Time is a slice of forever. God lives in forever but put us in time in order to protect us from forever. Time was given to us to live life in doses and measure our life. Time prevents us from hurting forever, time changes our situation because time is measured in past, present and future (Myles Munroe). Time is so powerful that whatever you invest it in is what you become. Time can be spent, invested or squandered. It is more important than money, it can depreciate or be devalued based on how you spend it. It can be controlled, managed, converted, exchanged and used to change your life. It can be redeemed - which means it can be bought back, reclaimed. It is measured in results. The success of your day is based on your seeds not on your harvest.

The best time to plant a tree is twenty years ago. The second-best time is now. (Chinese proverb)

If you have a project to execute, first assess your resources and determine how to leverage them to the greatest advantage. Time is often your most limited resource. Look at the time available to accomplish the task. Decide how best to use your effort in the available time and work backward from the deadlines to the present situation. Stop and think so you can think of stopping.

The number-one time waster for most people is looking for things that are lost. You have 86,400 seconds daily: how are you using yours? To waste time is to spend it on what is pointless and has little or no value.

I never lost a game; I just ran out of time. (Vince Lombardi)

In sport it is evident that there is a race against the clock and it is the team that is most productive in the allotted time that wins the game. In real life, however, the race against time is not immediately striking. Hence people tend to waste time not knowing that they are wasting life. The truth, however, is that in sport the clock can be temporarily halted or a timeout can be offered. But in real life, there is no respite, no recess, no halftime; every minute counts, the stakes are way higher in the game of life, and when the Divine Umpire blows the whistle, it's not time out - it's lights out!

69. Visions and dreams

The only thing worse than being blind is having sight but no vision.
(Helen Keller)

There was a six-year-old boy called Steve from a low-income family. One day in class the teacher asked all the children to write what they wanted to become when they grew up. Steve wrote, 'I want to be on TV making people laugh.' The next day the teacher read out loud what each child had written. When she came to Steve's paper she asked him to come to the front of the class. She asked Steve whether he had ever been on TV or whether anyone in his family had ever been on TV. Steve answered: 'No, ma'am.' So the teacher said he should take the paper back and write something more realistic. Steve went home confused because this was the first time anyone had told him what he could or couldn't become. He shared this with his father and his father told him to keep his paper and read it aloud to himself every morning thanking God that he would be on TV. That boy was Steve Harvey, one of the foremost comedians in America. He is a television host, producer, radio personality, actor and author. Steve kept his vision before his eyes daily and he achieved it.

Another young man wrote an essay in college for an economics exam on his vision for overnight mail. The professor took a red pen and gave him a C, with the comment: 'Do not dream of things that cannot happen.' The young man left school and started Federal Express.

The poorest man is not the man without money but the man without a dream. (Harry Kemp)

In his book, *Dare to Dream*, John Maxwell writes: 'Daring dreams can be great things. Daring dreams have changed the world. Galileo had daring dreams to see the planets and developed the first telescope. Lindbergh had a daring dream and flew solo across the Atlantic ocean. Ford had a daring dream, so did Ray Kroc, John F. Kennedy and Martin Luther King Jr. Daring dreams change the world. But there is a difference between a daring dream and a mere daydream. One fires you up and moves you forward. The other is nothing more than wishful thinking. Daring dreams are worth dying on the hill to take them. Daydreams do little more than make you want to take a nap.'

Never measure the height of a mountain until you have reached the top. Then you will see how low it was. (Dag Hammarskjold, Swedish diplomat)

Walt Disney was a dreamer. Even though he had already created Disneyland in California, he dreamed of something much grander and magical. He considered many locations around the country for his new dream and eventually settled on what most believed was unusable swampland in central Florida. Disney saw what other could not see: great roads and interstates, an airport nearby, fine weather all year round and an abundance of cheap land. His advisors were hesitant about the site because of the challenges of swampland and construction, but Disney was not dissuaded and the rest is history. Disney World is a dream that seemed impossible to many people, but not for a dreamer like Walt Disney.

Dream seeds

When you ask God for an oak-tree, He gives you an acorn because the oak tree is in the acorn; it's just a matter of time before what's inside bursts out. Whatever God has promised you, the seeds are already within you. Could it be that the overall reason you are really outstanding at one thing and scarcely have a smattering of talent in other areas is simply that you have been perfectly matched to fulfil the dream in your heart? Your dream is located right in the heart of your greatest strengths, your most amazing talents and your strongest desires: not where you have weakness, not where you struggle to be even average, not where you hate doing things. That's why everyone who finally finds and lives their dream is so fulfilled and joyful. Why? They finally fit perfectly. They were born for this! You were born to live out your dream. [47]

The rung of the ladder was never meant to rest upon but only to hold a man's foot long enough to enable him to put the other somewhat higher. (Thomas Henry Huxley)

What do you see?

When you take time to think about your future - to visualise and see the invisible - you are one step closer to making it happen. Therefore create a daily routine of visualising your future. Your life is constantly moving towards the dominating images in your mind. If you're going around day by day with no dream inside you, you're like a dead person walking. Without a vision people perish; they run riot; their lives run amok.

Vision is the capacity to see further than your eyes can see.

To fulfil your vision you need clarity. Clarity is the ability to determine what it is you want to be and do or achieve. Clarity comes by writing things down. 'And then God answered: "Write this. Write what you see. Write it out in big block letters so that it can be read on the run. This vision-message is a witness pointing to what's coming. It aches for the coming—it can hardly wait! And it doesn't lie. If it seems slow in coming, wait. It's on its way. It will come right on time"' (Habakkuk 2:2-3 MSG). I challenge you to believe that God has a bigger vision for your life than you've ever known. A dream that can only take God to fulfil it. That God-sized dream will pull you forward! It will give you a reason to jump out of bed in the morning. It will bring purpose to your days.

Oral Roberts is the founder, first president and chancellor of Oral Roberts University in Tulsa, Oklahoma, USA. A plaque on his desk reads *'Make No Little Plans Here'*. I recommend we take his advice because small plans have no power to stir people's blood; and they will probably go unrealised. Dream big, imagine big, think big! There's magic in thinking big!

If it doesn't scare you, it's not big enough .(Joel Osteen)

70. Wealth

Wealth is a consequence not a purpose.

In ancient Babylon there lived a very wealthy man named Algamish. A young man called Arkad consulted him for advice on becoming wealthy. What Algamish gave to Arkad, I pass on directly to you today: 'I found the road to wealth when I decided that a part of all I earned was mine to keep. And so will you.' Every gold piece you save is like a slave that works for you. Every copper it earns is like its child that can also earn for you. If you wish to become wealthy, then what you save must earn, and its children must earn, and its children's children must earn, so that you may acquire the abundance you crave. Pay yourself first.

Wealth, like a tree, grows from a tiny seed. The first copper you save is the seed from which your tree of wealth will grow. The sooner you plant that seed, the sooner the tree can grow. And the more faithfully you nourish and water that tree with consistent savings, the sooner may you bask in contentment under its shade.[50]

Financial freedom is when the return on your investment can pay your bills. (Sam Adeyemi)

To be wealthy is to be financially independent. Financial independence is the ability to live on the income from your own resources. Wealth is financial freedom. It comes from a conversion of effort and enterprise into currency and equity, into freedom from financial pressures, freedom to create, to share and to have choice. It is having enough resources to improve the quality of your life and live with dignity.

Profits are better than wages. Wages make you a living, profits make you a fortune. (Jim Rohn)

Anyone with a reputation for reliability can create – build - wealth. Money is a numeric analogue for how you run your life and what you have done for others. We do not get paid for time, we get paid for value. The only real way to build wealth is to attend diligently to the needs of others and conduct oneself in an honourable and trustworthy fashion. If you are wealthy you won't need to show it. The truly wealthy don't need to show it – it shows naturally.

Poor people pursue money, rich people pursue things, wealthy people pursue ideas, and ideas attract money. Learning is the beginning of wealth. Your income is directly related to your philosophy, not to the economy. Here is the philosophy of the wealthy: invest your money and spend what is left.

The absence of money does not make you poor: it is the absence of ideas. (Sam Adeyemi) [51]

Wealth is not simply acquisition of money. What makes you wealthy is more valuable than the money you accumulate. The greatest value is not the millions you acquire: it is who you have become in the process. When you become a millionaire, it's not the money that is important, it's the person you have become in the process of getting it. If you lose the million or, better still, if you give it all away, you can get it all back because you have become a person with the mindset, skill-set or philosophy of a millionaire who is capable of making a million; so you can make it again and again. That is why the greater percentage of those who win the lottery become bankrupt in a short time: they could not keep the millions they won because, although they had a million, they had not become millionaires: they did not have the mindset or philosophy of a wealthy person, so they were quickly parted from their money (the saying, 'A fool and his money are soon parted,' comes to mind). Money is always looking for a good place to call home.

Set a goal to become a millionaire, for what it will make of you to achieve it! (Jim Rohn)

Set a goal that will make something of you to achieve it. It's not about what you get from it. It's about what it makes of you; what you will become in the process of achieving it. Set a goal that will stretch you and help you to develop and achieve your full potential; for what it will make of you to achieve it - the skills, character and attributes you could and would develop in the process of achieving it.

Wealth is what you accumulate, not what you spend. (Thomas J. Stanley)

According to Napoleon Hill in his book *Think and Grow Rich*, acquisition of wealth begins with a state of mind and definiteness of purpose because our brains become magnetised with the dominating thoughts which we hold in our minds. Mysteriously these magnets attract to us the forces, the people, the circumstances of life which are in perfect harmony with the nature of our dominating thoughts. To accumulate riches we must magnetise our minds with intense desire for riches so that we become money-conscious until that desire drives us to create definite plans for acquiring it. [52]

Compound interest is the most powerful force in the universe. Compound interest is the eighth wonder of the world. He who understands it, earns it; he who doesn't, pays it. (Albert Einstein)

Compound Interest

The best way to explain compound interest is to use a simple illustration. First, this is how compound interest can work against you. Assume you have a thirty-year mortgage of £200,000, and you are paying 5% interest. The principal and interest payment would be £1,073.64. That means that you will be making 360 payments of that amount. On that first payment of £1,073.64 only £240.31 of it goes to pay down the principal while £833.33 goes towards the interest. Each month a few more pennies goes towards knocking down the principal. In total over the 30 years life of the mortgage you would have paid a sum of £386,510.40 (360 x £1,073.64), £200,000 of which goes to pay the principal and £186,510.40 to pay the interest. Now for the sweet part! We can harness the incredible power of compound interest to build wealth. Using the same illustration above, if you were to save £1,073.64 per month for 30 years into an account earning 5% interest, guess what your money will be worth? Wait for it! The value of your savings will be £902,066!   With compound interest working against you, those payments would retire a debt of £200,000. With it working for you, they would grow to over £900,000.

If you could get a better interest, say 8% over thirty years, your money would be worth over £1.6 million and, if you invested in the stock market over that thirty-year period at about 10%, your investment would be worth almost £2.5 million. In all these cases, we are looking at the same thirty years and the same total amount of payments of £386,510.40. If the miracle of compound interest is working for you; you could have anything from £900,000 at 5% interest to almost £2.5 million at 10% growth.

Simple Wealth Building Tips

- Stay out of debt: debt kills your option because the borrower is the servant of the lender.

- Save! It is a necessary monthly expense achievable only by spending much less than you earn.

- Invest! Let the miracle of compound interest work for you.

- Be generous! Exchange your tangible money with the intangible blessings of God. When God blesses you with wealth, don't just give Him the credit for it: give Him some cash too.

- Keep the right company: if you hang around with nine broke people, you're the tenth one.

- Become financially literate and astute; a fool and his money are easily parted.

71. Wisdom

Every man is a damn fool for at least five minutes every day; wisdom consists in not exceeding the limit. (Elbert Hubbard)

The story is told about a wealthy man who had a foolish son and a wise slave. Not wanting to leave his entire estate to an unwise son, he decided he would leave his estate to his slave but give only one thing to the son. He told his son he could choose anything out of his vast estate, absolutely anything. The son was flummoxed and decided to seek counsel from a wise old man. The old sage advised him to choose his father's slave since the slave belonged to the father. He did as advised and consequently all that the slave inherited became the son's possessions. He took wise counsel and turned out not to be a fool after all. Moral of the story: even if your wisdom is limited, you'll turn out okay if you take wise counsel.

According to John Maxwell, the leadership expert, you are responsible for your growth, but you shouldn't go it alone. Why? Self-made leaders start with themselves and end with themselves. Teachable leaders start with themselves and sharpen themselves on the wisdom of others.

I have an acid-test for wisdom: a wise person is the one who appreciates those who correct and instruct them. No one is totally wise in all spheres of life. I think we all have a smattering of foolishness in us. However, if you are growing in wisdom, you will not despise constructive criticism or those who correct your indiscretions. That's not to say you won't feel emotionally sore about the criticism or rebuke, but you know it's for your own good; so you eat humble pie and take it with aplomb. Anyone who rebukes a mocker or a foolish man will get an insult in return. 'So don't bother correcting mockers; they will only hate you. But correct the wise, and they will love you. Instruct the wise, and they will be even wiser' (Pr 9:7-9). 'Wisdom will multiply your days and add years to your life. If you become wise, you will be the one to benefit. If you scorn wisdom, you will be the one to suffer' (Pr 9:11-12 NLT). [58]

Brian O'Driscoll humorously said, 'Knowledge is knowing that a tomato is a fruit. Wisdom is not putting it in a fruit salad!' Knowledge is horizontal. Wisdom is vertical. It comes down from above. It is far more important to grow in wisdom than to grow in wealth. Wisdom outweighs wealth.

The story is told of a consultant engineer who was invited to a factory to help fix a broken assembly line. As it was the factory's most productive line, the managers were really anxious to get it fixed quickly. The engineer had come highly recommended so they were quite hopeful. When the engineer arrived at the factory, he was taken straight to the production-line. The engineer paused for a few seconds, looked up and down the line, walked to a particular spot, tapped on the side of the machine with a hammer and the production-line sprang to life again. The production manager and director were delighted. They asked him to send an invoice for payment. The following day they received an invoice for £10,000. The director was annoyed: how can we pay £10,000 for just five minutes when all he did was tap on the assembly line with his hammer? So they sent the engineer a message asking him to forward an itemised bill. This is what he sent:

'For tapping on equipment with hammer £1.

For *knowing* where to tap £9999.

Total £10,000.'

So how does wisdom come? How do we become wise people? How do we grow in wisdom? Wisdom comes, I think, primarily by a willingness to listen to and learn from others. Ask good questions and listen to the answer: this will surely add to your wisdom. Read excellent books and listen to good audio messages from tried and tested wise men and women. When we are talking, we are usually merely repeating what we already know. When we are listening, we may learn something new. Often, those who know most speak least. Wisdom leads to simplicity and brings clarity. Wisdom is holistic and is shown not only in what we say but also in what we do not say and in how we live.

Mark Twain said: When I was a boy of fourteen, my father was so ignorant I could hardly stand to have the old man around. But when I got to be twenty-one, I was astonished at how much he had learned in seven years.

One day, after seeing the latest Disney Aladdin film on the big screen, I asked my twelve-year-old daughter what she would wish for if she had a genie in a lamp like Aladdin's. I told her she could not wish for unlimited wishes but could wish for anything else. She wished for unlimited genies. Hmm, out of the mouth of babes wisdom shines through.

We can learn from anyone, even people younger or less experienced than we are. We can also learn from fools: if nothing else, we can learn what not to do. If I place myself above the people I meet, they won't be able to pour their wisdom into my own cup. But if I place myself lower than them, their wisdom flows naturally into me, drawn by a kind of spiritual gravity.

Respect for parents is a mark of wisdom. Wise children should make their parents proud of them. An inquisitive mind is also a mark of wisdom; the spirit of wisdom gives you a hunger for truth and knowledge. Wisdom comes from deep within and is a kind of intuition. True wisdom comes from God, the fountain of wisdom and it is supremely acquired through your relationship with him. Knowledge is horizontal. But wisdom is vertical. It comes down from above. You will grow in wisdom as you learn, reflect and live in relationship with God.

We all desperately need wisdom. The Old Testament has several 'Books of Wisdom': *Proverbs, Job, Ecclesiastes* and *Song of Songs*. In addition, sprinkled throughout the Bible are various writings which can be described as 'Wisdom Literature', which covers a varied range of subjects such as the power of the tongue, the blessings of faithfulness, the dangers of adultery, the hazards of strong drink, the inequalities of life, the contrasts between the wise and the foolish, the skill of leadership and the art of parenting. This wisdom is a kind of sanctified common sense. It leads to greater self-understanding. It gives you the ability to cope in life and to steer through and master its challenges. Wisdom is the art of steering through the battles and blessings of life and living skilfully in whatever conditions you find yourself. It is the sort of legacy good parents want to hand on to their children. Where is wisdom to be found? True wisdom starts with a relationship with Jesus Christ. This is far more valuable than anything the world can offer.

Wisdom is not just about knowledge. It teaches that to be wise is to live well. An example of wisdom is excellence in speech: honest, truthful communication with words that are righteous and true. The first step in living well is to set the right goals and ambitions. In the book of *Ecclesiastes*, King Solomon notes that wisdom is better than strength. Wealth cannot secure your victory, and poverty cannot prevent it. Never let your lack of resources justify your lack of ambition. Never allow the measure of your wealth to be the measure of your life. Solomon was a man with both great wealth and great wisdom, but he could see clearly that only great wisdom ensures the best future.

The path toward wisdom is taken not by steps but by choices. We do not become fools because we lack the right information; we become fools because we love the wrong things. Wisdom is the ability to choose right over wrong. Before you swing your axe, choose your tree. Decide what your life is about; decide what is worth living for. Find your intention, and no matter what may come, never relinquish it.

Wisdom is choosing to do now what you will be happy with later on. (Joyce Meyer)

The art of being wise is the art of knowing what to overlook. (William James)

Knowledge is a process of piling up facts; wisdom lies in their simplification. (Martin H. Fischer)

72. Words

Never say anything about yourself you do not want to come true. (Brian Tracy)

The story is told about a young Thomas Edison who came home one day with a paper for his mother. He told her, 'My teacher told me to give this paper only to my mother.' Thomas' mother read the note and her eyes filled with tears. Thomas asked his mother what the note said, and she read aloud. 'Your son is a genius. This school is too small for him and doesn't have enough good teachers for training him. Please teach him yourself.' And that's exactly what Thomas' mother did; she home-schooled her child with devotion and dedication. As the story goes, many years later, after Thomas Edison's mother passed on and he was now one of the world's greatest inventors, he found a folded paper among other family items. He opened the very same paper that had been handed to him to give to his mother and read the following message: 'Your son is mentally ill. We won't let him come to school anymore.' At that moment, Edison realised what his mother had done for him so many years ago. He wrote in his diary: 'Thomas Alva Edison was an addled child that, by a hero mother, became the genius of the century.' Can you imagine what might have happened to Thomas Edison if his mother had read to him the reckless and hurtful words written by his unwise teacher? He might never have invented the light bulb or made his many other contributions to society. Thank God for the wisdom and wise words of his mother! She created the context in which her son could grow to his full potential.

Let's take this message to heart and resolve to use our words for healing today. You might be a parent: what do you say to your children? You might be a teacher: what do you say to your pupils - especially the ones that are not really performing well at present? What do you say about your parents, family, spouse, boss, subordinate, leader, colleague etc? Just as hurtful words can cause uncontrolled damage for life, so can wise words positively affect a person for life.

Sir Winston Churchill's impact on the twentieth century is difficult to overestimate. A master orator and writer, Churchill knew the power of words. Martin Gilbert, Churchill's official biographer, wrote a book called *Churchill: The Power of Words*. Churchill's words sing in a way that English-language leaders and politicians have tried unsuccessfully to match ever since.

Your words are powerful. With kind and encouraging words, you can change a person's day – or even their entire life. Political speeches, impassioned calls for revolution, commercial jingles etc. are all examples of the way words are used to influence and bring about change in the world today.

Words are wonderful, with tremendous power to produce reaction and emotion. Words are powerful, words paint pictures, words can make a difference between life and death. A few words spoken carelessly produce phenomenal damage. Never underestimate the power of words, particularly your own words. Your own words can make or break you because they have a more powerful effect on you in the long run than words spoken by others.

There is something mysterious or almost magical about words and how they work to bring about what is contained in them. It is not surprising that power should be attributed to God's word, but this same power is attributed to human words, particularly to blessings and curses. Words possess, in Hebrew thought, the quality of a magic spell. A word once uttered takes on a life of its own beyond the control of the speaker and achieves its effect by some kind of innate power.[53]

Words are like eggs: once spoken they cannot be unspoken. When words are spoken a sequence of events is activated; a ripple effect begins. Sometimes great damage is done that is difficult to amend. Your words attract good towards you - or evil - so don't speak the wrong words. Proverbs 6:2 says, 'Thou art snared with the word of thy mouth, thou art taken with the words of thy mouth.' The sheer number of Bible verses that deal with the issue of words is astounding. The Bible has a lot to say about speaking words because the words we speak affect us immensely. Proverb 18:21 says, 'Death and life are in the power of the tongue: and they that love it shall eat the fruit thereof.' And Psalm 34:12-13 reads: 'What man is he that desireth life, and loveth many days, that he might see good? Keep thy tongue from evil, and thy lips from speaking guile.'

One of the most important things you can do in life is to keep your heart full of the word of God. This is because whatever is in your heart in abundance is what you will speak. Faith filled words are the most powerful things in the universe.

Make Your Words Count

In the English language twenty-six letters rule your world. We all know the power of words. Words can inspire you and encourage you. Words can create a desire in you to be the biggest and brightest. And words can also tear you down, discourage you, demoralize, and dishearten you. Words are powerful. Words are important. Your biggest challenge in life will be controlling your words. There is power in your words. Be careful what you say.

Speak with the goal of building up, seeing the good in every circumstance and always making people better. There is great wisdom in pausing before you speak to measure your words against these standards: is it helpful? is it necessary? is it kind?

Kind words are like honey: sweet to the soul and healthy for the body. (Pr 16:24 NLT)[58]

Don't simply use your words to describe your situation or your life: use your words to design and shape your life and situation. A wise woman (Terri Savelle) has said: 'If you want to know where your life is headed, listen to the words that are coming out of your mouth.' Don't use your words just to convey information: use your words to create transformation.

Give thy thoughts no tongue. (William Shakespeare)

When it comes down to it, the most immediate gift of encouragement that we can give is through words. Words, whether they are written or spoken, drill deeply into our hearts. Why is this? I think it is because of the way we have been created. The saying, Sticks and stones may break my bones, but words can never hurt me, is total nonsense, a fallacy! We respond deeply to words, for we have been created to be affected by words, and especially God's words. When we speak words of encouragement and minister to someone with healing words, they respond to these words as surely as those words ministered to us. It is with these facts and perspective that we embrace our sacred responsibility to use our words to edify and strengthen the Church and to make disciples by our influence on our world around us.

Like apples of gold in settings of silver is a word spoken at the right time and in the right way. (Jewish proverb)

Power of words

Wars are started with words.

Love is communicated through words.

Instruction and education are shared by words.

Deception and confusion are propagated by words.

Kingdoms are built with words.

People are controlled motivated, inspired by words.

Lives are shattered and healed through words.

Worlds are created by words - the earth was and so is our personal world.

Words may very well be the most powerful conduit of authority and power in the world

You will have to eat your words if you're reckless with them. Spare yourself the humiliation. (Yomi Akinpelu)

73. Work

Work brings profit; empty talk brings poverty. (Proverbs 14:23)

Work is good! Don't be afraid of hard work! Work is the mechanism that allows you the self-respect of knowing that when you eat, you eat as a result of having done good for others in the world. Anyone unfortunate enough to be living off the sweat and perspiration from someone else's brow is said by Jewish wisdom to be eating ' the bread of shame'.

Hard work never killed anyone, but poverty kills. (African proverb)

Don't wait for inspiration before you work - get to work and be inspired by your working! Don't expect to be perfect - just expect to get it done! If you do what you must do only when you feel like it or when you are in the mood, you will never be successful. Anyone who does what he must only when it is convenient isn't going to be successful. The secret is following through. If you develop the habits of success you'll make success a habit.

Things may come to those who wait, but only things left over by those who hustle. (Abraham Lincoln)

There are things in life you have to work for, and there are things in life you have to wait for; don't confuse the two. So often, people neglect taking action because it requires actual work to be done. Stop wishing, start doing! Big achievements come along one small advantage at a time. You have the power to mould your life, to shape it and reshape it if you will consistently put in the work required and keep making improvements along the way.

Hustle beats talent when talent doesn't hustle! (John Maxwell)

When you put in the hard work, day in and day out, you begin to see measurable progress. Intelligence and talent is overrated. They are not the most important components of success. Diligence in putting in the hard work without slacking is the key to great achievement in the long run. I have seen hard working, average people achieve better results than more able ones because they put in the hard work and were not lazy. The way to make progress is just show up, put in your best and then do it again the next day. No slacking and not neglecting to do the necessary things daily. Yesterday's success will not bring you tomorrow's success only today's work will. Work diligently, on yourself and on your job or business or ministry and keep on finding creative ways to add value to your clients, this will lead to success.

Eighty per cent of life is just showing up. (Woody Allen)

Hard work is more important than innate talent. As Thomas Edison famously said, 'Genius is one percent inspiration, ninety-nine per cent perspiration.' John Wimber has been know to say, 'It's hard to sit still and be good.' We are much less likely to fall into temptation when we are fully occupied and in the right place.

Stress does not come from hard work, it comes from lack of necessary action - stress comes from ignoring things you shouldn't be ignoring. (Jeff Bezos CEO Amazon)

74. Worry

Worry is the dark room where negatives are developed.
(Wanda E. Brunstetter)

At the end of his life, Sir Winston Churchill said, 'When I look back on all these worries, I remember the story of the old man who said on his deathbed that he had had a lot of trouble in his life, most of which had never happened!' Churchill was speaking about the burden of worries that never materialise. However, there are many different types of 'burdens' in life, and some of them are very real.

Worry is a cycle of inefficient thoughts whirling around a centre of fear. (Corrie Ten Boom).

I think the most useless activity on earth is worry - it changes nothing but increases blood pressure! Don't worry, be happy! Too much analysis leads to paralysis. Worry means to strangle or choke off! Worry leads from somewhere to nowhere. In life you must cultivate a little 'I don't care attitude' don't worry about what people might think. When you try hard to be liked, you become overanxious; you look bad.

John Newton said, 'We can easily manage if we will only take, each day, the burden appointed to it. But the load will be too heavy for us if we carry yesterday's burden over again today, and then add the burden of the morrow before we are required to bear it.'

Concerning worry Jesus said, 'Come to me, all you who are weary and burdened, and I will give you rest. Take my yoke upon you... and you will find rest for your souls. For my yoke is easy and my burden is light' (Matthew 11:28–30). A yoke is something Jesus would have made in a carpenter's shop. It is a wooden frame joining two animals (usually oxen) at the neck, enabling them to pull a plough or wagon together. The function of the yoke is to make the burden easier to carry.

Eugene Peterson in *The Message Bible* translates Matthew 11:28–30 in this way: 'Are you tired? Worn out? Burned out on religion? Come to me. Get away with me and you'll recover your life. I will show you how to take a real rest. Walk with me and work with me – watch how I do it. Learn the unforced rhythms of grace. I won't lay anything heavy or ill-fitting on you. Keep company with me and you'll learn to live freely and lightly.'[57]

According to Jim Rohn, worry is fear painting negative pictures in your mind and if you watch that mental movie for too long, you get a false picture of how things really are. Worry is a mental broadcasting station and more often than not it is false or at least distorted propaganda. Worry has that sneaky way of stopping short of giving you all the facts, worry is often the trickery of mentally filtered facts on the negative side, and the bold declaration and impression that those are all the facts. Worry has the mental audacity to suggest that the elevator only runs one way: down. Many times worry is a five-alarm bell for a simple waste basket fire! Worry is a depletion of constructive emotion. It's wasted mental energy, it's like letting the starter run the battery down when the car won't start. Worry is most often due to a lack of all the facts. It's a lack of full understanding, a lack of complete information and also because of lack of planning or being unprepared for what lies ahead. When you feel inadequate ability, knowledge, talent, courage and faith, you feel anxious. Left unchecked, worry can become like a mad dog loose in the house. Don't let worry run amok in your life a moment longer, it's a burden you can get rid of. It's a monkey you must get off your back. Getting rid of worry starts with a decision - do it now, plan, be prepared. Get rid of that nagging, sinking feeling that you won't make it; that you can't do it; that things will not work out for the best. Worry is undue concern that takes too much of your emotional time. You should be concerned and careful about life's issues but not overly concerned. Worry is undue concern. Get rid of worry by consistent affirmation, by not neglecting to do what you should do at the right time. Remember all the things you worried about that never happened. Recall all the things you're grateful for. 90% of things you have worried about in the past never happened anyway. Analyse the worry to death by arguing against it based on all the positive experiences you have had and all the negatives that never happened. Talk to yourself persuasively about all the good you have experienced. Believe your beliefs and doubt your doubts, look at all the facts and silence the one sided negative propaganda of worry. The best answers to worry are gratitude for the blessings you've enjoyed, prayer and planning ahead. [42]

A lot of people suffer serious emotional distress, such as depression and anxiety, the most effective and powerful antidote for anxiety is thanksgiving and gratitude. When we feel anxiety coming on or even begin to think about the possibility of it coming on we want to nip it in the bud immediately by counting your blessings.

Worry is like a rocking chair: it keeps you going but you don't get anywhere. (Emma Bombeck)

75. Zenith of life

Things which matter most must never be at the mercy of things which matter least. (Goethe)

I read that Robbie Williams once went on a shopping spree in Los Angeles. He bought seven cars, including a brand-new Ferrari, a brand-new Porsche and a brand-new Mercedes. Within a week he wished he had not bought any of them. Robbie wrote this song 'Feel':

I just want to feel real love…

There's a hole in my soul

You can see it in my face

It's a real big place.

You've got to admire his openness. Robbie Williams is unashamedly open about himself. He is ruthlessly honest about his self-obsession and addictions.

This chapter is titled the zenith of life because I wanted it to be the last chapter and because this *topic is* the most important in life. Why am I here? What matters most? These are soul-searching questions which have been asked throughout the ages by sages and simpletons alike. God implants this desire 'to feel real love' in humanity. This 'hole in my soul' is common to all human beings. It's not a design flaw or glitch, it's God implanted, it's part of the manufacturer's design. It cannot be filled by fame, wealth, success, sex or drugs. It is a God-shaped hole. It is a spiritual hunger and thirst.

I recently bought a new HP printer after my old faithful printer gave up the ghost. I think the old printer had been a brand of HP in its former life. The new printer was wireless, smart and enviable.

The manufacturer warned that only the original HP ink-cartridge should be used not a compatible cartridge because the original one had perhaps a code, chip or sensor which is recognised by their printer but which would be missing on a compatible ink cartridge and so might malfunction or not print at all. That kind of reminded me that the God-shaped hole we all have cannot be filled by anything but God - our Creator.

Thou hast formed us for thyself, and our hearts are restless till they find rest in thee. (Augustine)

Billy Graham died on 21 February 2018 at the age of ninety-nine. In 1934, at the age of sixteen, he'd heard God's call and became a faithful messenger of the gospel. He spoke about Jesus to over 210 million people in person and to almost half the population of the world on TV or radio. As a messenger of God, he had planned his own funeral very carefully to be a call for people to put their faith in Jesus. He had said beforehand, 'Some day you will read or hear that Billy Graham is dead. Don't believe a word of it. I shall be more alive than I am now. I will just have changed my address. I will have gone into the presence of God.' He was determined to make the most of every opportunity, including his own funeral, to pass on God's message to the world.

Nicholas Glyn Paul Gumbel (born 1955) was educated at Eton College. He studied law at Cambridge. After graduating from university, Gumbel followed in his father's footsteps and became a practising barrister. At the age of eighteen Nicky Gumbel set out to read the entire New Testament in order to disprove Christianity. Here is an account of his experience in his own words:

> As I read, I was surprised to find that I became convinced that it was true. The last thing that I wanted to do was to 'become a Christian'. I thought that would ruin my life and make it boring by stopping me having any fun. Yet, knowing in my heart that it was true, I felt I had no option but to say 'yes' to Jesus. The moment I did so – to use the words that C.S. Lewis chose to describe his own experience of encountering Jesus – I was 'surprised by joy'. Ever since, Jesus has never ceased to surprise me.

Nicky Gumbel is the developer of the well-known Alpha Course, a basic introduction to Christianity supported by churches of many Christian traditions. Since 2005, he has been Vicar of Holy Trinity, Brompton, London, United Kingdom.

The way to find yourself is to seek God!

There is a phrase that we often hear, which goes something like this: 'There is something missing.' These words mostly come from those who, at least at first glance seem to have it all together. They are wealthy, in good health, have a great family, drive nice cars and have a great future ahead, yet deep down there is a relentless voice that gnaws at them about the emptiness in their souls. This profound emptiness put quite simply, is a deep longing for God. At the centre of our hearts, beneath all the other desires and yearnings, there exists this persistent and intense longing to know God. We should not be surprised, for we have been made by God, for love and to love. We are divinely designed for God's love. God has made us for Himself, as Augustine once said, and our hearts will always be restless until they find their rest in Him. This deepest longing is our bus ticket to the way home.[7]

Salvation to the wise

There are a lot of very intelligent people in this world who do not believe in God or the gospel of Jesus Christ. The reason for this might be that they have decided that the criterion for them to believe anything at all should be that it must make sense to them. It must be able to be verified in some way by reason based on empirical evidence apart from faith in biblical revelation. For some others, the problem of why a benevolent God allows evil is a stumbling block.

In your search for the truth, perhaps you could begin with C.S. Lewis' *Chronicles of Narnia*. I recommend it for several reasons. First, C.S. Lewis had been an atheist, and might therefore be able to answer your questions and objections. Secondly, for the intellectuals, C.S. Lewis was a man who had graduated from Oxford with Triple First Class Honours in Classics, Philosophy and

English, and was one of the greatest British academics of his generation. If he made the journey from atheism to Christianity, then it is logical to assume that you don't have to suspend your brain in order to believe in God. Thirdly, you couldn't accuse C.S. Lewis of being superficial or shallow about suffering. Having lost his mother at the age of 10, being unhappy at school, and then gone on to experience the horrors of trench warfare during the First World War, he was obviously only too aware of the problem of evil. His discussion of these issues are certainly illuminating in his books. If you read Lewis' three most important books, *Mere Christianity, Miracles and The Problem of Pain* (The Problem of Pain is a 1940 book on the problem of evil, in which Lewis argues that human pain, animal pain, and hell are not sufficient reasons to reject belief in a good and powerful God). Perhaps like Clive Staples Lewis, you also will discover intelligent and convincing answers to all your doubts.

We need the message of the cross, because it is revelation from the Creator of all things on how to get into proper relationship with Him. For those who accept the message by faith, it is 'the power of God to salvation' (Romans 1:16).

God is not mad at you; He's mad about you. When you get serious about finding God and want Him more than anything else, God will reveal Himself and will make sure you are not disappointed. There is nothing - absolutely nothing - more important than developing a friendship with God. It's a relationship that will last for eternity.

God not only loves you as you are, but also knows you as you are. Because of this you need only come as you are; no artificial religious cosmetics can make you presentable to Him. You can simply come as you are.

There are two kinds of people in this world: those who say to God, 'Thy will be done' and those to whom God says, 'All right, then, have it your way.' Be one of the former and not the latter. Do not let the theme song of your life be: 'I did it my way!'

Sources/References

1. Douglas G. Brinkley *Rosa Parks A Life* By Published by Viking Books 2000

2. Nick Vujicic, *Life Without Limits*, (Waterbrook, 2012) p.viii, 21.

3. Napoleon Hill, *Think and Grow Rich* Published by The Ballantine Publishing Group 1983 p.9

4. Mark Fisher, *The golfer and the Millionaire* Published by Cassell 1998

5. Ian Robertson *The Stress Test: How pressure can make you stronger and sharper* by, 2016 Bloomsbury Publishing pp. 150-180. 142-149.

6. Yomi Akinpelu, *Read and Soar* Pneuma Springs Publishing Dartford 2008

7. Nicky and Pippa Gumbel https://my.bible.com/en-GB/reading-plans/13685-bible-in-one-year-2019

8. UCB Word For Today, Free issues of the daily devotional are available for the UK and Republic of Ireland. Written by Bob and Debby Gass United Christian Broadcasters, Westport Road, Stoke-on-Trent, ST6 4JF

9. References - Joyce Meyer, New Day, New You (Faithwords, 2007), p.365

10. Darren Hardy *The Compound Effect* Audio

11. Bill Eckstrom 'Why *Comfort will ruin your life*' TedX Talk Audio

12. https://en.wikipedia.org/wiki/Cuban_Missile_Crisis (Assessed 03/10/19)

13. Nelson Mandela, *The Long Walk to Freedom*, (Abacus, 1995) p.748

14. Gary Keller & Jay Papasan *The One Thing*, John Murray (Publishers) 2014

15. Levi Lusko https://my.bible.com/en-GB/reading-plans/3816-swipe-right/day/1

16. Mason, John L., *Let Go of Whatever Makes you Stop*, (Tulsa, OK: Insight International, 1994);

17. Mason, John L., *You're Born an original, Don't Die a Copy*! (Tulsa, OK: Insight International, 1993)

18. Michelle Obama - *Becoming* Audible Amazon.co.uk

19. Merritt, James, *Still Standing: 8 Winning Strategies for Facing Tough Times*, (Eugene, OR: Harvest House, 2012), 121, 122)

20. Charles Dickens, *A Christmas Carol*, First published by Chapman & Hall London 19 December 1843

21. 'Interview with Mother Teresa', Hello, Issue 324, 1 October 1994

22. Rabbi Daniel Lapin *Thou Shall Prosper* Published by John Wiley & Sons 2010

23. Terry Savelle Foy *Imagine Big*, Published by Regal Books 2012

24. (https://medium.com/@adsactly/the-importance-of-writing-down-clearly-defined-goals-21d90ca78844) (Accessed 10/09/19))

25. James Clear - *Atomic Habits: An Easy and Proven Way to Build Good Habits and Break Bad Ones* - Random House Business (18 Oct. 2018)

26. Craig Groeschel *Habits* Bible App. YouVersion.com

27. Yomi Akinpelu *Wholesome truth about Healing* Pneuma Springs Publishing Dartford 2006

28. James Rampton, 'James Cameron: My Titanic obsession', The Independent, Monday 8 August 2005.

29. Rick Warren, Daily Hope with Rick Warren, 'Take the First Step to Integrity' November 2014, accessed via: http://rickwarren.org/devotional/english/take-the-first-step-to-integrity [last accessed 8 August 2019])

30. Nicky Gumbel, How to Avoid the Titanic Mistake https://www.bibleinoneyear.org/bioy/commentary/3270 14 April 2019)

31. Henry Cloud, *Integrity*, (HarperBusiness, 2009)

32. Dietrich Bonhoeffer, The Cost of Discipleship (New York: Macmillan Books, 1970) p.196

33. John C. Maxwell, *Intentional Living: Choosing a Life That Matters* Hachechett Book Group 2017

34. Adapted from the poem 'Fellowship of the Unashamed by Dr. Bob Moorehead)

35. Myles Monroe, How to write a book Audio.

36. Richard Bewes - Speaking Effectively in Public. Published by Christian Focus Publications Ltd, July 2005

37. Winston Churchill excerpt from address to Harrow School, 29 October 1941. https://www.nationalchurchillmuseum.org/never-give-in-never-never-never.html

38. Rick Warren YouVersion Bible App. YouVersion.com

39. Brendon Burchard *High Performance Habits* Hay House Inc. 2017

40. John Mason *You can do it even if others say you can't*, Published by Revell a division of Baker Publishing Group 2003.

41. John Maxwell, *The 15 Invaluable Laws of Growth: Live Them and Reach Your Potential* Kindle Edition November 2014

42. Jim Rohn - The Major KEY to Your Better Future is YOU - Full Seminar Audio

43. Myles Monroe Time Management and Planning Audio

44. Bill Hybels, *Too Busy not to pray* Interversity Press pp. 7, 11

45. St John Chrysostom, quoted in Leonard Ravenhill, Why Revival Tarries (Minneapolis: Bethany Fellowship, 1959), p.156

46. John Piper, *A Hunger For God* quoted in https://www.goodreads.com/work/quotes/200711-a-hunger-for-god-desiring-god-through-fasting-and-prayer (Accessed 11/9/19)

47. "Steven Spielberg: Synopsis," A& E Biography, 2012 http://www.biography.com/people/steven-spielberg-9490621 also quoted in Imagine big by Terry Savelle pp. 128, 136

48. Jack Canfield The Success Principles Element An Imprint of HarperCollins*Publishers* Ltd 2005

49. Bruce Wilkinson *Dream seeds* YouVersion Bible App. YouVersion.com

50. George S. Clason *The Richest Man in Babylon*, BN Publishing p.17

51. Sam Adeyemi The Real money Audio

52. Napoleon Hill, *Think & Grow Rich*, Published by Fawcett Books p.11

53. Yomi Akinpelu *A Matter of Life and Death* Pneuma Springs Publishing 2003

54. John Maxwell, *No Limits: Blow the CAP Off Your Capacity* Kindle Edition Hatchet Digital Mar 2017

55. John C. Maxwell, Developing the Leaders Around You, (Thomas Nelson Publishing, 2012) pp.2–3.

56. https://news.harvard.edu/gazette/story/2017/04/over-nearly-80-years-harvard-study-has-been-showing-how-to-live-a-healthy-and-happy-life/ (Assessed October 2019)

57. Scripture quotations identified MSG are taken from THE MESSAGE, copyright © 1993, 2002, 2018 by Eugene H. Peterson. Used by permission of NavPress. All rights reserved. Represented by Tyndale House Publishers, a Division of Tyndale House Ministries.

58. Scripture quotations identified NLT are taken from the Holy Bible, New Living Translation, copyright © 1996. Used by permission of Tyndale House Publishers, Inc., wheaton, Illinois 60189. All right reserved.

About Yomi Akinpelu

Yomi Akinpelu holds a Masters degree in Medical Immunology from the College of Medicine, University of London. She has undertaken Biblical studies at doctoral level and worked at a postgraduate college of medicine in London for over a decade before pursuing her passion for writing. She is the author of three books; A Matter of Life & Death – The Power of your words, The Wholesome Truth About Healing, Read and Soar, all available as paperbacks and ebooks.

Yomi is a wordsmith, passionate about books, reading, education, healing and health. She has appeared several times on television and radio; speaking about the subject of reading, healing and health. She is the publishing editor and a director at a UK based publishing company.

Yomi lives with her husband and three children: Joshua, Gloria and Hannah in Kent, England. She is available for interviews, speaking engagements and writing feature articles as well as guest blogs.

Other Book(s) by Yomi Akinpelu

A Matter of Life & Death ISBN 9780954551001

This book is about the power of the words you speak and how you can harness that power to chart the course of your life to your destination. In the pages of this book you will find out that the words you speak are powerful, consequential and therefore must be used deliberately.

You will never view the words you speak the same way again after reading this book, but will start to understand how the words you speak can affect your life. In the pages of the book you will find out that the words you speak are powerful, consequential and therefore must be used deliberately. As you read through this book your eyes will open to certain life changing truths, if you take hold of it and put it to use it will work for you.

This is one of the finest books on the power of our words. A matter of Life & Death is a must read for everyone who aspires to arrive at their ordained destiny. It is a very well written and practical book for every serious believer to own.

Praise for A Matter of Life & Death

Sometimes a book comes into your hands with a message so powerful and profound that you have to share its contents with those around you. "A Matter of Life and Death : The Power of Words" is such a book. So convinced was I of the positive life-changing principles held within every page, that even before I reached the final chapter I had purchased a copy for each of my friends. The book is written in an easy to read and friendly style. Full of biblical wisdom with practical advice, read this and let its message change the way you think about words forever."
Fiona M. Colclough, Water Engineer

You would have thought that this book was written by a combination of seven wise, dedicated and conscientious Christians who have had at least 30 years walk with God. It is a book, which all young people should be encouraged to read or better still their parents/guardians or even teachers should discuss with them the powerful gems contained in the book. This book has helped me to sharpen my verbal response, such that I consciously make sure that my words remains positive and a source of life. I recommend that this book be read at least twice a year, over many years. This is because to fully engrain the powerful truths in this book upon one's heart, it will require repeated assimilation. 'A matter of life and death' left an outstanding impression on me of all the books that I read in the last year.
Richard Oyin-Adeniji, Charity promotions manager

Despite being a student of the subject for many years I found 'A matter of life and death" quite inspiring and instructive. The author, Yomi Akinpelu has combined sound scriptural principles with her experiences of the creative power of words to make a compelling case in this book. In a concise and compelling manner she sets out her argument with the meticulousness that can be expected of a scientist. This book is good, not just for beginners, but also as a refresher for those who are familiar with the lifestyle of accountability with words. The best compliment one can pay an author is to testify to the change effected by her writing. I have thought more seriously about my speech since reading this book.
Kenny Ajayi, Injury Prevention Consultant

Wholesome Truth About Healing ISBN 0954551079

This book is for those who have questions and need answers. The Wholesome Truth about Healing was initiated as a result of a question; "Does God desire perfect health for all? If He does, why are some healed and others not healed"? The subject of these pages will always be poignantly up-to-date because sickness and disease are a fact of life, and Scripture is the highest 'court of appeal', where our thinking and faith must be fully anchored. Evidence from medical research showing that prayer plays a role in healing, and real life testimonies of God's healing power are superbly woven together with scriptural evidence to present a convincing case for healing. This book may well be the most thought-provoking and helpful presentation of this controversial subject you ever read. The Wholesome Truth about Healing tackles the tough questions, offers hope, and inspires faith in God's ability and willingness to heal. Well researched, edifying, exhilarating!

Read and Soar ISBN 9781905809189

There are very few simple habits in life that can have such an immediate and significant impact on your life like reading. Through reading you can share in the wisdom of the greatest minds that ever walked the earth. Although usually seen as a passive pursuit, reading has such a capacity to unlock a wealth of treasure and greatness from within an individual. This book seeks to describe how reading can enrich and even transform our lives.

Books are idea starters; they feed your mind and give you constructive material to think on. Books are like ladders they allow you to see beyond where you are to where you can be; from your present situation to future possibilities. Books capture your thoughts and take you on a journey to a place the author has been. Developing your mind through reading is a sure way to invest in a better future. Reading helps to mould your mind, challenge it and stimulate it. We can direct the course of our lives and shape our world by regularly exposing ourselves to good books.

www.ingramcontent.com/pod-product-compliance
Lightning Source LLC
LaVergne TN
LVHW091249080426
835510LV00007B/173